Chicken Soup for the Soul.

Christmas
in Canada

Chicken Soup for the Soul: Christmas in Canada
101 Stories about the Joy and Wonder of the Holidays
Amy Newmark, Janet Matthews
Published by Chicken Soup for the Soul Publishing, LLC www.chickensoup.com

The publisher gratefully acknowledges the many publishers and individuals who
granted Chicken Soup for the Soul permission to reprint the cited material.

Front cover photo courtesy of iStockPhoto.com/blamb (© blamb).
Back cover photo courtesy of iStockPhoto.com/IanChrisGraham (© IanChrisGraham).
Interior photo courtesy of iStockPhoto.com/meshaphoto (© meshaphoto).
Photo of Amy Newmark courtesy of Susan Morrow at SwickPix.
Photo of Janet Mattews courtesy of Brock Weir.

Cover and Interior Design & Layout by Brian Taylor, Pneuma Books, LLC

Distributed to the booktrade by Simon & Schuster. SAN: 200-2442

Publisher's Cataloging-in-Publication Data
(Prepared by The Donohue Group)

Chicken soup for the soul : Christmas in Canada : 101 stories about the
joy and wonder of the holidays / [compiled by] Amy Newmark [and] Janet
Matthews.

     pages ; cm

ISBN: 978-1-61159-943-5

   1. Christmas--Canada--Literary collections. 2. Christmas--Canada--Anecdotes.
3. Canada--Social life and customs--Literary collections. 4. Canada--Social life and
customs--Anecdotes. 5. Anecdotes. I. Newmark, Amy. II. Matthews, Janet, 1951-
III. Title: Christmas in Canada

GT4987.15 .C45 2014
394.26630971/02   2014946340

PRINTED IN THE UNITED STATES OF AMERICA
on acid∞free paper

24 23 22 21 20 19 18 17 16 15 14   01 02 03 04 05 06 07 08 09 10 11

Chicken Soup for the Soul.

Christmas in Canada

101 Stories about the Joy and Wonder of the Holidays

Amy Newmark & Janet Matthews

Chicken Soup for the Soul Publishing, LLC
Cos Cob, CT

Chicken Soup for the Soul

Changing your life one story at a time®
www.chickensoup.com

Contents

❶
~The Spirit of Christmas~

❷
~Holiday Celebrations & Traditions~

3

~Holiday Memories~

4

~O Christmas Tree!~

5

~The Santa Files~

❻
~A Winter Wonderland~

❼
~Taking Care of Each Other~

8
~Angels in Our Midst~

9
~The True Meaning of Christmas~

10
~The Spirit of Giving~

Introduction

Welcome to Christmas in Canada! If you live here, you know the Christmas holiday season in Canada is particularly special for many reasons—not the least of which is that Santa Claus himself is a Canadian. Yes, he is. Did you know that Canada Post receives letters from children all over the world written in dozens of different languages, and has, for many years, been forwarding them to Santa at the North Pole? It's true—Santa's famous H0H 0H0 postal code is recognized worldwide as belonging to Canada. Between one and two million letters addressed to Santa arrive in Canada every year and Canada Post makes sure that every single one is delivered to Santa and his helpers.

What else is special? Well, in addition to Santa being a Canadian, in most parts of the country you can generally expect or at least hope for a traditional white Christmas. It snows just about everywhere in Canada, and even in Vancouver and Victoria—it could happen....

Another thing special about Christmas in Canada is our multicultural identity; all across the country we find our roots from so many different traditions around the world. Yet, despite these differences, when it comes to the Christmas holiday season there seems to have developed a common experience based on a blend of our historically diverse Canadian heritage combined with our dependably challenging winter climate and... the fact that (as I've already mentioned) Santa Claus himself is clearly a Canadian.

Take for example, Lesley Marcovich who lives in Newmarket, Ontario. Lesley and her family came originally from South Africa and always had a dream of what experiencing a real Canadian Christmas might be like in a peaceful and free country. Her story in Chapter One, "A Christmas Dream," brought tears to my eyes the first time I read it, and each time since. It reminded me (despite the still recent Christmas 2013 Ice Storm), how grateful I am for this wonderful land of peace and freedom we call home.

Speaking of that Christmas 2013 Ice Storm, it was such a huge, dramatic event that impacted so many people, when we began this project only a few weeks later I knew I wanted stories about how people survived and helped each other through it. Imagine my delight when the EXACT story I was looking for arrived from a fourteen-year-old girl named Alexa Danielle Patino. Alexa's family lives in Toronto and like 600,000 other homes in Southern Ontario, their entire neighbourhood lost power on the Saturday morning before Christmas. But by some small miracle, after only a couple of hours their small bungalow was part of a strip of only six houses where the power was inexplicably restored. For the rest of those eight days her parents opened their doors to a steady stream of neighbours and friends to come in and warm up, have a hot shower or share a meal. Christmas Eve at their home was one big sleepover with ice storm refugees sleeping on every available surface. In Alexa's story, "Under One Roof," you will be so touched when you read how on Christmas morning, after a big community breakfast, the gift opening around the tree with friends and neighbours of all ages with everyone still in their pyjamas, created a very intimate and memorable experience!

Now, when it comes to memorable experiences, I think you will love Sharon Melnicer's story, "The Hanukkah Parade," about her feisty Austrian grandmother whose beloved silver menorah was stolen and then recovered just in time for Hanukkah. The vision of Sharon's tiny ninety-year-old "Baba" leading a parade of friends and neighbours along a wintry Calgary street triumphantly holding aloft her precious two-foot menorah is one I really wish I'd been there to see in person!

Our chapter on Holiday Celebrations & Traditions is full of stories about different traditions, sometimes within families, sometimes in communities, and sometimes traditions that have been blended in from other countries. We LOVED Caroline Sealey's story "The Farmers' Parade of Lights," an unusual and amazing annual community tradition in Rockwood, Ontario. We delighted and laughed at the wonderful images she shared about the parade and the experience she and her kids had, and I can assure you that next year—I plan to go!

In Holiday Memories you will find a collection of delightful stories, some touching and some that will make you laugh out loud. For most of us, family is a very important part of the Christmas season, and J.A. Gemmell's story "A Quebec Christmas" really brought that home. I don't want to spoil the surprise, but I think you will be truly moved when you read the lengths to which people will go to be with their loved ones at Christmas.

Then there is the tree. O Christmas Tree!—what would the season be without you? As I read through all the stories that came in, I came to realize that next to Santa, that Christmas tree may be one of the most important elements of a Canadian Christmas. Laura Snell sent us a lovely story entitled, "Our Special Christmas Tree." As a young single mother, she did her best with limited resources to create a special experience for her little boy. This included the best tree she could afford, which was a small "Charlie Brown" type artificial tree. But the experience of decorating it together with her son created a very special tree, which as the years passed became more and more special. Through family circumstances that special tree was retired and put in storage for a few years, and when it was finally brought forth once again, a very touching drama ensued, just not the one they were expecting. Once again I don't want to spoil the surprise, but this story—like all the others in this book—really does illustrate the overarching theme of the eternal power of love—always more powerful at Christmas.

Of course the tree is the focal point for Santa's visit on Christmas Eve to deliver all the presents. In The Santa Files you will find a collection of delightful stories about Santa, including "Christmas Coals" by Encina Roh, who emigrated with her family from China to Vancouver when she was only six. Now fifteen years old, Encina is easily able to recount her exultant experience as a six-year-old of her first Christmas in Canada, and her first experience with Santa — never having known this tradition in China. I was simply delighted with her excitement as she found proof positive that Santa had indeed come down their chimney during the night to bring presents, and then left the same way he had come in.

One theme that permeated many of the stories we received is the joy most people experience when they give; giving of course being love in expression. That theme is represented in every chapter in one way or another, but in Chapter 7, Taking Care of Each Other, Kristine Groskaufmanis delights us with her story "New Year's Eve Warmth." Having just suffered a broken heart, she was in no mood to celebrate anything, and wanted only to hunker down and stay home alone. But her friend would have none of it, and coaxed, coerced and tricked her into finally going out. The lovely experience that followed is artfully told by the author, reminding us all of the healing power of true friendship.

Again on the theme of giving, in The True Meaning of Christmas, Vera C. Teschow touches us with her lovely story "A Canadian 'Family' Christmas." As an only child, after losing her mother to cancer two days before Christmas, she realized she needed to create a new kind of Christmas in her home. At the time, she and her husband were volunteering at a local refugee reception centre, so the following Christmas they decided to participate in a program of inviting a refugee family into their home for a Canadian Christmas dinner. But instead of inviting just one, they opened their home to as many families as could get there. The turkey was donated, and she and her husband prepared the rest. On Christmas Day twenty-five refugees along with friends and volunteers filled their home, bringing the total count to over thirty. Gifts donated by local businesses ensured that every person in the room had at least one Christmas present with their name on it under the tree. Vera says what I know I feel in my heart each time I read her story — that sharing her home with thirty-two strangers turned out to be the best Christmas experience she ever had.

While Vera Teschow had thirty-two visitors in her home that Christmas, in the chapter Angels in Our Midst, veteran Canadian media personality Don Jackson has a different kind of story to share about "Mysterious Visitors." It seems that while his wife Lydia was in labour with their first child, his father passed away before he was able to meet his new granddaughter. Now, in their home, once each year at Christmas, the front door opens and closes of its own accord admitting what Don and Lydia believe is the essence of his father—come to visit. Beautifully written by one of Canada's foremost storytellers, I know you will love Don's touching contribution to this lovely collection of stories as much as I do.

No matter what Christmas tradition you come from, I hope you will find some time this busy holiday season to enjoy these stories. You may choose to read some of them out loud, and share them with your children and your family. Just so you know, Chicken Soup for the Soul's Christmas books are always appropriate for young readers or listeners—we all work closely with Santa to keep the magic alive.

I hope you will enjoy *Chicken Soup for the Soul: Christmas in Canada* as much we enjoyed gathering these stories together for you. From our family to yours, we wish you a very Merry Christmas, Happy Hanukkah, and the best New Year's ever!

~Janet Matthews
Aurora, Ontario

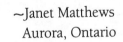

Chapter
1

Christmas in Canada

The Spirit of Christmas

Christmas, when observed with the right spirit, still has the power to call miracles from Heaven to Earth.

~Richelle E. Goodrich, Smile Anyway

I Was a Teenaged Reindeer

Christmas is perhaps the only time in the year when people
can obey their natural impulses and express their true sentiments without
feeling self-conscious and, perhaps, foolish.
~Francis C. Farley

I always wanted to be Santa Claus. When it's Christmas and you're in the make-believe business, who doesn't want to be the big guy? But as a gangly teenager—six foot two inches and maybe 170 pounds, even covered in a funny animal outfit—I was definitely built more like Rudolph.

My costumed adventures started when I was looking for my first job out of high school. Something impressive, I thought, something that suited my skills. Then I spotted this classified ad. The perfect job. Singing telegrams.

I arrived at the office of a company called Big One Fantasy and the place was filled with helium tanks and balloons and a whole bunch of oversized cartoon animal costumes. I was in love. I wanted this job.

The guy at the desk who looked a bit like Jimmy Cagney barely glanced up. "Who are you?"

"I'm Mark," I said.

"Mark, have you ever been a gorilla before?"

"No."

Then Cagney jumped up, said "This is what gorillas do," and proceeded to dance gorilla-style around the room occasionally stopping to scratch his armpits.

"And if you really want the crowd to go crazy sniff someone's pant leg. And if you see a bald guy, rub his head. Slays 'em every time."

"Got it," I said.

"And if the bald guy's wearing glasses, take the glasses and put them on top of his head. Never fails. I need you downtown in fifteen minutes. Just remember one thing—gorillas do not talk. Ever." Then he handed me the costume and a bouquet of balloons.

"Give these to Gary and sing 'Happy Birthday' to him."

"But I don't talk."

"Never."

"But I do sing 'Happy Birthday.'"

"You got it."

I grabbed the balloons, hopped in my car, raced to the Hyatt Hotel in downtown Vancouver, put on the gorilla suit, and ran into the ballroom where I couldn't believe my luck. Gary was bald and wore glasses.

I jumped around the room, I sniffed some pant legs, I rubbed the birthday boy's head, then topped his cranium with his glasses. The crowd went wild.

Gary was thrilled with me. But when I got back to the office the tall blond surfer dude standing next to Cagney wasn't.

"I'm Marc," he said.

It turns out I was not the Mark they were looking for.

The other Marc was a seasoned gorilla and he showed up thirty seconds after I ran off with the suit. So I not only had a new job, I had a new nemesis.

That summer Marc and I both worked almost non-stop.

I was a gorilla, a bunny rabbit, a chicken, a bear, a valentine. And the job was so much fun, and paid so well that I stuck around after summer was over. I was still dressing up when it was time for the Stanley Cup finals of the costumed critter biz: Christmas.

Since I was too svelte to play the real Christmas star, and too tall for elf-hood, Cagney handed me the costume for one of Santa's bigger helpers: Frosty.

"Snowmen can talk," he said.

I waded out into the crowd at the Bayshore Hotel and a bunch of little kids who were going to get everything they wanted for Christmas. One of the adorable little tykes who looked like a ten-year-old Jimmy Cagney came over and said, "Hey Frosty, sing us the Frosty song."

I hadn't heard the Frosty song since I was this kid's age, so I said, "Maybe we can sing it together."

The kid looked up at me and sneered. "No. *You* sing the Frosty song."

Great. "Uh… Frosty the Snowman was a very jolly soul. With a corncob pipe and a button nose and two eyes made out of coal." Yes!

"Keep going," he said.

By now a crowd was gathering, a Christmas mob.

"Frosty the Snowman was a really happy guy. With a carrot nose and a stovetop hat, and two corncobs for his eyes. Then one foggy Christmas Eve, Santa came to say, Frosty, with your nose so bright, would you guide my sleigh tonight."

And that's when the kid declared, "That's not Frosty," and the crowd disappeared to poke Santa's belly.

So, I was not exactly thrilled when I found out my next Christmas gig was at a downscale mall on Vancouver's Eastside. These kids were not gonna get everything they wanted for Christmas.

This time I was set to play Rudolph. The good news—I knew the Rudolph song. But just as I was getting ready to walk into the mall, Cagney came over to tell me, "Reindeer don't talk. Santa doesn't want to be upstaged." Great.

The other thing reindeer couldn't do? See. The mask had no peripheral vision. I stumbled out of the dressing room into the mall, trying not to bump into anything and, just as I reached the Christmas Village, I felt something grab my leg.

I looked down and saw a little three- or four-year-old ball of adorableness. And he looked up at me and shouted, "Rudoff!"

What could I do? I couldn't say anything. I could barely move without accidentally punting my pint-sized admirer. The only thing I could think of…

I knelt down and let the kid hug me.

As soon as the kid let go I started to get up, then another kid threw his arms around me, then another, then another — all shouting, "Rudolph! Rudolph!" And they were all at exactly that age when they were over the moon because Santa was coming on Christmas Eve in a sleigh pulled by eight reindeer. With Rudolph guiding the way…

Finally, it was time for my break so I got up and made my way back to our dressing room, glowing with Christmas cheer. But when I finally removed my mask, Marc and Cagney were furious. Not only didn't they like the little kids hugging me, they weren't particularly keen on kids.

After promising that I wouldn't let anyone else hug me, ever, the mall manager stormed into the dressing room shouting, "Where's Rudolph?"

The other two guys looked straight at me and I knew what this meant: I was so fired. And that's when the mall boss said, "Get back out there! All the little kids are asking for Rudolph!"

I put on my Rudolph head, stumbled back to Santa's Village, knelt down and let the little kids climb all over me. And that afternoon I knew just what it felt like to be Santa Claus.

~Mark Leiren-Young
Vancouver, British Columbia

Under One Roof

Christmas waves a magic wand over this world, and behold,
everything is softer and more beautiful.
~Norman Vincent Peale

On the day of my fourteenth birthday, in late October 2013, a huge winter storm rolled in as if from thin air. So instead of celebrating outside around our backyard fire pit the way we'd done the year before I had to move my party inside our small Toronto bungalow. Then, on the heels of the chill that disrupted my birthday came a frost that covered the lawns in early November. It was our first sign of the long, cold winter ahead. By mid-November, snow already covered the porches and driveways of Toronto homes. Although it was early, I was absolutely delighted because I loved snow. It was already starting to feel like Christmas!

I was in my first year of high school, majoring in vocal at a special school for the performing arts. It was now mid-December, and our annual Christmas Concert was finally finished. This followed weeks of high tension and struggles simply getting to, and especially home from late rehearsals because of the intense early winter weather, and the continuous, large quantities of snow. Every morning I would wake up surprised to find it had snowed yet again. The holiday season was finally in full gear, and everyone in my family was ready for the Christmas break.

Despite the excitement of Christmas fast approaching, people around me were getting edgy. As the presents and parties grew in numbers, so did the fears that a power outage could occur at any time. Short summer outages in Toronto aren't uncommon, but losing power in the summer seemed more of an inconvenience than a hardship. A day or two of barbequing was fun, and my family found it was a good excuse to go camping at Sauble Beach!

This time it was different. The snow was piling up, the thermometer showed negative numbers, and worst of all was the biting wind chill. With all this non-stop snow the possibility of losing electricity was becoming a real concern. A power outage in winter meant no heat, no lights, no cooking—and often no hot water. And there would definitely be no barbequing outside, or going camping to escape. I began reconsidering my thoughts about snow and how much I loved it.

It was the Saturday before Christmas when the freezing rain started. I woke up to a cold house and an eerie silence. My dad is an electrician and a sound engineer, so our home is filled with electronic devices that announce things—like the house is at the right temperature. But the house was silent... and cold. It had finally happened.

When my parents told me that most of Toronto was without power and covered in ice, I had no clue what to do. So, being a lazy teenager, I decided to just sleep through it. I figured it would last an hour at most. Hopefully by the time I woke up from my nap the lights and the heat would be back on. Surely people wouldn't be able to last long without heat in these temperatures. I just assumed the city was already doing everything they could to restore the electricity. Like everyone else I could only hope.

Miraculously, in our home, that hope was fulfilled! Suddenly, after only a few hours, the electricity in six houses on my street, including ours, came back on, bringing this small strip of neighbourhood back to life. We were so thankful to once again have power, and along with it lights and heat, and the ability to take a hot shower and cook a meal. Unfortunately, this wasn't the case for everyone.

When I tried to keep in touch with my friends I discovered their cellphones and laptops were all dying. One friend told me that recharging his phone meant going to a mall (or someplace else with power) and sitting on a wet floor. After three days the freezing rain finally stopped, but the streets were now littered with fallen trees and broken branches all coated with ice. And they continued to fall. Then the temperatures plummeted, causing everything to freeze solid. Then it started snowing again on top of the ice, making driving and walking conditions even more treacherous.

Over the days leading up to Christmas Eve many people came in and out of our home to find shelter from the bitter cold for a few hours, or just hang around to charge their phones. Their own homes were still cold, and without lights or hot water. My family was more than thrilled with all the company.

By the time Christmas Eve arrived on Wednesday, our small bungalow was packed with at least fifteen people from four different families, along with friends of mine and two of my sister's classmates. Their homes had now been dark and cold for five days. Again, the snow fell heavily that night. Desperate for relief, friends and neighbours streamed into our home seeking refuge—and my folks welcomed them all.

In our small living room we all shared stories over cups of coffee and hot chocolate. Children ran around and, after bringing their presents from their own homes, they set them under our Christmas tree hoping that even though they weren't at home Santa would still find them. Late Christmas Eve my house turned into a motel, with people sleeping on anything that looked relatively comfortable. Despite the reason, it felt so intimate spending Christmas Eve with so many people in such a compact space. When everyone was finally settled, beds, couches, even padded chairs were covered with balls of comforters. It was just one big sleepover!

I gave up my double bed to a couple who hadn't slept well in days. One of my sister's classmates slept in the second bed in her room, and I slept on the floor between them. Knowing that everyone in the house was snug and warm for the first time in many days allowed me to do that with a lot more acceptance. I hadn't had to deal with the cold and discomfort that they had.

I woke up early that Christmas morning to a house full of happy faces from a proper night of sleep in a warm house. Someone had brought a real evergreen wreath and the fragrance permeated the room. There was heat, and light, and water to wash sleepy faces. The huge breakfast made by the combined efforts of all the parents filled everyone with laughter and joy. Christmas morning is always magical, but opening my presents that morning with other teens and younger kids and everyone still in their pyjamas made Christmas seem more magical than ever. My mom had back-up gifts on hand which she gave to my sister's classmates so they had something to open as well. With everybody warm and full and laughing and hugging, overnight my family had turned from four people into fifteen. I don't remember ever before having such a heart-warming feeling. It was extraordinary!

That experience was a real turning point for me. Before this I hadn't really thought about Christmas in such an intimate way. And even though this amazing experience came out of hardship and misfortune, it renewed for me, and still does, the magic of Christmas that I'd had as a small child. Whenever I think of Christmas now, it includes the memory of the smell of sweet evergreen, hot chocolate, piles of snow and the laughter of many—all under one roof. This experience brought me face to face with the true spirit of Christmas.

~Alexa Danielle Patino
Toronto, Ontario

Christmas Elves

I slept and I dreamed that life is all joy. I woke and I saw that
life is all service. I served and I saw that service is joy.
~Khalil Gibran

When my husband Ray and I were still newlyweds, there were a few forlorn Christmas seasons with just the two of us. Then, in early fall, a new family moved into our little town in central Alberta and they attended our church. There was Mom, Dad and about six kids, all under the age of ten. I learnt that Dad was a labourer and Mom stayed at home with the four youngest kids, while the older ones attended school.

It was obvious there was not a lot of money for extras for this family. In November I overheard the eldest girl saying she wanted a Cabbage Patch doll for Christmas. This was quickly followed by the unkind words of two church ladies who were struggling to find just such a doll for their own children: "Not going to happen." Those Cabbage Patch dolls were hugely popular that year, and selling out everywhere.

"Well, why not?" I thought. Commuting to Edmonton for work, I felt sure I could find just such a treasure. But it turned out to be not an easy quest. I began casting farther afield and enlisted the help of family and friends to widen the search.

Meanwhile Ray and I began making sure we sat close to the family in church, and shamelessly spied on them to discover what else might be needed for Christmas. We soon realized that everything was on the list. Again, we enlisted the help of our closest friends—two other young couples, also as yet without children. Everyone was given a list and, of course, the first item on all the lists was that Cabbage Patch doll.

I took on the task of making Christmas stockings and filling them. My spying paid off in garnering the names of all the family members, and another friend kindly embroidered the names on the stockings for us. I had fun finding all kinds of wonderful small toys, books, crayons, puzzles and candy for the stockings.

Ray took on the task of overseeing the gifts for each child. Our friends, Paul and Karen, helped him out with this. Bruce and Sue took on the task of putting together a traditional Christmas food hamper with a turkey, cooked ham, cranberry sauce, potatoes, vegetables, fruit, and lots of home baking. Their goal was to make sure that family ate well for weeks.

The quest for the Cabbage Patch doll was proving difficult. I did find and purchase a Cabbage Patch doll set that consisted of a child-sized doll carrier and baby bottle. Meanwhile the toys for all the other children had been gathered so we began gift-wrapping. But it was now December 19th and we were becoming anxious about that doll. I began thinking we'd have to make one. But while I was a good tailor, I had never ventured into sewing crafts and did not think I could pull it off. Nevertheless, determined to fulfill this child's wish I went to the fabric store and then to the Army & Navy store for thread.

Guess what I found there? Yes, the Cabbage Patch doll! I couldn't believe it! Choosing the best one of the four on the shelf, I could barely let go of it to pay at the cash register, and drove home elated. As I had already purchased the fabric, I then made up a little coat and an extra outfit for the doll.

Our next problem was how to deliver everything. Ray suggested we package it all up in big boxes. "We can probably sneak it onto their front step," he said.

We decided everyone would meet at our place Christmas Eve, and we'd make our delivery together. Bruce and Sue arrived in their pickup truck with Paul and Karen squished into the cab with them.

The food hamper was packed into three boxes in the back. Bruce also had a Christmas tree, totally decorated with ornaments and lights, tied in the back of his truck. Karen and Paul had filled a few extra boxes with warm coats, sweaters, mittens and scarves for everyone.

"Just in case they don't have one," Bruce explained, catching me staring at the tree. After we loaded the five boxes of gifts and stockings into the back of his pickup, Bruce covered everything with a tarp. We followed them in our car across town. It then began to snow and we became anxious, worrying if our boxes would keep everything dry.

When we arrived at the house, the only light we could see came from the kitchen. Through the window, we could see Dad sitting there, looking dejected.

Very quietly we sneaked everything onto the front steps. There were three boxes of food with candy and bright cookie tins on top, then five boxes of toys and four boxes of clothing sitting on the steps. We placed the Christmas tree, ready to be plugged in, at the bottom of the steps.

Giggling, we ran back to our vehicles. The snow was still falling. Bruce honked his horn.

The house remained dark. We honked our horn and Bruce answered with his. No action. After fifteen minutes we finally pulled away and met on the main street. We walked over to the truck and Ray phoned on speakerphone.

"Hello," answered the dad.

"There's a package of toys on your front step for the children," Ray said.

The voice at the other end picked up immediately.

"Who's this? Santa Claus?"

Ray was grinning from ear to ear. He repeated that there was a package on the front steps for them.

The voice on the other end of the phone had totally come alive.

"Why Dasher!" he said. "I was not expecting your call."

We now could hear movement in the house. Dad's excitement obviously was contagious.

"You say there's a parcel on the steps?"

"Yes, well, the chimney is old in this house."

We could now hear children's voices, and Dad moving across the room and opening the front door. There was a hush, and then a huge shriek with the children all talking at once.

"There's even a tree!" one of them shouted excitedly.

Dad came back on the line, his voice faltering.

"God bless you."

Ray hung up then. Abashed now by the emotions we had heard over the phone, we quietly said our goodnights and returned home.

The next morning, all six of us went to church for the Christmas Day service and sat about two rows behind the family. All of them seemed to glow, standing proudly, and at peace in their world. I noticed that Dad wore a coat for the first time to church. And the little girl had that Cabbage Patch doll strapped in its baby carrier, and was as attentive to it as any new mother. That image continues to warm my heart every Christmas Day, along with the memory of the happiness on all our faces as we realized the full impact of our actions.

And while we certainly enjoyed our Christmas brunch together after church, it wasn't the gift exchange that kept us smiling and regaling each other with stories. No, it was the recounting of the hunt for the Cabbage Patch doll, Bruce's inspiration to get a tree and decorate it, and the baking and gathering of warm clothing for others who needed it. Our shared experience of giving had brought Christmas to life for us in a way it had never been before.

~Jan Piers
Edmonton, Alberta

A Christmas Dream

Canada is not a starting point, it's a goal.
~Jean-Claude Falardeau

It's stinking hot in KwaZulu-Natal. And drizzling. The air thick. My skin clammy. Our two children sit playing on the parquet flooring next to our South African Christmas tree, the tree we bought in a box ten years ago. Decorations are the dream of Canada. White cotton wool balls nestled between lifeless pine needles. A small red plastic bird. A knitted snowman with a black stitched grin.

I walk over to the tree; pull out a miniature brass wreath with the word "Peace" engraved on it. I caress the words gently between my fingers. I want peace. And our transfer to Canada will bring it.

South Africa has no diplomatic ties with Canada at this point and immigration is impossible unless my husband's company transfers us. The company is reluctant. Its local staff is shrinking. Only magic can save us.

Out the corner of my eye I see the living room curtain ripple. Just once. I draw it open. Little rivers of raindrops trickle down the glass behind the burglar guards. Tears for a country lost.

We have sold our family home and are renting a townhouse. We are portable. And we wait. For days, weeks, months. I try to imagine Canadian life. Do people there spend a lot of time outdoors? How many fireplaces does each house have? Do Mounties patrol the streets? Is there dust there? And how cold is cold, really?

Restlessness brews in South Africa. May Day brings a tension, hanging thick in the air like the time before a storm. Pressure, power, passion. Change is coming and there will be thunder.

Finally, we leave South Africa during the African winter. Twenty-five degrees. I love my homeland but I don't look back.

We arrive in damp dismal England where we visit the Canadian Embassy every morning to see if our Canadian work permit papers have arrived. We are stuck in no man's land with two little children clinging to our hands on the overcrowded tube trains. Two weeks later we board the plane for Toronto and arrive during the Canadian summer.

The hot months are spent outdoors. In local and provincial parks, in lakes, and back yards. In no time at all the children have acquired Canadian accents, we have a new baby on the way, my husband is working and our feet are planted firmly on our new land. We buy a link home that doesn't have even one fireplace and yes, although I don't come across any Mounties, there is tons of dust.

Cold comes. And now we know what it is. Our noses tingle. Our denim jeans freeze against our skin. What a strange feeling! And then comes the snow, that first sprinkling in November. I scream to the kids, who rush outside and try to scrape it together. The neighbours start gathering to watch.

We jump right into winter in the north… skating, sleigh rides, and tobogganing. Cuddling under down-filled duvets with hot chocolate to watch TV specials.

The Sears Christmas Catalogue arrives and my six-year-old son gets to work on his letter to Father Christmas—sorry, I mean "Santa."

"Dear Santa, How is Mrs. Claus? Please can you bring me 75849a, 75929b, 87332a…"

We have a lot still to learn about this festive time in Canada.

It's just a few days until Christmas and memories of South Africa seem distant. Blurry. A time of days long gone.

Children's giggles come from their rooms. I stroke my pregnant belly. The smell of gingerbread wafts in the air. The grocery cupboard is stocked and I am ready for the season. I walk over to the window and look outside.

The world is snow covered, fresh and white, iced onto lampposts and sagging green pines. All gleaming in the late afternoon light. A bright red cardinal hops onto the fence, shakes, and cocks its head as if listening intently. A round cheerful snowman sits in the front yard. Carrot nose, long woolly scarf, pom-pom hat. A crooked twiggy grin on his face. A huge Christmas wreath adorns the front door of the house across the street with the word "Peace" written below it.

Our South African Christmas tree has been brought to life.

A magic wand has been waved over the world and everything is beautiful, perfect. And free.

~Lesley Marcovich
Newmarket, Ontario

Christmas in Cadotte Lake

Every gift which is given, even though it be small,
is in reality great, if it is given with affection.
~Pindar

Decades ago I taught in Cadotte Lake, an impoverished Métis Colony located close to Peace River in northwestern Alberta. There seemed little sense of their culture, with no traditional dancing or clothing, nor signs of a connection to the spirituality of their ancestors. Some could not even speak their Cree language. It was as if they had been displaced when an oil company moved them off their original land.

I was young, naïve and unprepared for this life. I was friendly, but wary, and the community took a "watch and wait" attitude towards me. In my classroom, I felt overwhelmed. Teacher training had not prepared me for a room with three grades, five age groups and ten learning levels. One little girl named Harriet spent the first few days with her head on her desk looking defiant and I wanted to follow suit. Lesson preparation was a puzzle with missing pieces. I used the materials provided by the district, but soon found it easier and more fitting to teach through instinct and base my lessons on my students' world. My superiors didn't approve, but my kids did learn that year.

One example of their learning was evident when the principal stopped by and was speaking quietly to me. A student called out, directing my attention to a gathering of animals that were migrating across the lake. After the principal left, we grabbed our boots and coats and headed outside for a closer look at this incredible sight. The kids explained why the creatures must be wolves, as coyotes don't travel in packs. This was one of the many lessons on nature that I was taught by my students that year. We used journals regularly, as I felt instinctively that they were better teaching tools than textbooks, which the students could not relate to much of the time. Through journaling, they learned self-expression, developed writing skills, and found ways to describe the beauty in the world around them, something I was finally beginning to see with their guidance. I was not deliberately rejecting the ways of the school district, just finding my own path.

One of my most significant and touching memories was of our Christmas together. Decorating the classroom drew in all of the kids. With few supplies in the school, I relied on memories from my own childhood to get the fun started with simple materials. Bells were made from egg cartons and tin foil. Tin foil also made glittering angels. We made pretty chains with red and green paper that I scrounged from the nearly empty supply cabinet. Whiffs of glue mingled with marker and crayon and wafted through the air, riding on the excitement of the kids as they worked. Most were very artistic and I was always amazed by their ability to create beauty. As they worked, they switched between English and Cree. Grins and sixteen pairs of brown eyes shone like Christmas lights. They were in awe of their Christmas-making. I was in awe of them.

On the day we were all going to hunt for a tree, a boy brought an axe from home. This would never happen in urban life, but these kids were well practiced in the safe chopping of wood. Off we went in search of the perfect tree. I don't remember asking if they had ever had a tree before but in retrospect I don't think it was part of their Christmas. This is not sad, just different. They didn't put icing on cakes either. The small community had a simple lifestyle and I accepted their ways of doing things.

Laughter and carols mixed in with the crunching of snow as we walked. Santa was only mentioned in song, as he was never found in Cadotte Lake. Little was said about the Christian basis of the holiday, though I touched on it through song and story. Many kids had been introduced to Christianity and the story of Baby Jesus, but formal religion was not part of their everyday lives and conversion was not my role. We kept things simple, but joyous. I am sure Jesus would have approved.

We found the perfect tree and the grade five boys took turns with an axe, cutting it down. Back it came with us, leaving a trail of green needles on the pure and crisp white snow. It was propped against the school and we headed inside for a hot lunch. The next day, we brought the tree inside and I popped it into an old metal garbage can that was almost green. The fresh scent of evergreen added to the festivities as we went to work. Paper chains were hung on the tree and around the room. Christmas balls and bells, stars and angels were placed carefully on the tree. The work that everyone had put into the creations made everything so bright and cheery. Happy chatter and more singing completed the atmosphere. I had never seen them look so happy. Nor had I felt so happy since driving into the community that first day, to experience things I could never have expected.

On the day before Christmas break, everyone arrived full of excitement. I had grown accustomed to the morning ruckus, but it was different that day. Kids dropped off coats and boots and hustled into the classroom. They smiled at me, and then suddenly all was quiet. They stared and whispered, then quickly flew to their seats. They had spotted tiny gifts that had been wrapped and placed under their beautiful tree. They had no idea what to say or to expect. I was the only one smiling as I took in their sense of wonder. Gifts were not unheard of, but this way was different. They sat, squirming in anticipation of what would happen next.

"I bet it's books," Stacey shouted with an intense look on his face. Nobody laughed and I shook my head. When they could wait no longer, I called each child up to accept a tiny package. Wrappings were gone even before they made it to their desks and, judging by their reactions, they were well pleased with the tiny gifts I had selected. I stood and watched. It was my turn to be speechless. There was so much to take in that magic is the only word that comes to mind, as

I relive the best moments of that year. They were thrilled with little combs, pens shaped like tools, fancy note pads and other small items. Their excited chatter almost rattled the windows, as they compared their treasures. It became a hum, like a furnace spreading a warm glow between the children, through the room and into my heart. That was their gift to me. I returned to the front of the classroom. No words were used to thank me for these small offerings. It came through those eyes and those smiles; the joy that bound us together. Over thirty years later, it is still the best Christmas I have ever had.

~Paula Gillis
Edmonton, Alberta

Secret Santa

Sometimes beautiful things come into our lives out of nowhere. We can't always understand them, but we have to trust in them. I know you want to question everything, but sometimes it pays to just have a little faith.
~Lauren Kate

I was scrambling again. It was Sunday, December 10th, my brother's fortieth birthday party, and I was struggling, as usual. The kids and I were trying to get out the door and on our way to this family celebration, but my mind was spinning a bit. Okay a lot. It was overflowing with worries and concerns about the upcoming holidays, and just how I was going to guide us through them.

Freelance employment sounds very appealing in theory, but the financial reality can frequently be daunting. I'd had very little work in the previous few months. We'd been on our own for about two years, having finally managed to escape a life filled with controlling abuse and violence. I had expected — or at least hoped for — life to be less challenging by now, but in fact, it had become overwhelming. I had been running on pure adrenaline for the last few years, keeping myself incredibly busy with family court, criminal court, lawyers and custody assessors. That was in addition to being busy with work, raising two beautiful children, maintaining a house and focusing on everyone else's struggles. I would find myself counselling friends, nursing sick or injured neighbours, finding employment for my peers and coming to the rescue of just about anyone I came in contact with. For some reason I felt a responsibility to help solve problems and ease the struggles of others. This made me feel good of course, but it also allowed me to avoid focussing on my own problems. Tending to others left me no time to think about myself, and that's the way I liked it.

This was an unusual day because my own challenges were finally consuming me. Work had slowed down and I wasn't even sure how I would pay the mortgage, let alone create a Christmas. As I was preparing to visit my family my thoughts were full of kids' Christmas lists, Santa visits, how I would pay my bills and even just buy groceries this month. Successfully leaving a destructive family situation with my kids intact had made me realize that I am much stronger than I'd ever realized, but on this day I was not feeling strong at all; I was worn down and very worried.

As the kids slipped on their boots and coats I opened the door to go start the car. And that's when I saw it. Stuck between my old wooden door and the storm door was a cardboard FedEx envelope. I hadn't heard anyone come to the door, so I peeked my head outside hoping the driver might still be out front. The street was quiet. I was not expecting anything, and I was trying to recall if FedEx even delivered on Sunday. I turned the envelope over to examine the packing slip. The sender had addressed it to my married last name (and misspelled it) but it was clearly meant for me. I noticed the sender's name listed as "Saint Nick from 'Northern Products.'" The return address was latitude 0.00 longitude 180.00, Baffin Island Post. Obviously this was a gag gift. The contents description read "Christmas making products."

I zipped it open and found two smaller envelopes inside. One, a small manila bubble wrap envelope, and the other a crisp white letter sized envelope that read "Merry Christmas Suzanne." The script was large, flowing and artistically beautiful. I didn't recognize the handwriting, but marvelled at the penmanship. I opened this envelope first and found a typewritten note signed "The Spirit of Christmas."

My Dear Suzanne,
Well, over the last year you have truly captured the market on giving

to others, almost to a point that I did not have a job. Well, enough giving, it is now time to receive.

Your kindness and caring of this world around you and your family are exemplary. You need to know it does not go unobserved or unappreciated by those who receive your kindness but also by those who observe your unconditional giving.

In your heart and in your soul there exists such a priceless love for all, even though life's trials and tribulations sometimes can wear one down. The fact that you could stay true to your heart and do the best you could is an example of how special you truly are.

I hope you do not mind me dropping off your gift now, in order to help you do, what comes so natural to you—GIVING.

I know that with this gift, your first thoughts will be what you can do for those you love. Please, do what comes naturally and I hope you will.

However, there is one stipulation that goes with this Christmas gift and it is not negotiable! I know it may be hard for you to do, I know it will go against your natural spirit, but this Christmas, just this Christmas, I also want you to give to the most difficult person for you to give to, YOU!!

Wishing you, family, friends and all dear to you the very best and God's blessings in the year to come.

From The Spirit of Christmas

I was overwhelmed by these words. The writer was correct in knowing I was much more comfortable as a giver, and found receiving very difficult. I quickly opened the bubble wrap envelope and found a fistful of cash—much more than I had seen for some time. I did a quick count. Two thousand dollars. My mortgage payment. The kids had been standing with me through this entire experience. It felt like a long time, when in fact it had been only a few moments. The kids were confused. Santa had been here? My mind was racing. Who was this Spirit of Christmas? My family lived in another city and as we were on our way to see them, I knew it couldn't be from them. I have some beautiful friends, but none were in a financial position to be so generous. I do have a couple of people in my life in a position to do such a thing, but not only is it not in their character, I doubt them capable of writing from the heart the way this writer had done.

After the excitement of that day had passed, I spent many days trying to track down my Secret Santa to no avail. I was baffled. My family was baffled. My friends were baffled. Finally my mother's wise words made me stop searching. She pointed out how the sender had obviously gone to a great deal of trouble to remain anonymous, and it was not my place to take away his/her pleasure in giving by exposing them.

Realizing she was right, I put a public "thank you" status on my Facebook page. No explanation. Just thank you. If my Secret Santa happened to be a Facebook friend I hoped he recognized the message as being for him. I desperately wanted to thank my benefactor, for this person had truly made a difference in my life. Not only was I able to provide Christmas for my children without worrying about the immediate bills being paid, I managed to honour the condition to give to myself by—for the first time in my life—turning down work during the holidays so I could actually enjoy some family time. That was the best Christmas gift ever.

But in addition to those immediate and intended gifts I now carry this incredibly renewed faith in my fellow man. I have literally carried this symbol of faith with me now for six years. Both the handwritten envelope containing the heartfelt letter and FedEx packing slip go with me everywhere. If at any point I'm having an overwhelming day, I have only to look at the envelope or slip my hand in my bag to touch it and I feel better. It makes me smile. It reminds me to have faith. It reminds me to believe in the Spirit of Christmas, and of course to continue to share, with gratitude, my blessings with others.

~Suzanne Lindsay
Toronto, Ontario

Lela's First Christmas

It takes hands to build a house, but only hearts can build a home.
~Author Unknown

When I first met Jesse, I knew he had a three-and-a-half-year-old daughter somewhere in Indonesia. Lela lived with her mother and, believing she was well cared for, Jesse sent generous monthly support. As our relationship progressed into a life partnership, Jesse and I talked about going together to visit Lela. But I could never have guessed that this unknown child would become my cherished daughter.

On September 8, 2012, Jesse received a shocking letter from an Australian missionary in a small Indonesian village informing him that Lela had somehow been abandoned, and was now living hand to mouth on the streets. Horrified, we immediately made arrangements to fly to Indonesia. I knew that if I was going to spend the rest of my life with Jesse, that life would now include Lela, and I had to be part of this. We were determined to bring her home to Canada.

When we arrived, to our joy and amazement, Lela quickly and immediately identified Jesse as her father, and accepted me as her mother. After three long months in Indonesia dealing with the government bureaucracy and immigration laws, frequently despairing that we would ever be successful, we finally gained full custody of Lela. Once we had the necessary documents to allow us to leave with her we began our long journey home. On December 8, 2012, we landed safely on Canadian soil, a day we will never forget.

Having arrived in Canada in December, everywhere we looked we were surrounded by reminders of Christmas, which was fast approaching. Lela, having been born into the Muslim culture, had no concept at all of what Christmas was. Here was this four-year-old little girl with no idea who Santa Claus and his reindeer were, nor the joy they would bring children on Christmas Day.

Luckily, Lela spoke a little English, because her home had been in an area frequented by English-speaking tourists. She quickly learned more, and we spent hours teaching her English.

We also had something else to teach Lela! In the few weeks left before the big day our goal became to teach Lela everything about Christmas that a Canadian child should know. She got to see snow for the very first time on the drive home from the airport. We actually got out of the car with her to make snow angels, and we even built a snowman!

We quickly got a real Christmas tree and decorated it together as a family. It was so much fun to see Lela's pure delight! We sang Christmas carols together, and Lela even got to meet Santa for the very first time. It was amazing how much she absorbed as she watched Christmas movies—completely in awe. She quickly caught on to all the details and fun involved in a Canadian Christmas, including Santa and his elves, and even learned all the names of the reindeer! She was excited to be celebrating a new holiday with her new family, even though she was surrounded by people she had never met. She seemed to adapt to Canada and our holiday traditions right away.

We knew that over the holidays she was going to be meeting a lot of new family members, all of whom had played vital roles in the effort to bring her home. To help prepare her, we began to build the excitement about who was coming with phone calls, and familiarizing her with their faces in photos. No matter who she was introduced to, she immediately welcomed them into her life. She was so excited about all the family she had never met, but who had really always been there.

As we did our Christmas shopping for family and friends and began wrapping the gifts, Lela set aside a shoebox and put it under the tree. As Christmas got closer she would add small items to it: gifts she had already been given, or things from her bedroom. Since we were always shopping for everyone else, she just assumed there would be nothing under the tree for her. Her plan was to just keep adding things to her shoebox so she would have gifts at Christmas too. She never complained or asked where her gifts were; she was happy helping to pick out gifts for the rest of her new family and friends.

Finally, a few days before Christmas, relatives began to arrive to spend the holiday with us. Lela was excited as she sat at the window waiting for people she had never met, but she knew were her family. As soon as they pulled in she ran out with open arms. She knew exactly who everyone was, and was anxious to show them her very own bedroom, and the toys we had accumulated for her since she had arrived. At every meal she would lead the prayer before we ate, insisting that everyone hold hands, and saying, "I love all my family." It was so humbling to see her cherish a simple family dynamic that we had all just taken for granted.

When Christmas morning arrived Lela was up early with the excitement of Santa and Christmas. She first went to the coffee table where we had left a few treats for Santa and a carrot for Rudolph. She immediately commented that they only took a few bites out of everything, and this was a waste so she proceeded to eat the treats and carrot herself. She explained by sharing a nugget of wisdom from her own four years of life, "You should always eat everything you get."

After that, the gift opening began. This happened a lot slower than in most Canadian homes where there are young children. There was no frenzy of ripping open gifts. When she was handed a present she would open it so slowly and carefully. Then, after it was unwrapped, she would just sit there and stare at it, want to open it further or play with it. She was in no rush to move on to the next gift. We would tell her there was more under the tree for her and she would say "for me?" in English, with evidence of her Indonesian language still present. Every time she opened a gift with multiples (like a four-pack of lip balm) she would want to share it with everyone else; this little girl who was so used to having nothing could not understand that four of the same thing were all for her.

After all the gifts were finally opened, and Lela at last understood that there were, indeed, gifts for her under the tree, she took the shoebox and filled it with a few of the items she had just received. When asked what she was doing she replied, "I am going to send these to Indonesia. I got a lot of gifts for Christmas, and my friends there don't have any." It was hard to imagine that this little girl who had come from nothing was willing to give away some of her gifts from her very first Christmas.

Jesse just sat back in awe; this was a day he had long been waiting for. His little girl was finally home in Canada with him, his family circle was growing, and this was going to be the first of many happy Christmases as a family.

~Kendra Rice
Tofino, British Columbia

The Best Gift

Each should give according to what he has decided in his heart,
not grudgingly or under compulsion, for God loves a cheerful giver.
~2 Corinthians 9:7

December 1969 was a bittersweet time for us. Paul and I had been married about four months. Despite a struggle to make ends meet, we delighted in our life together. We lived in an old apartment in central Winnipeg and did our best to put aside some money. Our savings plan was simple—we put our loose change into a bag, which we stowed in the glove compartment of our six-year-old Oldsmobile.

It was a time of economic recession and high unemployment, which affected many, including us. While my husband faced the situation squarely, searched the newspaper ads and headed out to apply for jobs, I was inclined to feel sorry for myself. We had dreamed of much better things.

After a business venture proved unsuccessful, Paul signed up to train as a pots-and-pans salesman. The morning he left for his first training session, I remained alone in our apartment. I completed a few chores and took stock of the food in the cupboard and the refrigerator—a lot of hamburger, wieners and macaroni. We didn't regret the economical groceries, but what bothered me most was the looming fear that we would not be able to buy Christmas gifts for our family. I had been raised on thrift, but not on poverty. I didn't want to face the relatives on Christmas day without gifts. That would mark me as the family loser.

Paul had not planned to come home for lunch, but he surprised me by walking in the door, followed by a thin, fair-haired man in his thirties. He introduced me to Hans, another sales trainee. A friendly, cheerful man, he greeted me cordially and explained he was an immigrant from The Netherlands. He and his family had lived in Canada only a few months. Paul had obviously invited him home to lunch. I served soup and sandwiches, while making a mental note to advise Paul not to bring guests home for meals until we were better off financially.

Later that day, after Paul arrived home, he shared some information with me.

"Linda, we think we are hard up, but Hans and his family have no money to buy groceries. His wife has sugar and flour in the house, so she has been making biscuits for them, but I don't think he has been eating at all. He's leaving all the food for his wife and kids. I couldn't afford to take him to a restaurant, so I brought him home to lunch."

My self-pity vanished in one instant.

My good-hearted and resourceful husband had already made a plan. The next day he drove Hans to the Salvation Army. Hans was embarrassed. "I have never begged for anything before; I have always worked."

"Let me do the talking," advised Paul. "Pretend you don't speak English."

The Salvation Army worker listened sympathetically as Paul told of his friend's hardship; he willingly offered a food voucher. Next the two men went shopping. Paul, who was more comfortable in a grocery store, chose healthy vegetables, fruit, meat and milk.

At Hans' small rented house, his wife Anna and their four lively children were overwhelmed with surprise. Now they would have well-rounded meals, certainly better than eating biscuits all the time.

Since pots-and-pans sales were not as brisk as the two men had hoped, they turned their attention back to job applications. When

Paul and I visited Hans and Anna two days before Christmas, Hans had good news. He had found work in his field of building maintenance, and his job would start on Christmas Day.

By this time the Salvation Army groceries were depleted. Hans, as usual, was unwilling to ask for handouts. Paul had no such qualms.

"I'm going to the Christmas Cheer Board tomorrow and ask them for a hamper for you," he said. "That will give you food for few more days. Why don't you ask your employer for an advance on your pay?"

"Would he do that?" asked Hans with surprise.

"If you explained why you need it, he would probably give it to you. It doesn't hurt to ask."

The next morning, true to his word, Paul and I drove to the Christmas Cheer Board office. Unfortunately, we learned they had just sent out the last hamper.

Disappointed, we went back to the car, and headed out of town on our planned visit to my parents' home.

"I feel bad," remarked Paul sadly. "I wish we had something to give them."

I glanced at the glove compartment. "We have the money that we saved," I said brightly. I opened the glove compartment, pulled out the bag of change, and started to count it.

"There's over seventeen dollars here," I announced. "Let's go shopping."

It was enough to buy a bag of groceries. We stopped at a market and purchased a small turkey, fruit, vegetables and milk, as well as a bag of candy canes for the children. With happy hearts, we took them to our friends.

They received our gift with both relief and gratitude.

Hans quietly led Paul into another room. "You don't know how much this means to us," he said when they were alone. "I was ready to go out and rob a grocery store."

After a short visit we continued our journey out of town, with a feeling of contentment. It was the only gift we gave that Christmas, a small present from one penniless family to another. To our regret, we had no gifts to offer our family members, but looking back from more prosperous times, we realize that the small bag of food that we gave to Hans and Anna and their children that day was without question the best gift we have ever given.

~Linda M. Carpentier
Swan River, Manitoba

A Simple Gift of Song

There is nothing in the world so much like prayer as music is.
~William P. Merrill

Christmas, for my family, was a magical time, and our home was filled every day of the season with the music of Christmas. In my early teens I discovered, quite by accident, that I was very musically inclined. My parents ensured this was developed and one of the instruments I learned to play was the flute. I learned to play classical, jazz and other styles and grew as a musician throughout my teens. During this time a new and exciting "folk group" had been introduced at our church. I didn't consider myself to be a singer, but I longed to play my flute with this group. One day my opportunity came.

I was at the church when I happened upon the leader of the group, Cora. When I told her I played the flute she responded, "I'd love to hear it." I immediately left the church, climbed the ten-foot fence behind it, crossed the five sets of railway tracks between the church and my home, and then returned the same way with my flute. I played for her, and she invited me to become part of that ensemble. I was elated.

I loved to play. In classical ensembles, rock bands, school bands... wherever I could play any or all of my instruments. But no situation brought me greater joy than playing with our little church folk group in a suburb of Toronto. And no time of the year was more precious, more wonderful, than playing at the Christmas midnight mass with this group.

Our participation in this service became a tradition for quite a few years. A couple of months before Christmas we would begin to rehearse our Christmas music. We learned traditional carols, and then Cora would introduce something new—or even something very old—to enhance the program. On Christmas Eve we would begin to play before the service as people were arriving, and then we played throughout the service. I can honestly say that nothing has ever matched the sheer joy of this event.

Early in this experience we began to play "What Child Is This?" which is based on the old English folk song "Greensleeves." Each year we would perform it, and I was blessed to play a flute solo between the third and final verses. A simple rendition of the melody, it was very easy to play. For the first couple of years I simply played it, but never noticed anything special.

Then one year, Joe, an elderly member of our church, who I had known for many years, approached me. Joe suffered from a terrible skin affliction that made people avoid him, but I knew there was nothing to fear. A week before Christmas Joe asked, "Are you going to play the flute this year?" I said yes and he continued, "And are you going to play 'What Child Is This?'" and again I answered yes. Then he said, "Peter, when you play that song it just makes Christmas for me." This man was lonely and isolated, but the look in his eyes hit me like a truck at full speed. Somehow this one song that I played a solo verse of each year had come to really mean something to him.

Over the next year, other friends mentioned that "What Child Is This?" and the flute part really meant something to them. One described how the notes would seem to "float above the crowded church," and how everyone seemed to be truly listening when that happened. I wasn't sure how to handle this. This wasn't a complicated or impressive part that I had learned and performed at a conservatory recital, nor was it some glorious original piece that I had composed to great acclaim. This was the melody of an old folk song, performed simply. But when I played this simple tune, it seemed to somehow reach all kinds of people at the Christmas celebration.

Nearly a year after Joe had spoken to me I was sitting with the choir while the Christmas music was being planned. As expected, "What Child Is This?" was again included. I said nothing, but as it was mentioned I found myself overcome with emotion. I felt the strongest bond I had ever felt to a number of people who apparently considered that moment when it was played to be something of a "shining star" over their Christmas. While it was me they thanked, I realized that anyone could have played it. I felt an incredible rise in my heart, that I had been given the privilege of playing this song; I knew this was my gift.

For a few more years I continued to play it, and then I went off on my musical career. About seven years later I returned and reunited with a small group of church friends. For several years we once again provided the music for the Christmas midnight mass. To my great joy "What Child Is This?" was always included, along with my simple flute solo. During my years away I had found my voice, written my own Christmas songs and played a variety of instruments, but nothing meant as much to me as the flute solo in that simple song.

Joe has long since passed, likely now dwelling in the company of He whose birth we celebrate. Cora and I keep in touch, and other friends have come and gone. I now live in the United States but I still keep in touch with some friends at my old church, now surrounded by further suburbs of the growing city of Toronto. Perhaps I can go back one day, even Christmas Day, and once again share that gift of song with friends and family there. The gift of that song has never left me. Like the shining star over Bethlehem, it has guided me to places I never knew possible.

~Peter J. Green
Kenmore, New York

Our Christmas Eve with Max

Wherever there is a human being, there is an opportunity for a kindness.
~Seneca

The year was 1942. Thousands of airmen training in Canada were boarded into private homes, and Max was one of these "aircrafters" who came to our house. He was short, with dark, curly hair and a cheerful smile. His family were Polish immigrants who lived in Sudbury, in Northern Ontario. I was very young, starry-eyed with excitement waiting for Santa to bring me something wonderful, but had to sit quietly as Lorne Greene—The Voice of Doom—read the war news on the radio.

Early on December 24th, Max left for Toronto's Malton airport to fly home for his Christmas leave. He returned with a long face. Mum was ironing and I was drawing with crayons at the kitchen table. My brother Howard, five years older, sat opposite me, gluing a model Spitfire together.

"Bad luck, Mrs. B," Max said, shrugging off his blue uniform greatcoat. "A blizzard has closed every airport in the north. Tomorrow I may get out, but…" He sighed. "I'll eat downtown and go to a movie." He tried for nonchalance, but only looked forlorn. He was eighteen, and had never before been away from home.

"No," said Mum, "you'll stay here with us. There's more than enough."

"Are you sure?" He looked cautious but keen, as if a lifeline thrown his way might be snatched back. "I won't be a bother? I know Christmas Eve dinner is special."

Mum looked at him. "Our big meal is tomorrow. Is tonight's dinner special to your family?"

Max nodded. "It's called *Wigilia*."

Mum put the kettle on, a sign for tea and a chat. "Tell us about it, Max."

His face lit up as he sat at the table. "Well, before dinner, there is *Gwiazdka*—looking for the first star. An extra place at the table and a lit candle in a window invite any wandering stranger to join us." He told of other customs and listed a meatless menu of mushroom soup, fish, and strange-sounding foods like *pierogi*, *babka*, *kartofle*, and *oplatek*.

Max stopped for breath and a cup of tea.

"*Oplatek* is the bread of love," he went on, "thin, square wafers stamped with holy figures. We break the wafers with everyone at the table, and wish them health, wealth, and happiness. Then we eat."

He smiled, drank his tea, and munched shortbread. A soft light glowed in his eyes.

My brother and I had listened, enthralled. "What else do you do?" Howard asked. "After, I mean."

"Well, we sing carols, and then go to a special mass called *Pasterka*, or Shepherds' Mass. That's when animals can talk."

"Wow," Howard breathed. "Did you ever hear any talking?"

Max smiled. "No, and I don't know anyone who has. But that doesn't mean it doesn't happen."

"Gee, I guess not."

"Now, Mrs. B," Max said, rising, "I'll go out and shovel the sidewalks. We didn't get much snow, but enough."

"Thank you, Max," Mum said.

After Max went out, Mum sat for a moment, then grabbed a pencil and paper and began writing. I went back to my crayons and Howard to his Spitfire. In a few minutes, Mum spoke again.

"Howard, you're to go downtown to Despond's Fish store. I'll give you money and a list. Don't tell Max where you're going."

Howard looked up, holding a tiny wheel with tweezers. "Huh?"

Mum smiled. "We're going to give Max his *Wigilia*," she said. "At least, as best we can. Now bundle up well. A bus will be at the corner in a few minutes."

After Howard left, I started setting the dining room table. "Mum," I cried, "there are only five of us. Max said an uneven number was bad luck."

"Don't worry, Patsy. I phoned Mrs. Donaldson, and she's joining us."

I liked Mrs. Donaldson, who lived three houses up from us. Her hair was almost all white and she wore it in a bun at the back. Mr. Donaldson had died recently, and she was alone. She was coming for Christmas dinner tomorrow, along with all our relatives.

So, in the early dark, Max, beaming with surprised delight, lit a candle in the window. Outside, the wind had dropped. In the clear cobalt sky, one star hung glowing in the West. The beauty of it took my breath away.

"That's Venus," Howard said importantly. "Venus is a planet, not a star."

Dad smiled. "Tonight it's our Christmas Star."

Mrs. Donaldson had tears in her eyes. I thought in my young ignorance that the cold caused them.

At the table, we joined hands while Dad said grace. We said amen, and Max made the sign of the cross. For *oplatek*, Mum had graham wafers; big squares that separated into four smaller squares. Max laughed, and called them perfect.

"Like breaking a wishbone," said Howard, breaking his wafer with Mrs. Donaldson. "Health, wealth, and happiness, everybody."

We ate mushroom soup, Despond's fresh fish fried in butter, pickled herring, boiled potatoes, vegetables, and Mum's homemade pickles. Dessert was Spanish Cream and fruitcake. For Max, Mum added a compote of plums, raisins, and apples simmered in a syrup of sugar and cinnamon. Everything was delicious, even the pickled herring.

Max started to thank Mum, but she shushed him. "We thank you, Max, for showing us a wonderfully different aspect of Christmas. I'm glad if it reminded you a little of home."

A strange notion popped into my head. "Max, is your family up in Sudbury eating like this right now?"

"Yes, Patsy, right now."

"Gosh." My imagination suddenly broadened, widening far away. "And your relatives in Poland, are they eating too?"

"Well, time is different there, you know, and the Germans have taken Poland over. But, yes, somehow, they will celebrate too."

I couldn't speak, for my mind had flooded with images. Max's people in Ontario and Poland, looking at the same bright star, sitting at a table, saying the same things, singing carols, thinking of Christmas and of absent loved ones.

Why, they were all just like us. Had some of Max's Polish relatives been forced to flee like the refugees in the newsreels? To me, those scenes had seemed a fantasy, something in a Hollywood movie.

But no, they showed real people, real families. What if Canada was invaded and we had to escape with only what we could carry? How could Mrs. Donaldson manage?

Young as I was, the reality of war had come to me, and I was frightened.

Dad leaned toward me. "Don't worry, Patsy," he said. "You're safe here. Many brave men have gone to fight to keep us safe. Men like Max. Tonight we won't think of fighting, but about the birth of Jesus. Remember his other name?"

"The Prince of Peace," I murmured.

"Then that's what we'll think of—peace."

Soon we were all laughing and singing carols. My fear was gone, and I had grown up a little.

Our Christmas Eve dinners became special, more meaningful, and our mother, as I did later, always made some of the dishes we had that night. Our lives changed a bit for the better after our Christmas Eve with Max.

~Patricia Harrison
New Hamburg, Ontario

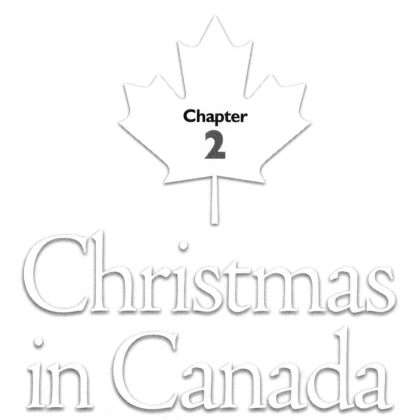

Chapter 2

Christmas in Canada

Holiday Celebrations & Traditions

Happy, happy Christmas, that can win us back to the delusions of our childish days; that can recall to the old man the pleasures of his youth; that can transport the sailor and the traveller, thousands of miles away, back to his own fire-side and his quiet home!

~*Charles Dickens*, The Pickwick Papers

A Christmas Box
Bigger than Me

Unselfish and noble actions are the most radiant pages
in the biography of souls.
~David Thomas

"Christmas won't be a lot this year. Try to be grateful for what you get and set an example for your sisters." I don't know whether my parents actually said this, or whether it was just something that I knew. I was ten years old, living in Calgary, Alberta, the oldest of four girls. I wanted to do my best to help my sisters enjoy celebrating Christ's birth, and be together as a family. I wanted to show them how to be kind and have joy.

I also wanted to help my parents understand that I wouldn't be unhappy on Christmas morning, even if there were very few presents. I knew we had enough funds for our needs, but my father had just finished optometry school and hadn't been working for long.

A few days before Christmas we were all sitting around the dinner table when suddenly there was a loud banging on our front door, followed by the clanging of the doorbell. My sisters and I clambered over each other, all racing to answer it first and see who'd come to visit. But there was no one there. Instead, on the front stoop, sitting in the round circle of porch light, was one of the biggest boxes I'd ever seen, beautifully wrapped in bright Christmas paper. The box was so huge I could've climbed in and fit comfortably.

"Mom! Dad!" we screamed and shouted. We dragged the ginormous box inside and then opened it quickly. Inside we found individual presents for all of us, ham, turkey, potatoes, all the Christmas dinner fixings, candy canes, small toys, books, gingerbread and so many more wonderful things.

"I can't believe they did this," I heard my mother whisper. I realized then she knew who had helped us, yet it didn't matter. The sheer joy and relief on my parents' faces was what truly spoke to me. Each girl had been given a beautiful Christmas dress, which we immediately tried on, twirling around and pressing the fabric to our faces in sheer delight. My dress had a magnificent pattern of holly with deep reds and greens. The frills and pleats of such a dress made me excited just to put it on. The generosity we experienced that Christmas had a big impact on all of us, one that would change how I celebrated Christmas when I had my own household.

Many Christmases later, my husband and I patiently gave our almost two-year-old son individual potatoes to place into the large box that stood open in our kitchen. His small hands couldn't hold much, but he loved helping us pack it all anyway. With a start we realized we hadn't wrapped the box before putting everything in it. So, with help from his small hands we taped sparkly snowman paper all over, a job that took twice as long because our son wasn't quite sure how to tape, but it was an important experience to share nonetheless.

We had asked the bishop of our church for the name of a family in need, and we truly enjoyed choosing individual gifts for them, as well as delicious food: oranges, chocolate, stuffing, pumpkin pie. It all had to be included. When it came time to carry it out to our van, it was so full my husband could barely lift the box and had to be extremely careful not to let the bottom give out.

When we arrived at the family's house we carefully drove past it and parked a little ways down the road, with the van facing away from the house to allow us to make a fast escape. I helped my husband load the box onto the porch and, after checking to make sure there was a light on inside, I snuck back to our van and had it ready and waiting. Then my husband banged on the door, rang the bell, and took off!

As I watched from the driver's seat he appeared around the corner of the house like an Olympic runner, moving so fast he nearly fell on the slippery snow. He then hurdled the neighbour's shrubs before leaping into the passenger seat and slamming the door. I felt like the getaway driver for a gang of bank robbers. We made it away unseen.

As often as my family is able I will build this box. I want to be the person who gives children the same joy I had so many years ago. I want kids' eyes to go wide as they see a box as big as themselves on their front porch. I love being a Canadian, but even more I love the fact that I live in a place where someone saw my family's need and responded, and because of their generous gift so many years ago I was touched and my life forever changed. I will continue to pass that on — pay it forward — and touch other lives.

~Danielle Mathieson Pederson
Kamloops, British Columbia

Christmas in Philips Head

It is Christmas in the heart that puts Christmas in the air.
~W.T. Ellis

Just before classes ended for the day, an eighth-grader named Marie raised her hand and quietly asked, "Teacher, what will we do in our Christmas concert this year?" She was one of my sixteen students ranging from grade five to grade nine in the "high room," in our two-room school. "We will have one, won't we?" she continued with concern. "We always have a concert."

"A concert?" I replied, caught off guard. "Well yes, of course," I managed to get out. "We must have a concert. What would Christmas be without a concert? Let's start making plans after school today."

Just two and a half months into my first year of teaching, I had soon learned the "high room" teacher was in charge of organizing everything from making sure the school's winter wood was stockpiled, to planning socials and scheduling parents to scrub the school. Now, it seemed, I was in charge of the Christmas concert as well!

After classes finished that day several students and I stayed behind and began making our plans. We looked at Christmas concert skits used in other years, and they laughed and reminisced about past successes and flops.

"Tomorrow," I suggested, "we'll write a business letter and order a book of plays."

"Yes, great," responded Edward and Verna, "and we can get started on making streamers and decorations tonight."

The little meeting ended. Darkness came early to Newfoundland in November, and as I lit the two Aladdin lamps on the classroom wall, I couldn't help but think how these two lamps wouldn't provide much light for the concert. Philips Head, a small community in the Bay of Exploits, was some distance from other larger towns and still isolated enough that electricity had not yet reached it. But concerns about lighting on concert night would have to wait. At that moment, there were other more pressing items that needed to be arranged.

The new concert material arrived on time, and by early December the program itself was beginning to come together, which included opening and closing recitations, a drill, a short play, and some songs that were copied and passed out to be practised. Young Sarah found the ideal drama for the grade nines and gave it to me to look over.

"Sarah," I said with some concern, "it calls for several speaking roles. We don't have enough students here to cover all the characters!" That's when I received another lesson about life in Philips Head.

"Don't worry," she laughed. "People here have always played in the concert. Some of them finished school here years ago, and they still perform in the Christmas concert. And when we sing the closing carols, most of them will leave the audience and come right up on stage to sing."

"Like who?" I asked a bit dubiously.

"Well, there's Uncle Jim, and you know Mrs. Baker the postmistress? She's always telling funny stories, and Norm and... they'll all want to play a part."

Now my greatest concern became making sure everyone had something to do! They came after school and practised. Roland's older brother could play the guitar, and provided the music we needed for "The First Noel" and "Good King Wenceslas." Then, one Saturday before the concert men armed with hammer and saw arrived and built our stage complete with two bed sheet-type curtains that could be opened and closed with a drawstring. "Teacher's only a young feller," they joked. "We'll get him through."

School closed early on December 22nd. Mothers came to give the school a thorough cleaning. Roland and Uncle Jim removed the folding doors between the two classrooms, and arranged the seating. Someone went into the woods and brought back a huge Christmas tree. Before 3:30 rolled around the woodsy smell of balsam fir filled the room, and the branches drooped with gifts for Santa to give out after the closing carol. But then came the final surprise. Verna's father, home from his work as an electrician in the Grand Falls paper mill, arrived at the school with his truck. He proceeded to string wires from his portable generator into the school, and then attached several light fixtures to the ceiling.

"Don't bother with those old Aladdin lamps," he said with a grin. "You won't be needing them now!"

When he threw the switch an hour before show time, the Philips Head Christmas Concert was lit by electricity for the first time.

Norm, who was slated to play Santa later in the evening, sidled over and said, "Well Teacher, the place is full already, and everything is going like clockwork."

"Yes," I laughed, as much in relief as excitement. "From home-made decorations and curtains, to music, songs and skits, even Santa will be jollier tonight. And with those electric lights, this year he won't have as much trouble seeing the names on the gift tags!"

Much later in the evening, as the final curtain closed on an over-crowded stage, I looked around the tiny schoolroom where Christmas traditions were being shared and passed on. Young and old alike had helped the new teacher transform our little school into a bright, festive concert hall. I knew I would never forget the lights of that special year, my first Christmas in Philips Head, Newfoundland.

~Robert C. Parsons
Grand Bank, Newfoundland and Labrador

A Canadian Christmas
After All

There are no strangers on Christmas Eve.
~Adele Comandini

By October of my second year at the University of Guelph my grades were in trouble, for sure. Beyond the help of even Coles Notes, I dropped my courses instead of flunking out.

Unsure of what to do next, I decided a few weeks in Mexico working on my Molson muscle would re-energize me. I packed my knapsack and drove my beater the fifty-or-so kilometres to Kitchener to let my mum know what I was doing. She asked where I was going.

"Oh, I don't know. The States, then somewhere in Mexico," I said, not realizing how that vague answer must have alarmed her.

"But don't worry, Mum," I added quickly, trying to reassure her. "No way will I miss Christmas, eh?"

She wasn't convinced, but I was determined to go. Besides, I already had my ticket to fly from Toronto to Atlanta, where I would visit a friend and then head south by bus. After a few weeks away I planned to be back for Christmas with enough time to spare to enroll for January classes.

But somewhere between Atlanta and Ciudad Juarez I came down with a bad case of wanderlust. By the time I crossed the Mexican border I was determined to stay away as long as my money held out. I figured with some miserly spending that might be a couple of months. With that decision, getting home to Canada for Christmas took a back seat.

An entry in my *Fodor's* about San Blas convinced me that it might be a nice stop. Described as small, quiet and out-of-the-way, it was a once prominent vacation spot but now just a run-down resort town on the Pacific Coast. It sounded ideal.

In early December I stepped off the bus in the centre of town and knew immediately this place was right for me. Transported back in time by its dusty, cobblestone streets, central church of peeling-plaster skin, and the sight of old men and dogs napping under shade trees in the *zócalo* I was convinced I'd found paradise.

Seeking cheap accommodations, the guidebook led me to the Playa Hermosa Hotel. Located on the outskirts of town it used to be a high-end inn but was now a run-down shell, and possibly not even open anymore. I headed towards the harbour and turned left to follow a rutted, overgrown path that ran parallel to the beach, and found the hotel at the end of the road. After waiting in the empty lobby for a while, the middle-aged housekeeper and her daughter finally appeared and rented me a room on the deserted second floor. It overlooked the entire grounds to the beach, had meagre furniture and an odd odour. There was no hot water or even electricity!

As the days passed a few more travellers checked in, and soon an interesting group was residing there. Bonded by our adventures we felt at home away-from-home, but as Christmas drew closer and I realized I wouldn't make it back in time I began to feel bad.

To lift my spirits I suggested we organize our very own Christmas celebration right there at the hotel. Everyone was excited and got into the spirit of the occasion as we divvied up the chores and set about planning a Christmas Eve feast.

In charge of obtaining much of the food, I realized my memory of a traditional Canadian Christmas dinner was out of the question, with its fare of pineapple-glazed ham, broiled back bacon, mashed potatoes smothered in beef gravy, tourtière, homemade beans baked in a crock of molasses and brown sugar, butter tarts and minced meat pie for dessert, and all washed down with near-frozen homo milk. Instead we settled for rice and beans, tortillas, pork, chicken, locally grown vegetables and a variety of fresh-caught seafood. While shopping for these ingredients I also bought some inexpensive gifts and, as there were only a few in our group, it didn't cost much for these trinkets. Anyway, what was Christmas if not a time for gift giving?

Christmas Eve day we gathered on the unkempt grass courtyard. Wood tables from the abandoned dining room were strung together and dressed with an embroidered tablecloth borrowed from the housekeeper; cooking utensils and place settings were scavenged from the hotel kitchen; candle remnants from unused rooms lit the night and tropical flowers were arranged in an assortment of vases. Everyone contributed to the holiday atmosphere with whatever fun and festive items could be found or supplied from our own belongings. The scene was thus set with a colourful collection of bandanas, bikinis, scarves and T-shirts along with an imaginative assortment of scraps and strips of everyday things like tin foil, ribbon, twine and shoelaces.

Anointing a nearby shrub as our official Christmas tree we decorated it with all manner of dangling, sparkling jewelry, accessories, washed-up shells and other castoffs from the beach. Beneath it we placed presents wrapped in assorted paper and cloth.

As Christmas Eve folded itself into a black night of winking stars, we cooked dinner over a large stone fire pit and watched the firefly sparks escape. We feasted on the food purchased fresh that day in town, drank plenty of pop, wine, beer and tequila and enjoyed a dessert of iced-sugar treats. Sated, we gathered around the Christmas shrub to exchange gifts, sing, play games and tell stories of Christmas past. Friendship deepened while we sipped coffee brewed over the dying fire pit embers. We relaxed, full of food and Christmas spirit.

For sure, it was a very different Christmas than back home in Canada, with its rambunctious hustle and bustle, last minute shopping and Boxing Day hangover. We were without the traditional evergreen tree dressed in expensive glass baubles, ornaments, keepsakes and mementos, wrapped in endless strings of popcorn and glittering lights and proudly displayed in the living room window. Of course, no snow blanketed our Christmas scene and I missed that most. Unable to peer out from a frosty window upon a billowy blanket of fluff, tinged moon-blue and stretching far out to the horizon of dreams, I really pined for home.

Yet for all the contrasts of place and time it turned out to be a very Canadian Christmas after all. We had friendship, kindness, caring, and more; we were no longer strangers thrown together in a small corner of the world but had become a true family at a bountiful table, getting—and more important—giving gifts. For a short time on a most memorable day we shared a meal, a moment and a prayer; for ourselves gathered there and for the rest of the world so very far away.

~Brian Wettlaufer
Franklin, Wisconsin

The Farmers' Parade of Lights

They called me and the Mrs. at the North Pole, to see if we'd join them on
their tour. It's a highlight of our season, and we wouldn't want to miss it!
~Mr. Santa Claus at Farmers' Parade of Lights

In big red letters the headlines of a local newspaper boldly
announced: Farmers' Parade of Lights. Overwhelmed by curiosity I hurried back to the house from the mailbox. A parade that
involved farmers was something I needed to know more about.

The article said the Farmers' Parade of Lights began as a spontaneous, informal event on the 2nd Thursday of December, by "The
3rd and 4th Line March Blahs Committee" and friends of Rockwood,
Ontario. Local farmers dressed up their farm equipment for the
Christmas season and rode through the village of Rockwood. A
holiday gesture of goodwill from the farmers to their non-farming
neighbours.

Over the years, the tradition continued. Twenty area farms joined
in the celebration, and two hundred farmers, their families, employees and friends rode on floats. This was an "invitation only" local
event that involved no advertisements, no fundraisers and no fees.
The parade route began on the 5th Line and travelled along Highway
7 to the 4th Line, with The North Pole as the final destination. The
article suggested an early arrival for spectators, as visitors had been
known to attend from various locations in Ontario, all across Canada

and numerous countries around the globe! Everyone from babies to seniors filled the streets of Rockwood to enjoy the decorated farm equipment.

When the school bus dropped my children off late that afternoon, I excitedly told them about the parade. A unanimous vote confirmed we were going!

On the afternoon of the parade, we sat around the kitchen table and enjoyed a simple meal. Grilled cheese sandwiches, tomato soup, celery and carrot sticks disappeared within minutes. At five o'clock, we began to prepare for the journey to Rockwood.

"Put on your snowsuits, warmest boots, toques, scarves and snowmobile mitts. It's going to be cold tonight, and the parade is supposed to be long," I told my children.

Bundled up and ready, we left our home in Pilkington Township for the forty-five minute drive to Rockwood. A slight breeze blew, snow was in the air, and temperatures hovered around -10 degree C.

Excited about our adventure, my children tried to imagine what the parade would be like.

"How do they put the lights on the tractors and light them up?" they wanted to know.

"How big will the tractors and equipment be?"

"Will Santa and Mrs. Claus be in the parade?"

The newspaper article offered answers to some of their questions, but the remainder would have to be a surprise!

Five miles outside of Rockwood we joined a long line of cars that were headed to the parade. The number of cars parked along the side of the road caused concern about parking, but closer to the village a few spots opened up. With the car parked, we walked a mile into the village.

After a short search for the perfect spot to stand and watch the parade, we settled in front of one of the local parks. The newspaper article had warned that a large number of spectators attended, but I was astonished by the crowds. Literally thousands of people filled the streets of Rockwood that night.

Leading the parade was a police cruiser with flashing lights.

Sirens wailing, a policeman waved to the crowd. We stood in awe as the first float passed in front of us. A John Deere tractor pulled a hay wagon with a nativity scene perched on top. The size of the float and the number of Christmas lights that decorated it overwhelmed us. Garland, tinsel, ribbons, wreaths, bows and banners added to the collection of lights.

The second float, a well-decorated Massey Ferguson tractor, towed a manure spreader covered in thousands of lights. Gold coloured tinsel hung from the spreader's beater bars. A generator-powered fan blew the tinsel into the air to resemble manure as it was tossed from the spreader. A group of local "cloggers" clogged to Christmas music on the bed of a hay wagon pulled by an antique Ford tractor. Clowns and firefighters waved to the spectators, shook children's hands and passed out candy canes as they walked the parade route. Christmas music provided by each float filled the air. The spirit of Christmas took over the crowd as parade goers joined in and sang Christmas songs.

The chute and auger on a snow blower mounted on a dual-wheeled Case tractor was decorated with white lights. Two short horizontal rows of icicle lights protruded from the chute. Creative minds had designed the lights to look like snow as it blew out of the snow blower.

Cheers erupted from the crowd as a skid steer named The Dancing Christmas Tree performed its version of a square dance down the main street. Covered in multi-coloured balloons with a flashing red light on its roof, the skid steer spun around, dipped and dived and doe-see-doed to the delight of the crowds on the street. Other floats contained stars mounted inside tractor tires, sprayer arms lit with red and green coloured lights, and hay elevators that displayed green and red candy canes.

Christmas trees of all shapes, sizes and colours were mounted on tractor fenders, cabs and hoods. Last but not least, as in every parade at Christmastime, Santa and Mrs. Claus rode high in the cab of a John Deere combine. Santa's shouts of "HO HO HO Merry Christmas" resounded into the night air. Mrs. Claus's rosy red cheeks and smile delighted young and old alike, while the crowds cheered and shouted "Merry Christmas."

Tired but excited, my children chatted about their favourite floats on the drive home. The Dancing Christmas Tree was voted number one. Candy cane-filled pockets were emptied as we satisfied our sweet tooth. With tired voices and sleep filled eyes, they asked if we could go to the Farmers' Parade the next year.

Attendance at the Farmers' Parade became a Christmas tradition for my family. Each year the floats become more imaginative than the year before. Participants wrap themselves in Christmas lights and wear Christmas tree-shaped hats. Plastic blow-up Frostys, Santas and reindeer have been added to the floats. Elvis made an appearance one year and entertained the crowds. Some floats remain the same, while others make minor changes. The more adventurous, creative farmers display new ideas each year.

Farm machinery has gotten larger over the years, but is restricted to the width of the roads and streets in and around Rockwood. Most years, the weather has cooperated and been ideal. As long as it does, we go. And each time we've joined the crowds at this spectacular event we have experienced what the organizers have set out to accomplish: to catch the spirit of Christmas—in a farmer's way. As long as Santa and Mrs. Claus have their crops harvested they will be back the next year with the combine. That way Rudolph and his reindeer team get well rested before the big night!

~Caroline Sealey
Alma, Ontario

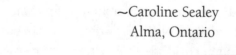

Editor's note: To see the Rockwood, Ontario Farmers' Santa Claus Parade of Lights, view this video on YouTube: https://www.youtube.com/watch?v=1yyCPCATpBM

Rudolph's Shiny Red Nose

*The Government of Canada wishes Santa the very best
in his Christmas Eve duties, and wants to let him know that,
as a Canadian citizen, he has the automatic right
to re-enter Canada once his trip around the world is complete.*
~Jason Kenney, as Minster of Citizenship,
Immigration and Multiculturalism

I didn't figure it out until I was nearly twenty-one years old. Every Christmas Eve Santa would visit the grandparents before we got there and, no matter how much I begged, he never once showed up at our house until Christmas morning. Dad said it was because some people (like Grandpa) negotiated Christmas Eve with Santa when they were small. Some people (like Grandpa) thought turkey was better before opening presents, not after. Since Mom never contradicted him, we accepted it without another thought. As envious as I was that they went first, I didn't mind getting two Christmases out of the deal.

The tradition was familiar, and special because of it. Our grandparents opened gifts pulled from beneath icicle tinsel dripping from the crannies of the small and weirdly silver tree that was tucked into a corner of their apartment. After Eight wafers and an abundance of Christmas oranges filled our bellies. Orange, mint, dark chocolate—there were probably other flavours to sample, but I can't recall them.

Grandpa's recliner was the same shade of Christmas orange, and it squeaked with considerable protest every time he moved. The Irish Rovers belted out the unicorn song through a stereo that took up an entire wall. With as much enthusiasm as we could muster, we sang the lyrics along with Grandpa.

The kids got one gift each, which may in fact have been a box of After Eights. When all the wrappings were disposed of and all the goodnights said, our family of six smushed back into the old station wagon for the eighteen-kilometre drive from Regina to Lumsden. The youngest brother fit nicely between Mom and Dad in the front, while the rest of us fought to avoid the dreaded hump in the middle of the back seat. We were squished, tired, and cranky kids by then. We still had a good thirty minutes to drive before we'd be home.

Without fail, before the halfway mark Dad would say, "You better quit bickering back there or Santa won't be coming to our house."

His warning bought perhaps three minutes of peace.

As the complaints about the tight seating mounted anew, Mom would add, "And you'll have to go to bed as soon as you get home. There won't be gifts for kids who are still awake."

My older brother refused. He was, after all, the eldest and the biggest, and clearly, the most mature. Going to sleep, that was for babies. I could, and our sister could but—

"Look!" said Dad, pointing out the window. "What is that? See that red light? I think... could it be? Yes, I'm sure it is. Rudolph's nose!"

Sure enough, there it was, a blinking red beacon in the sky guiding the way for eight more reindeer and of course, for Santa. We squinted to see the sleigh, but it was always lost in the blackness of night. We tried to climb over each other for a better look out the back window, but it didn't take long before Rudolph's nose vanished from view completely.

Missed it again.

When we got home, we hastily took to our beds. Santa was close! My sister and I shared a tiny room in our tiny house and shushed each other while we pretended to fall asleep. We listened intently for reindeer hooves on the roof. I have no idea if my older brother slept or not, but we dozed off in spite of our determined efforts to stay awake long enough to sneak out and see Santa transforming the front room.

In the morning, gifts would cascade from under the tree to the centre of the room, carefully piled so the biggest ones were at the back. The spicy fragrance of warm and gooey cinnamon buns coming out of the oven mingled with the distinctive aroma of Mom and Dad's coffee. Both sets of grandparents would come to our home, and we would spend the morning in a paper and ribbon frenzy. We never succeeded at waiting patiently to see what someone else may have gotten. We were however, quite adept at ripping apart a package in nanoseconds.

We left that house and moved a province away just as I was entering my teen years. When it was time for university, I went back to Regina in no small part because my grandparents still lived there.

One day, I decided to show off small-town Saskatchewan living to my Australian classmate. At the midpoint of our drive to Lumsden, a familiar red glow blinked slowly in the blue sky of spring. Had I imagined it? Surely Rudolph only flew in the night sky. With excuses to my Aussie friend, I pulled over, then backed up on the shoulder until I found the light again. I began to laugh.

"What's so funny?" she asked.

"That's Rudolph." I giggled again.

She looked at me as though I had somehow stomped on all my brain cells.

"That's a radio tower," she said.

"True enough. Sorry. It's kind of hard to explain."

I told her the story, and it took some time before it was as funny to her as it had been for me. After showing her my town and the house where I used to live, we made the return trip back to Regina. This time, we both waved and giggled at Rudolph as we passed by, asking him to say hello to Donner and Blitzen for us and to put in a good word with the big guy.

I phoned my parents. "Dad," I said, "did you know Rudolph hangs out in the same place every day of the year?"

After a long pause, he said, "Well kiddo, you better get to sleep right quick, or Santa won't find you."

"It's May," I said.

"I know," he said. "Always good to plan ahead."

~Crystal Thieringer
Ottawa, Ontario

A Perfect Present

You must never feel that you are less than anybody else.
You must always feel that you are somebody.
~Alberta Williams King,
mother of Martin Luther King, Jr.

When my three-year-old son Paul was first diagnosed with autism, pictures of him in an institution, sitting in a corner rocking back and forth, flashed through my mind. Somehow I managed to see through my tears well enough to drive us home after the assessment. I had never anticipated even for one second that I'd be confronted with such devastating news, otherwise I would have asked my husband to accompany us.

For three years I had somehow managed to deny the fact that my quiet little boy was always lost in his own world. I had steadfastly overlooked all the times that, when I spoke to him, he would never even look at me, let alone answer me. Now there was no more denial. The diagnosis of autism had slapped me solidly in the face.

I remembered hearing parents of special needs children say the silver lining in their clouds of sorrow is that these kids have the biggest hearts in the world. If that were true, I thought, as I lifted Paul out of his car seat that day, I would never know it. Paul would never be able to tell me or show me how he felt. When I set him down on the driveway, I watched as he ambled into the house without so much as a glance back at my tear-stained face.

After an entire week of crying and praying, I began reading as many books on autism as I could get my hands on. The more recent the book, I soon realized, the more hope it offered for finding my little lost boy. The Cobequid Centre just outside Halifax proved to be a great resource. It was there we found Judy Smith, a wonderful speech and language therapist. Judy gave me reason to believe that Paul could and would be helped.

Within a few months Judy was getting him to respond to her verbally with basic commands such as "more" when he wanted her to blow more bubbles. She forced him to look at her when he talked, although he wanted nothing more than to look away. She was patient but firm, which was just what Paul needed.

Faith plays an integral part in our family and we always looked forward to the Sunday school Christmas pageant at our church in Sackville. My three older children were very excited about the songs they were singing, but I wondered if I should sit Paul out when his class went on stage to perform. What if he wandered off? What if he just stood there without opening his mouth? My husband and I didn't want to segregate him, but we didn't want our little boy to be embarrassed either.

Paul's mental strengths soon proved to make up for much of his verbal weakness. He easily memorized the words of the song his class was to perform, as we sang it together in the car and at bedtime for the few weeks before the pageant. When the time came, I video-taped my brave boy standing straight and still, and singing "Away in a Manger" along with the rest of his Sunday school class, just like there was nothing to it.

The next day, when I took the video with me to share with Judy, we both stared at it in tears. We were amazed that our little Paul could blend into a group of such smart, well-behaved kids so easily.

"You did that," I whispered.

She hugged me in the emotion of the moment.

"WE did that — Paul, you and me," she insisted. "We're a team."

What a priceless Christmas present that moment was for me. To realize that my little boy, despite his limitations, had such a strong talent for memorization. With very little help from me he had mastered the words to what has become my favourite Christmas carol.

This event gave us reason to believe our son was exceptionally intelligent in ways that would eventually help him overcome his disability. Through this wonderful Christmas experience — God gave us hope.

~Jayne Thurber-Smith
Chesapeake, Virginia

Welcoming the Ghosts

"Bear but a touch of my hand there," said the spirit,
laying it upon his heart, "and you shall be upheld in more than this!"
~Charles Dickens, A Christmas Carol

Christmas had lost a bit of sparkle. I was on my fifth tired trip from the basement, wondering if all this hoopla was necessary anymore. My arms were loaded with snowmen, pinecones and other festive knickknacks. A large jingle bell slipped my grasp, fell on my toe, and bounced across the floor, frightening the yuletide out of my cat.

It had been easy to feel the magic of Christmas when my children were young. It was all there in the misspelled letters to Santa and the worn pages of the Sears *Christmas Wish Book*. It was infused in school pageants and gold spray-painted macaroni crafts. It melted like marshmallows into hot chocolate as we watched The Grinch, Rudolph, Frosty and Charlie Brown.

It's harder to feel the magic now that the kids are young adults. We keep up many of our traditions, but some have fallen by the wayside. We no longer attend the annual Christmas magic show sponsored by the local fire fighters. Coordinating everyone's weekend work schedules simply became too complicated. And the kids don't get up to open their stockings before the sun anymore. It's more likely I'm waking everyone up by setting the coffee to brew.

I have my own steadfast tradition though: for years I've read Charles Dickens' *A Christmas Carol* by the light of the Christmas tree.

You can't read that story over twenty-five times (not to mention the many versions of it I've seen in films) and not start noticing the three ghosts in your own life. But they don't visit me the way they did Mr. Scrooge over the course of one night. They settle in for the season.

The ghost of Christmas Past demands the same Christmas meal every year: turkey, mashed potatoes, peas, sage and onion stuffing, baby carrots, rich gravy and canned cranberry sauce. It isn't so much sauce as jelly, and it's important that the can rings are visible as it jiggles in the glass serving-dish.

His voice is heard in the stories told across the dinner table, and in the tiny mince tarts made from my grandmother's recipe. He is a ghost as light and fragrant as the memory of my grandfather's pipe smoke, yet he is the ghost that anchors us together. Those we have lost from our table rest in his shadows and our hearts.

The ghost of Christmas Present arrives long before the meal if I am willing to slow down and welcome her. Yes, for me, if not for Dickens, the ghost of Christmas present is a woman. She turns up the Christmas music and opens a bottle of wine. She reminds me to remain calm in long checkout lines. She keeps me company and reminds me why I am baking pie after cookie after lemon square when I'd rather be feet up by the fire. And on Christmas Day when dinner is finally served, she is the laughter at our table, the stories shared for the first time, the new neighbour who stops by with cinnamon maple scones.

The hardest ghost to recognize is the ghost of Christmas Yet-To-Be. It has no gender, no shape or solid promise, but it breathes softly in my daughter's voice as she shares her hope to act on stage at Stratford one day. It darts through the light in my son's eyes when he looks toward his girlfriend. It reminds us that the worries and the joys that fill our days will pass. But it whispers too, that there will be new joys and new worries to take their place.

So when that jingle bell bounced off my toe, it sparked the memory of my son finding it nestled in the snow on our deck. It was a Christmas morning eighteen years ago. His eyes were wide with wonder and I had smiled and winked at my husband. "It must have fallen from Santa's sleigh," I told my son. We hung it on our tree that year, and every year since.

That memory reminded me why I was lugging all those decorations up the stairs. The Christmas ghosts would be arriving any day now. I soothed the startled cat, and wondered whose turn it was to hang the jingle bell on the tree.

~Kim Reynolds
Orleans, Ontario

Striking Chaos

Three phrases that sum up Christmas are: Peace on Earth,
Goodwill to Men, and Batteries Not Included.
~Author Unknown

My husband and I pushed our shopping cart through the department store aisles, each colourful display trumpeting festive cheer.

"Think we'll find anything as good as the singing clock under our tree this year?" I asked.

"We can always add it to Santa's list," Paul said. He wasn't really listening, too transfixed by the array of holiday chocolates and candies.

The singing clock was one of those items popular for about ten minutes in the late 1990s. The clock was supposed to chime a different bird song every hour.

My mother had clipped a magazine ad and ordered the clock for my father, who had recently entered a care home.

Paul and I had been sharing a Sunday dinner with her when she showed us the ad.

"You know how Dad loves all feathered and furred creatures, so I'm sure he'll enjoy the sound of birds in his room," Mom said, confidently nodding her head and pushing second helpings on anyone within range. "The ones advertised on TV sound incredibly life-like."

She should have ordered from the TV ad because the makers of this clock from her magazine had apparently never listened to a real bird! I was there when the package finally arrived in the mail with only a day to spare before Christmas. Together we tore open the box and slipped in a handful of batteries, ready to be transported to a tranquil summer garden in the Canadian Prairies.

Our garden vision quickly wilted. Oh, the birds did "sing" on the hour all right, but instead of melodious chirps and tweets, the clock's mechanical noises were closer to a loud pinball machine than a meadowlark. One birdcall sounded like a machine gun's rapid fire.

"Mom, you can't give this to Dad!" I shrieked. "He'll think he's under enemy attack!" At first I figured she was crying when her head tilted downward as we sat side by side at the kitchen table. But no, I soon realized, she couldn't answer because she was laughing too hard.

"But I don't have time to shop for a new gift!" she said through her giggles.

Another unusual detail about the clock was its face. Except for two obvious bird species, the robin and the blue jay, we couldn't identify any other drawings. And all the names were printed in Latin.

If, when referring to songbirds, you use words like Turdis Chrysolaus or Zosterops Japonica, then you shouldn't be reading this story. You should be filling out your application to Mensa.

"Look through the packaging," Mom said. "Maybe there's an English translation."

After a thorough search no translation could be found, although I did find instructions, and here they are, exactly as written:

ADJUST THE HANDS MUST BE CLOCKWISE TO AVOID STRIKING CHAOS. IF STRIKING CHAOS, RESET CLOCK ACCORDING UP-ON. FROM PM 10:00 TO AM 5:00 SILENCE WITHOUT ANY VOICE. IF BIRD'S TWITTER SOUND MODULATING, CHANGE NEW BATTIES.

I really tried, but this time it was me who simply couldn't continue reading aloud. Along with my mom I was laughing so hard I was crying.

Of course the clock never made it to Dad's care home, so on

Christmas Day he received much of the chocolate Paul had purchased. Instead, Mom kept the clock for herself and retrieved it from the closet every time friends and relatives came for a visit. Each guest was treated to a demo, followed by waves of laughter from young and old alike. The $29.95 plus shipping was the best Christmas money Mom ever spent.

I hope to receive that clock myself one Christmas. It sure would be more fun than another fruitcake!

~Shannon Kernaghan
Leduc, Alberta

The Christmas Orange

I wish we could put up some of the Christmas spirit in jars and
open a jar of it every month.
~Harlan Miller

Christmas always makes me think about a story that became a tradition in our family. It's the story of The Christmas Orange. I think that most families have a story like this. My father would tell it in response to us children explaining how life as we knew it would end, if on Christmas morning we did not find The Mountain of Death Battle Station with a dungeon that really screams (batteries and extra severed limbs not included) under the tree.

"When I was your age," as began all Dad's stories that were intended to teach a valuable lesson, "we didn't have store-bought toys." The preamble to the story would be accompanied by much rolling of children's eyes and a look around the room for the surest route to a quick escape.

I should also point out at this juncture that we children didn't believe for a second that there was a time before toy stores. "When we were little," Dad would continue in spite of the children's eyes glazing over like a Christmas ham and our breathing becoming increasingly shallow and erratic, "most of our toys were handmade." What followed was a totally unbelievable account of toy race cars being made out of sardine tins and dolls patched together from socks full of dog hair.

We children, now almost catatonic and making the same sounds as the dungeon in The Mountain of Death Battle Station, were further regaled with the story of how Aunt Minnie's best Christmas present ever was a hat her husband made out of a tinfoil turkey roasting pan. Not only did one size fit all, but since it hadn't been rinsed after its last use, Aunt Minnie also saved on perfume.

At this point our hopes of getting our Galactic Warriors or Barbie's Off-Road Hair Salon began to fade. They were replaced with the fear that we would come down Christmas morning and instead of finding expensive and easily breakable toys under the tree, we'd discover a stick with a string tied to the end, wrapped in tinfoil.

Having succeeded in rendering the children immobile, it was now time for my father to bring out the story of The Christmas Orange.

As the story goes, as a kid Dad would open all his presents under the tree—a new block of wood for carving, or hand-me-down clothes originally worn by an older member of the opposite sex. Then the unmarried and slightly shady uncle who played the ponies would appear later in the day, and if the horse he had bet on the previous week had been full of the Christmas spirit, he would produce from behind his back... an orange.

To hear my Dad talk, back then when someone in Canada received an orange for Christmas people would travel for days just to get a glimpse of it nestled under the Christmas tree. In fact, even I am old enough to recall the days when people returning from a Florida vacation would lug a giant mesh bag of oranges back with them to hand out one at a time as family gifts. It didn't matter that by the time you drove home half of them were soft and mushy, and home to a couple million fruit flies.

Unless you think I'm getting like my father as I settle comfortably into middle age myself, I do remember a time when you couldn't get your hands on out-of-season fruit in Canada. Given the Canadian climate, that was pretty much ten and a half months of the year.

So it's not surprising that rather than eat it, the Christmas orange would be put on display in various prominent locations around the house for envious guests to admire until at least New Year's Day. Only when it was getting soft on one side and developing a colourful antibiotic patch of fuzzy green on the other did the family peel and pass sections of it around, and think of how lucky they were.

I have checked with my friends of a certain age, and every single one of them has a story from their father about the magic of getting an orange for Christmas. By my calculations, instead of being a rare and much envied event in the olden days, there must have been hundreds of thousands of oranges in circulation on Christmas Day.

Whatever the truth, to this day my wife and I still put an orange in the end of each other's Christmas stockings to remind ourselves of how lucky we are. Last year we put one in my son's Christmas stocking too, underneath all the candy, batteries and toys.

"What's this?" he asked, eyeing it suspiciously after trying to figure out how to turn it on.

"Have I ever told you," I asked, "the story of The Christmas Orange?"

~Stephen Lautens
Toronto, Ontario

Finding My Perfect Christmas

*One of the most glorious messes in the world is the mess created in the living
room on Christmas Day. Don't clean it up too quickly.*
~Andy Rooney

My parents were both born and raised in India. They married in 1976 and moved to Victoria, British Columbia, excited to start a new life together as Canadians. After my brother and I started grade school we wanted to share in the festivities of the holiday season that all our friends talked about with such excitement.

So my parents started their own version of Canadian holiday traditions, doing their best to create Christmas memories for our little family. Every year on December 25th we would wake up and eat a big breakfast, then get washed up and put on our finest outfits before we could even think about opening any of our gifts. We would then pose for coordinated pictures with the neatly stacked presents lined up under the tree. Everything was done in an orderly fashion, and we each patiently waited our turn to open gifts. It was the only way I knew how to do Christmas, and I waited for this day all year long. It was perfect for our family.

In my mid-twenties I married the love of my life and I was blessed to become a part of his wonderful family. He came from a background rooted in Canadian heritage with an upbringing very different from my own. For our first Christmas together as a married couple we flew on Christmas Eve from British Columbia to Burlington, Ontario to spend the holidays with his entire family. Still trying to overcome the three-hour time difference, we eventually got up on Christmas morning and groggily joined the family in the living room. Without wasting any time, everyone immediately dove into the stockings that Santa had left the night before. Then, after putting on silly elf hats, we jumped right in and started working our way through the giant mountain of gifts that were piled under the tree. Crumpled balls of wrapping paper were being thrown at each other, and the room was filled with chaos and laughter as the dog tried to dig out his doggy snack from Santa—which was hidden deep under the sea of gifts.

This Christmas morning was so different from anything I'd ever experienced—and I loved it. That night, as we were joined by aunts, uncles, cousins, and friends to share a delicious feast, I felt that I had finally experienced a true Canadian Christmas.

Four years later, and home in Vancouver, we found ourselves in the middle of an exceptionally busy holiday season. Our daughter was now two years old, I was seven months pregnant with our second, and we were getting ready to move into a new house on December 22nd—just three days before Christmas. Thankfully, my in-laws came out to British Columbia to help with the big move, and planned to stay and spend Christmas with us in our new home. One of the first boxes to be opened as we unpacked was our Christmas tree. We got all of our decorations up so that we could be ready for Santa's arrival two nights later.

Christmas morning arrived. With our young daughter, our unborn son still in my belly, and both sets of our parents there with us, we celebrated our first Christmas in our new home. Our daughter was the first and only grandchild for both families, and watching her sheer excitement that Christmas morning made all of us teary eyed. In that moment, as I looked around the room, it hit me. Surrounded by all the people I loved most, seeing Christmas through my young daughter's eyes, in the home where we planned to raise our family, my heart completely overflowed with happiness. I had finally found my perfect Christmas!

~Ritu Shannon
Surrey, British Columbia

Eight Candles

May the lights of Hanukkah usher in a better world for all humankind.
~Author Unknown

Five days into Hanukkah, my friend Susan and I were having our usual Sunday breakfast at a local deli. In honour of the holiday, I had ordered eggs with latkes instead of home fries. I took a bite, savouring the contrast of the cold sour cream against the warm, crunchy potato pancake.

"So, did you bring potato latkes to school?" Susan asked as she spooned applesauce onto hers.

I shook my head. "Nope. I may love eating them but I'm not willing to spend an hour shredding potatoes and onions and then frying them up. Too messy and I usually shred at least one finger in the process." I shrugged. "None of the stores near me sell them already made. So, my students will have to wait 'til Passover when I bring in a box of matzoh for a taste of traditional Jewish food."

I smiled as I remembered my adult English as Second Language students' reaction to last year's taste test. If you're not used to it, matzoh tastes like cardboard. Actually, it pretty much tastes like cardboard even if you are used to it.

"My principal laughs," I continued, "saying I'm the only Jewish teacher she knows who also brings in hot cross buns for Easter and candy canes for Christmas. Hey, this is Toronto, the most multicultural city in the world. I figure it's my job to introduce newcomers to some of the major holidays in this country."

"How do you handle the other holidays?" Susan asked.

I took another bite of latke and pictured the bulletin board that ran the length of the classroom. "After twenty years of teaching, I've found pictures of almost every major holiday in every religion and culture in the world, plus some fun ones like the tomato-tossing festival in Italy. Every December I cover the entire wall with pictures and brief explanations and title it 'Holidays from Around the World.' They don't even have to be December holidays. Then each student does a short presentation about a celebration from his or her own country. That way, no one is excluded and everyone gets to be an expert."

I sighed, thinking back to what it felt like being excluded around Christmastime. I wasn't an immigrant, but at the public school I attended, December meant Christmas, complete with a tree in the main lobby, decorations throughout the school and a Christmas concert. Although the school was about ten percent Jewish, Hanukkah simply didn't exist at school back then. I told Susan how glad I was that it was different now.

Susan shook her head. "Maybe not so different."

"What do you mean?" I asked before popping another mouthful of latke.

"Now that I'm a principal," she began, "I make sure that our school decorations include Hanukkah dreidels as well as Christmas trees. I even bring in an electric menorah for the main office. You just tighten one more light bulb every day until all eight candles are lit."

"That's great. So what's the problem? Is the school board complaining about the extra electricity you're using?"

"It's not the school board," Susan said. "It's the police."

"The police? Now if it had been the Fire Department, and the menorah used real candles, I could see how that would be a potential fire hazard. But an electric menorah? No way."

"Yes way," Susan said. "Now be quiet and listen." She gave me the look she'd honed as a teacher and now used just as effectively as a principal. "It all started with Officer Mike. I've told you about him. He's the community police liaison, a really sweet guy and the kids like him. He brought his sergeant in for a surprise visit and the menorah was sitting on the counter with two of the bulbs screwed in so they lit up. We chatted for a few minutes before I had to take a phone call in my office. By the time I finished the call, they'd left."

"I'm still not seeing a problem," I interjected, and then thought the better of it. "Sorry, your story. Me eat. No talk." I smothered the last of my latke with sour cream, sighed in anticipation, and chowed down.

"Neither did I until a few minutes later when Officer Mike came rushing back into the office without his sergeant and went straight for the menorah. That's when I noticed all eight candles were lit when it was only the second day of Hanukkah. He grinned sheepishly at me, and then began unscrewing six of the lights."

She rolled her eyes. "Turns out his sergeant had never seen a menorah before and thought it was some new type of Christmas decoration. He didn't know we light one more bulb on each of the eight days, and that it was only Day Two. He figured the unlit candles hadn't been screwed in properly so he tightened them until they lit up. I guess he thought he was doing his manly thing in an office filled with women. Officer Mike didn't want to embarrass him by correcting him in front of the office staff."

I snorted. "Manly and parochial. So much for the most multicultural city in the world. I just hope Officer Mike had a quiet talk with his sergeant afterwards so you don't get a repeat of this next year. Hmmm, when Passover rolls around, maybe the sergeant would like some matzoh as a friendly ecumenical gesture. What do you think?"

"Definitely," Susan said, "and I'll make sure Officer Mike gets some, too."

~Harriet Cooper
Toronto, Ontario

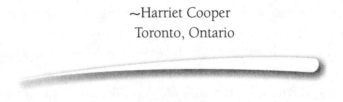

Our New Year's Eve Tradition

One resolution I have made, and try always to keep, is this:
To rise above the little things.
~John Burroughs

Like most young couples, my husband and I felt that being out on the town on New Year's Eve was the climax of the year. One year however, we decided to forgo the cost of dining out and hiring a babysitter and instead chose to cook our own fabulous meal! Joining us was a friend of ours who, like me, enjoyed cooking.

The menu consisted of steamed lobster and crab, mussels and shrimp sautéed in white wine and garlic, a homemade red sauce with a few added mussels and shrimp for flavour, mixed salad, angel hair pasta and a baguette to sop up all the wonderful juices. Dessert was homemade Tiramisu. This was going to be great!

The night started out perfectly. I had set the table beforehand and everything was in place. My mother-in-law had made us two beautiful tablecloths for our large oak table. One of the cloths had poinsettias in shades of red and pink, and the other was a deep shade of red with a small pattern of Santa Claus and holly. I chose the Santa tablecloth because it was a favourite and more importantly, would hide any spills the children might make. After all, they were sitting at the "big" table tonight and since they were all aged between two and four years, spills were to be expected!

Messes weren't a big issue with this table, but there were definitely issues. From the time we had purchased it three years earlier, we had found nearly everything made a mark on it. Whether it was a hot cup of tea or a warm plate, it left a mark. We had even paid an extra fifty dollars for a special stain resistant coating. But that table had been back to the shop twice to be refinished, and I vowed I would never send it out again. I was vigilant about cleaning up spills and protecting its finish. So far so good.

Music played in the living room as we picked up the children, twirled them and dipped them, and blew little paper horns and kazoos. And of course we took the occasional breather to visit the bathroom to check on the live lobsters and crab in our bathtub. And we laughed, all the while taking turns in the kitchen.

It was during one of these turns in the kitchen that I noticed it. It didn't catch my eye immediately, but the glow from the dining room seemed odd and I took a second look. To my horror, I saw that the tablecloth was on fire! "Fire." I said it quietly as I stood there immobile. I suppose I didn't want to alarm anyone.

My husband turned and looked at me. "What did you say?"

"Fire!" I said it a little louder this time as I quickly turned and filled a large glass with water. Too late—the gig was up; the fire had been spotted and children were jumping and pointing at the flame as it spread across the middle of the table. My beautiful table and tablecloth! I ran, glass in hand and doused the flames.

I don't want to give the impression that it wasn't a big deal to me as I stood there looking at the candelabrum. Apparently, one of the candleholders was loose and melted wax had slid down the side of the candlestick to the bottom. The softened candle had tipped and gently fell upon the table. I will admit, after a moment of staring at the scene, calmness did settle on me and our friend spoke the truest words: "Guess you won't be worrying about stains anymore." He was right.

We placed tea towels on the wet area, removed the candelabrum and continued with dinner. We had lots of fun as music played and wonderful aromas drifted from the kitchen. We celebrated with hoots and hollers around 10 p.m. and saw the kids off to bed. We adults stayed up and chatted and watched the New Year arrive in both Toronto and New York on TV.

We have kept the tradition of staying home on New Year's Eve for eighteen years. We still look forward to our seafood dinner, with the addition of a chicken breast for my son who won't eat seafood. We dress the table, play board or card games and listen to music. Sometimes we dance. Some years we host many friends; some years it is just us. And every year, I look at that old table and see the burn marks that share space with fork marks, water rings and dents. And I remember that night when the table was on fire, and smile when I remember the words: "Guess you won't be worrying about stains anymore."

~Cheryl-Anne Iacobellis
Barrie, Ontario

Chapter 3

Christmas in Canada

Holiday Memories

*Blessed is the season which engages the whole world
in a conspiracy of love!*

~Hamilton Wright Mabie

The Hanukkah Parade

May love and light fill your home and heart at Hanukkah.
~Author Unknown

Originally from Austria, my sweet grandmother was a small woman, barely five feet tall. Her two-foot-tall candelabrum was more than just a candleholder. It was a family symbol, a magnet that brought us all together. On Shabbat evenings, Baba (Jewish for grandmother) would don a special Shabbat kerchief, a white linen square with a border of delicate lace. With great fanfare she would light each candle. Once she had finished lighting the last candle she would stand in front of the candelabrum and close her eyes. Tears ran down her cheeks. She prayed for her husband, her married children and for us, her grandchildren. She spoke in Yiddish, *"Her mein tier tata, hiet oif mein man, kinder un di eyniklach."* (My Dear Father, watch over my husband, my children and my grandchildren.)

We all stood by the Shabbat table in awe. Baba looked like a queen speaking to the King of Kings, to Almighty God himself. When she finished her prayer, we began our Shabbat.

As our family grew, my grandmother spent more time with her candles. By the time she reached her ninetieth birthday she had many married grandchildren with children of their own. There were now five generations in my baba's family. Before every Shabbat, Baba would shine her silver candelabrum and pray, "May my *mazel* (luck) always shine!" When lighting the candles, she prayed for each family member, never omitting any of us.

Her candelabrum was made of solid silver with a heavy silver base. All year it had three branches, each with two candlesticks. In the middle was a stem for another candle. The traditional custom for Shabbat is to light one candle each for the father, mother and children. As each child is born, another candle is added to the Shabbat lighting. For most of the year Baba's candelabrum was fitted for six candles.

But during the week of Hanukkah, she would add another branch of two candlesticks each, making a total of ten candles. Her candelabrum was built in such a way that the candleholders could be removed so that oil cups could be inserted for the special lighting on Hanukkah. Our Shabbat candelabrum was thus transformed into a beautiful Hanukkah menorah.

During the eight days of Hanukkah, she turned over her prized menorah to my Zaida (Jewish for grandfather) to light the candles for the holiday. Hanukkah was our happiest time. All of us children, grandchildren and great-grandchildren came to Baba and Zaida to receive Hanukkah *gelt* (a small gift of money, usually a fifty-cent-piece or two) and join in the lighting of the menorah.

Imagine the two-foot menorah with ten candles shining in all its glory. Zaida stood proudly like a *Kohain*, the high priest in the temple, when he lit the candles.

When my Zaida died, Baba sold their two-story house in Winnipeg's north end to move to a tiny, one-bedroom apartment not far away. Although she couldn't take all of her cherished things, of course she packed her precious candelabrum. First she wrapped it in a large piece of worn, cotton flannel and then again in tissue paper. Then she placed it gently into the box she had made a special trip to get from California Fruit on Main Street.

But when the van drove away from her new apartment that day, after the movers had piled all the cardboard boxes containing her possessions in the middle of the living-room floor she was horrified to discover her treasured menorah was not there. Her first thought was it had accidentally been left in the back of the truck, or perhaps it was still at the old house. But after a call to the moving company and a visit back to the old house, it was clear that someone had stolen her menorah.

My baba was livid. Her small body shook like a willow in a storm as she spoke about her most prized possession. How could anyone take it? How would she light her candles?

But Baba believed her menorah would return. "I have prayed that the menorah would protect us, and I'm sure the menorah has done just that. Now I pray that the menorah protect itself and be returned to me." With silent determination she prayed and prayed. The family did not know what to do. The weather was growing colder and Hanukkah was fast approaching.

Then, one day in November, a childhood friend from Austria unexpectedly came to visit her. They had been friends for years, both here in Winnipeg after they married, and before that, as young girls in the old country. Upon arrival Mrs. Stern announced, "I never saw another menorah like yours until today. My mouth fell wide open when I saw a menorah exactly the same, in the window of the pawn shop I passed on Main Street, while walking here."

Baba immediately called my mother and her siblings. We were dumbfounded. Could it be that Baba's friend had actually seen the stolen menorah? Baba was now geared up and ready for action. "Let's get my menorah!" she declared. "It soon will be Hanukkah—and I need it back!"

Then she hastily pulled on her winter coat. Once we were all gathered, Baba, my parents and I, Aunty Tzeril and Uncle Simcha, Mrs. Stern, and our friendly neighbourhood policeman from the North-central Precinct made our way to the pawn shop. Baba was so excited she forgot to put on her headscarf, her gloves and her overshoes.

Her eyes sparkling, and with a shout of confirmation and sheer joy, when we arrived at the shop Baba pointed to her beloved menorah standing in the window just as Mrs. Stern had reported. With a quick movement, she bent her head toward it and spoke softly to it like an old and trusted friend. In Yiddish she whispered, "Yes, you have done well. You have protected us and now you have protected yourself. *Kim a haim mit mere.*" (Come home with me.)

Before anyone could say anything, Baba grabbed the menorah off the shelf and held it close to her heart. Nobody could stop her.

"Baba," I protested, "you can't just take it. That's stealing! It's against the law!" Much to my confusion, my mother clamped her hand over my mouth and imperiously marched me out of the store. Meanwhile, Aunty Tzeril stayed behind with the policeman and pawn shop owner "to do the paperwork."

By this time, the commotion had attracted quite a crowd. Neighbours, both Jewish and non-Jewish, joined my grandmother in her triumphant walk home. Along the way, the closer we got to her apartment building, more and more people joined us. My diminutive baba, still wearing her apron and house-slippers, marched proudly home, the menorah she was carrying almost as big as she was. She was followed by our ragtag procession of excited family, neighbours and friends. What a sight to see! It truly was a grand Hanukkah parade!

Today my baba's cherished menorah sits on my own mantle, right in the center, holding the position of honour. I polish it daily, making sure that it gleams, like she so lovingly did all those years ago.

~Sharon Melnicer
Winnipeg, Manitoba

A Quebec Christmas

Christmas is a time when you get homesick—even when you're home.
~Carol Nelson

My wife and I were spending our second year in Eastern Canada and were really starting to miss our families, who were spread across Europe. Her brother lives in Scotland with his family, while my sister and her brood live in Spain. It was hard being so far apart, and it became even more difficult at Christmas. We had been accustomed to spending holiday time with our brother and sister ever since our parents had passed on a number of years ago. When we moved to Canada we knew there would be a bit of a social hiatus before we managed to establish a new circle of friends, but it took us a while to realize we would never find a substitute for family. This lack of family connection really hit home during the holidays. To make matters worse, all of our Canadian friends were busy with their own families at Christmas and New Year's, leaving us feeling quite isolated.

Back in Europe, our families were well aware that we had spent a pretty lonely holiday period the previous year. It was my sister, Joan, who suggested that we take a trip to the Chateau Montebello to celebrate Christmas, explaining that there we would likely be holidaying among people who found themselves in a similar situation. The thought of spending another Christmas at home just the two of us was not appealing, so we booked ourselves into the Chateau Montebello for the holidays.

Winter had started early in this part of Quebec. Heading out of Ottawa the roads were clear for driving, but everything else had a healthy covering of fresh white snow. Our first impression as we turned off the main road toward the chateau was of the black and red painted log entrance gate straddling the driveway entrance. From there the driveway wound its way toward the main building through huge mature pine trees, all beautifully decked out with Christmas wreaths and lights. We felt this was a good start to our mini vacation.

Overlooking the Ottawa River, the majestic four-storied log building stood quietly amid the newly fallen snow. Smoke curled slowly out of the central chimney as it rose to meet the grey and overcast sky. The main building was enormous; surely there cannot be a larger or more impressive log structure anywhere in the world.

As we entered the foyer we were delighted to discover a two-story-high Christmas tree decorated and lit in such a spectacular manner it could have made the New York Rockefeller Center tree look like a Charlie Brown special. Surrounding us were three stories of wooden balconies draped with festive decorations. These rose up around a central hall supported by a massive, twenty-metre-high, six-sided stone fireplace. Three of the fireplaces blazed invitingly while small groups of people sat in cozy looking chairs and couches reading or quietly talking, just soaking in the delightful atmosphere.

Our room turned out to be a wonderful large end suite with a fabulous view out over the skating rink and the frozen Ottawa River. Leaving our unpacking for later, we headed out to explore the chateau. Originally built as a private club for a rich fishing and hunting clientele, no expense was spared in its construction. Every room is beautifully appointed with a great view of the extensive grounds.

Picking up an activity listing at the main desk we discovered to our delight that cross-country skiing, curling, skating, tobogganing and horse-drawn sleigh rides were all available to guests. Not being particularly adept at any of these activities we vowed to try them all, just hoping not to embarrass ourselves in the process. We had brought cross-country skis and ice skates with us, so we headed off to try out the skating rink before darkness fell. But we need not have rushed as it turned out the rink was lit at night for evening skaters, providing those in the dining room with a ringside seat to the colourful activity.

Despite all the beauty surrounding us, I realized that my wife really seemed to be missing her family this year. It had been a while since we'd been home on what was called the "five-thousand-dollar cure for homesickness." I was the one who had initiated the move to Canada, so I felt a weight of responsibility for us being so far away from our families. We soon discovered that many family groups seemed to be using the hotel as a holiday meeting place, and this only made us all the more aware of missing our own families. A few times I caught my wife staring wistfully at family groups seated at adjacent dining room tables. Nevertheless, we both began to look forward to Christmas morning. We had not brought many gifts with us, just a few token ones to exchange on Christmas Eve.

On our second evening we were feeling up to trying something new, so we signed up for a curling bonspiel. Fortunately we were teamed up with a husband and wife who had played many times before. So in spite of my contribution we won the bonspiel and were led into the main hall to be presented with our medals and a token bottle of rum. Standing on the podium, as I looked around the room I suddenly noticed four familiar faces that were smiling much broader than any others. Somehow, there stood my sister and her husband along with my wife's brother and his wife—smiling broadly and applauding loudly! I don't think I have ever been more surprised in my life!

My wife and I let out yells and bounded off the stage into their open arms, with tears of joy streaming down our faces. It turned out my sister had suggested the chateau to us because she had already booked herself and the others into the hotel for Christmas. They had just flown in from Europe that very morning. Knowing how much we missed them they had made the supreme effort to join us on our home turf. The miracle was that she had managed to do it without us having even the faintest idea of what was being planned.

Needless to say we ended up spending a wonderful Christmas

together. We all agreed it was the most memorable Christmas ever. For the rest of our lives the Chateau Montebello will hold a very special place in all of our hearts.

~J.A. Gemmell
Ottawa, Ontario

My White Christmas Sleigh

A good time to laugh is any time you can.
~Linda Ellerbee

It was the night before Christmas Eve, an ideal night for shopping, with large soft snowflakes floating down and Christmas music drifting from every doorway. The air was crispy cool and you could see your breath. Sidewalks creaked with every step and the coloured lights blinked a Merry Christmas greeting as the sparkling snowflakes blinked back at them.

If I was ever going to be in the mood for Christmas shopping this was the time! I still had last-minute gifts to purchase and I talked my husband into going with me. We began adventurously elbowing our way through the masses of shoppers.

Last-minute shopping was not my husband's idea of a great way to spend an evening, so he finally said he'd wait for me in the car. We owned a white Dodge 600 in those days and he had parked at the meter in front of the downtown department store where I was spending my last few dollars. I went about my task, humming along with the music, threading my way through the throng or waiting in long checkout lines.

Eventually I could buy and carry no more, so I decided to join my husband and head for home. I pushed open the doors, spotted the white Dodge with the patient male behind the wheel, and crawled in with my load of parcels. Reaching blindly over the top of the front seat, I unceremoniously dumped the packages on the seat behind me and proceeded to adjust the bungled fabric of my long winter coat. When I had it comfortably in place, it dawned on me that the key had not even been turned in the ignition.

"Well? What are you waiting for? Christmas?" I asked as I adjusted my over-wadded shoulder bag on my lap. Still no response. I turned quickly to look at—a stranger!

"Oh, no!! I thought this was our car," I blurted as, red-faced, I began to paw for the packages on the back seat.

The strange driver was looking at me with a peculiar half-smile on his face and it was obvious he was having difficulty holding back a chuckle. Two car lengths behind, my husband was sitting in our identical car splitting his sides with laughter. From this vantage point, he had watched the entire episode unfold in front of him from the moment I came out of the store.

~Joyce MacBeth Morehouse
Ripples, New Brunswick

Love, Shania and the Whispered Wish

Go confidently in the direction of your dreams.
Live the life you have imagined.
~Henry David Thoreau

The sun was low in the sky by the time I stepped out of the limousine into the slush of mid-December downtown Ottawa. I gingerly gathered up the frothy layers of white tulle and lace, exposing my clunky winter boots, my only nod to practicality on a day filled with hope, beauty, and joy.

I stopped for a moment, looking up at the ornate doors, and took a deep breath. This was the church my parents were married in over thirty years ago. And today, less than a week before Christmas, I was about to enter into my own wedded bliss.

Inside, it was warm and welcoming. The flames of the candles swayed and flickered, beckoning me forward. The enchanting scene in front of me was simply delightful.

Quickly replacing my boots with my white satin pumps, and gently resting my hand on my father's arm, I walked down the aisle amidst the smiles and whispers of fifty close friends and relatives, ready to pledge my heart to my soul mate. Perhaps because I had a bad cold—always a potential peril for a winter wedding, and evidenced by a chapped nose in otherwise lovely photographs—the ceremony was a bit of a blur. Nonetheless, my friend assured me later that she had never heard anyone say her vows with such certainty. In turn, I teased my new husband that, in his nervousness, he said his vows to the reverend instead of me! We all chuckled about the "help me" painted on the shoe soles of the best man, exposed for all to see as we knelt down for the final blessing.

After our first night together as husband and wife at the stately Chateau Laurier, we headed west to continue our honeymoon at Deerhurst Resort in the heart of Muskoka country. The highway was shrouded in fog almost the whole way, but we were too blissfully content to feel any fear. With the big city lights long behind us, the hush of the Canadian boreal forest enveloped us with a surreal peace and calm.

Arriving at the resort, we were struck by the contrast between the rugged scenery surrounding the property and the spectacular Christmas lights of the main lodge. We were surprised to see how deserted it was, realizing only later that we had arrived in the lull before the Christmas crowds arrived. We had our own charming little honeymoon cabin, but for that first night we decided to dine at the lodge restaurant.

The food was excellent, and as we lingered over after-dinner tea, a petite, beautifully dressed brunette with a lovely voice serenaded us with seasonal music. I leaned over to my husband and shyly whispered my very first wish as a newly married woman: "That's what I want to do one day!"

I had always loved to sing and play piano but I was too shy to do so publicly, and too focused on my professional editing career to really have time to pursue it. But even as I was starting a new life as a wife, that simple confession of my heart's desire would just as dramatically shape and define who I would become.

Two babies and a move across the country later, I started singing in a church band. At about the same time, there was an explosion of outstanding female artists coming on the scene, including the soon-to-be Canadian icon Shania Twain. Gorgeous and a little mysterious, Shania was from Timmins, a small northern Ontario city I had visited once years before. I read that her first break in show business had been at Deerhurst Inn—the very resort where I had spent my honeymoon, at around the same time. Could it be that I saw music history in the making that Christmas weekend I got married?

Over the years I followed Shania's career, searching for the unequivocal answer to my question, at the same time never giving up my own dream of pursuing singing. Being a wife and mother, and working outside the home often placed my personal aspirations on the back burner. But I continued to sing at church, work on my craft, and eventually write my own songs.

In 2011, I entered a recording studio for the first time to record my first album. While still knee-deep in the process, I read Shania's recently released autobiography, hoping to solve the mystery once and for all. Finally, I came to the conclusion that I may never know if Shania was that young singer I saw so many years ago. But my belief that it was, and her phenomenal success, has kept me inspired all these years as I carve out my own little niche in the music world.

Two years later, I finally quit my day job. By the end of the year I had released my second CD, fittingly a Christmas album, a nod to my most favourite time of year.

We can't really understand until we look back through the eyes of the future how one snapshot in time can impact our life so profoundly. For me, on this last weekend before Christmas the year I got married, I not only received the beautiful gift of a lifelong partner, but the seeds of a dream that, to this day, is still growing.

~Sally Meadows
Saskatoon, Saskatchewan

Christmas Poop for the Soul

The belly rules the mind.
~Spanish Proverb

Our morning started off with the usual bustling around to get everything together before we ran out the door to school and work. My husband had left an hour earlier to beat rush hour. I took my last bites of breakfast and threw together two more lunches for my son and me. I called out little reminders to help him pack his bag for school and he wandered down from his room fully dressed, backpack in hand with tousled hair. The last thing we always did before leaving was let the dog out. We had quite a solid routine, even down to the gravelled area where Oliver was trained to go to the loo. On this particular morning I was feeling quite pleased with myself because, with only a few days left of school and work, we were leading up to our most well budgeted holiday season yet. I'd finished my shopping by October, we'd made a few handmade gifts, and I'd actually cut our holiday spending almost in half.

But, on this frigid Winnipeg morning, that was about to change. First, Oliver didn't want to go out. For him this was very unusual. Normally he rang the dog bell we'd trained him to use if he needed to go out. He was even known to bark at us as we were leaving to make us realize we'd forgotten to let him out! I thought perhaps the cold hit him at the door, but being an eighty-pound Lab who loved the snow, that had never stopped him before. I nudged him out the side door and headed back to the kitchen to gather our things to put by the front door. I had a habit, from his puppyhood, of always glancing out the window to be sure he'd had time to go, but this time I could see that he was struggling.

I had no idea at that moment that we would need to unravel the mystery of what our dog had ingested the previous day. I stopped cold at the window because he was trying and trying, but wasn't able to poop. And then suddenly his breakfast came right back out the way it went in. At least he was outside. We hollered him back in and confined him to the floor space in the back hall, giving him plenty of water. My son Gavin dragged down Oliver's huge pillow from the bedroom to make him comfy. The plan? Drop my son at school, tell my office I'd be late and scoot Ollie off to the vet for a check-up.

Several hundred dollars later he'd been poked and prodded, given a chalky substance to swallow with X-rays and the surgery was booked for two days later to remove whatever was blocking his stomach. The parting words from the vet? Pray for poop.

When we got home that day, Oliver was his usual happy self, although ravenously hungry, so he scarfed down the tiny bowl of rice suggested by the vet. Our goal was to figure out what he'd eaten. We knew that he could not resist socks because socks went missing often and we'd even found Gavin's little Baby Gap socks in Ollie's poop. But over the years, we'd become vigilant with our socks. Our slogan was "always in the drawer, never on the floor." So we searched around the house to figure out what else could be missing.

The entire house was decorated with holiday ornaments; the tree was trimmed; the garland was out. Every Christmas book and stuffed animal with a Santa hat was on display but everything seemed to be in order. We even had an adorable fabric storybook nativity scene all laid out on the hearth. Everything looked normal at first glance, but it was Gavin who noticed that something was missing. The fabric book was unfolded as the backdrop to the manger, and the little characters of Mary and Joseph were softly stuffed little egg-shaped fabric prints. The tiny cradle was nestled perfectly between them. But yes, something was definitely missing. My husband called Oliver over in a low voice saying, "What did you do?" Ollie's ears went down and he looked away as he always did when he was in trouble. Oliver had eaten baby Jesus!

The vet confirmed that the X-ray did look like a wad of batting that was caught up inside and all we could do was wait. The next day we continued to give Oliver small portions of rice, hoping that the fabric and batting would break down a bit more so he could pass it. I came home every few hours to check on him. The night before the surgery we lay in bed thinking that what was initially going to be our least expensive Christmas ever was turning out to be a financial disaster. The surgery was going to bring us well over the thousand-dollar mark. We both closed our eyes with the same wish that night as we drifted off to sleep.

The next morning we awoke a bit earlier than usual. We both stirred, hearing Oliver's bell and rolled towards each other hoping to nudge the other person into hopping out of bed first. At once we both realized that this was one bell we had both wanted to hear and we bolted downstairs together to get Oliver outside. What a sight we must have been in our housecoats and winter boots hooting and hollering with joy at 5 a.m. as our dog pooped out baby Jesus.

~Brandy Lynn Maslowski
Summerland, British Columbia

The Church Organ

Life is a shipwreck but we must not forget to sing in the lifeboats.
~Voltaire

Angel decorations adorned the Christmas tree beside the pulpit. Dozens of poinsettia plants covered the floor in front of the altar. Candles flickered on windowsills. Thirty minutes before the Christmas Eve service was scheduled to begin the sanctuary was already half-filled. Children, clad in fancy dresses and dress shirts, fidgeted. Adults wished each other the best of the season.

My husband, daughter, and I would spend Christmas Day with my in-laws, a large, exuberant gathering that included a lot of excited children, presents, and an abundance of food. On Boxing Day we would drive to the country to celebrate with my parents and my brother's family. But Christmas Eve belonged to our church family.

We'd been members of this small congregation for several years, drawn by its open, accepting welcome, its caring attitude, and the willingness of members to step forward and do what needed to be done. The sense of community in this city church felt like that of the small town I'd grown up in.

More families filtered in, some with three or four generations celebrating together. We greeted friends as they walked by. My daughter raced to the back of the church to meet a friend. Ushers added extra chairs. Smiles filled the room. Above the buzz of happy anticipation,

Donna, the organist, played a selection of Christmas carols. On this cold, winter evening, I felt warm and blessed.

The Christmas Eve service has always been an important part of the season for me. As a child I always performed in the children's pageant and, after the service, visited with my cousins. This Christmas Eve, as an adult, I sat and enjoyed the beautiful prelude of carols. Donna knew how to really make that old organ come alive, and the choir had been practicing for weeks. I looked forward to hearing them sing, and to the climax of the service, when the lights would be dimmed, candles distributed, and we would all sing "Silent Night."

Suddenly, the organ boomed. Well, it was actually more like an explosion. Donna threw her hands into the air and shouted, "Oh my God!" These were words not unfamiliar in a church setting, but meant to be used in a somewhat different context. The stunned congregation collapsed into silence. A wisp of smoke ascended from the organ. Donna stared at it with shock and disbelief, as if she'd been betrayed by a trusted friend. Clearly, the old organ was done.

My blissful feeling turned to unease as I wondered what would happen to the service now. Would the entire service be stopped, or, would it continue minus music? We could easily sing the familiar carols a cappella. Could the choir still perform? Would we skip some planned hymns? Perhaps our minister could accompany the candlelit singing of "Silent Night" on his guitar, the instrument the carol was composed for and originally played on.

A movement in the sanctuary interrupted my private re-planning of the service. Val, a member of the church, dashed across the room, quickly sat down at the piano and immediately began playing where Donna had left off. The congregation breathed again. A hum of relief accompanied the piano as people whispered to each other.

The service proceeded as per plan. We sang carols. The choir performed. The minister spoke of the meaning and miracle of Christmas. Near the end of the service, with lights dimmed and candles in our hands, we sang "Silent Night" with joyous awe and with gratitude for the miracle of helping hands among us.

Shortly after Christmas, fundraising for a new organ began.

We have used the new organ for many years now. But the story of that evening has become part of our folklore, recounted from time to time when someone asks, "Do you remember the Christmas Eve when the church organ blew up?"

~Donna Janke
Winnipeg, Manitoba

A Very Cherry Christmas

Stop worrying about the potholes in the road and celebrate the journey.
~Fitzhugh Mullan

I t was a cherry car. A shiny red 1977 Checker cab with black vinyl roof, dark tinted windows, and large silver wheels ringed with thick whitewall tires. The used car salesman said that it had been a taxicab in Niagara Falls, New York. The odometer read 450,000 miles, but he proudly announced that it was probably 1,450,000. In 1981, even though the Checker was no longer being manufactured, everyone knew that the car was indestructible. The smiling chrome grille and glowing red paint job sold me. It looked so cool!

I named the car Big Red, and after a wash and wax I would take the kids out for frozen yogurt. We'd count the heads that turned as we drove by. In the mile-and-a-half journey we counted twenty-two gawkers one day.

I featured the family grouped around the grinning grille on our 1981 Christmas card. That year, Jake and Kristen, aged eight and five respectively, were excited about the ride to their grandparents' house in Sault Ste. Marie for a guaranteed white Christmas. I was excited about the first highway test of the new car. The cavernous backseat area was like a large playroom, big enough to keep both kids out of each other's hair for the eight-hour drive from Toronto. My wife Brenda was looking forward to riding up front in peace. She packed games, sandwiches, coffee and juice so we could just keep moving.

Big Red sat tall and floated northward across the frozen brown landscape. Cocooned in a chunky mass of heavy plate steel, pulled along by a big six Chevy truck engine with an Oldsmobile transmission and heavy duty Cadillac brakes, I felt a wonderful sense of security. Still no snow as we entered Canadian Shield country. Out came the snacks. This was happy motoring.

With darkness falling I noticed a White Rose gas station north of Britt that would come in handy on our return journey. Gas stations were scarce in the North so you had to keep alert. And just how was our mileage doing? Our last vehicle, a VW van, could make it within an hour and a half of our destination on one tank. With night upon us we had just passed the halfway point, the zone where the kids normally started to get on each other's nerves. To my alarm, I realized the old engine had really been sucking up the gas.

The fighting in the back seat started. Then the sleet started. The meagre defroster barely melted the ice accumulating on the windshield and the hard rubber wipers were smearing my severely limited vision. There was nowhere to pull over. The gas needle was on E. My hands grew tight on the wheel.

Whack!

"She hit me."

"Ouch."

"He hit me first."

In frustration, I reflexively reached back to grab one or other of the kids, but they were so far back in that cavernous expanse they easily evaded my grasps. While pointlessly groping with my right hand, my left hand stayed oh so steady on the wheel. My right foot was doing the heel and toe dance between the accelerator and brake, and my left foot was tapping because of the thermos of coffee that I had finished 150 miles back.

We were on the Sudbury bypass with no gas stations or rest stops for miles. Creeping along at twenty miles per hour I jockeyed to keep the car from sliding off the road in the now raging full-blown blizzard. "Why didn't I buy snow tires?" I asked myself. I prayed that the reserve tank would pull us through. Brenda used all of her mollifying skills to calm the kids. My left foot was really bouncing now.

Suddenly, above the swirling white headlight glare, a shining red star appeared in the sky. It was a Christmas miracle! Below the star, the sign read: Texaco OPEN.

Stepping into the deep snow in my slippery city shoes, I heard the gas station attendant say over my shoulder, "Washroom's busted. There's an outhouse out back." I nearly ripped the door in half trying to open it against a snowdrift. During that long interval of heaven-sent relief, I realized I was still wearing light clothing. Outside the wind howled and the storm hit hard. I hobbled back to the car aching and shivering.

Invigorated, but slightly debilitated, I wheeled Big Red back into the storm. Comfort came from the car radio. Thank heaven for the CBC. It was Fireside Al, Alan Maitland on *As It Happens*, reading a story of a returning British jet fighter pilot lost at night over the North Sea. Out of the fog, a mysterious World War II Mosquito aircraft appeared off his wingtip and acted as his shepherd to guide him back to home base. Our family was entranced. Fireside Al and the shepherd became my control tower, guiding me, a wounded pilot through the storm.

Yes, we had a merry Christmas up in the Sault. The car did develop an electrical problem, but battery boosts for every start kept us dashing through the snow to visit kinfolk and friends. The big ex-cab was cheerily waved through every R.I.D.E. road check.

We headed home with the car packed with presents and Grandma's snacks. Back on the road, the return trip in Big Red was filled with even more edge-of-your-seat drama. What I initially thought was ground fog turned out to be smoke drifting up from between my legs. The floor was on fire! We coasted to a stop near an open ditch. I ran out, scooped water into the thermos and doused the flaming floor carpet. We crept along in the gathering dusk to find a garage minutes before closing time. The mechanic easily replaced the burnt out headlight dimmer switch, the cause of our predicament. This, plus finally running completely out of gas and having to call a tow truck ultimately made for some great Christmas memories.

Since that eventful Christmas trip in 1981 I have driven the

Toronto to Northern Ontario route many, many times. Each time I am thankful for a clear highway, a reliable vehicle, and a full tank of gas. And always, on the long night runs, I think of the shepherd, just off my right wing tip, guiding me home.

~Lloyd Walton
Orillia, Ontario

The Little Red Wagon

Memory is a way of holding onto the things you love, the things you are, the things you never want to lose.

~From the television show, The Wonder Years

"It's almost Christmas, Julie. Do you know what that means?" my mother asked as we trudged home from school in the deep snow.

"Yes! It means I will get a little red wagon from Canadian Tire for Christmas!" I announced, full of five-year-old confidence.

"Well, you will certainly get some lovely things, but..."

"But a little red wagon is the best present," I interrupted.

"For a boy, maybe," Mom shrugged. "But I thought you wanted a dollhouse!"

I thought about that. I had wanted a dollhouse very much. But now I wasn't so sure.

Mom noticed my hesitation. "What made you think about a wagon?"

"Mrs. McHendrick read us a story today," I explained, "and the boy wanted a little red wagon so much that he was good for months before Christmas, and then on Christmas morning he got his red wagon, and it said 'Canadian Tire' on it and everything was wonderful!" I had stopped walking and stood there, in my big rubber galoshes, staring up at my mother.

She smiled. "Oh! I see. Well then. Let's give that some thought, shall we?"

"Okay." I nodded happily and we continued walking home.

The Christmas season progressed, filled with school concerts and a nativity play featuring some very funny looking sheep and donkeys. Dad and I put up the tree, and I helped Mom with her baking. We wrapped gifts together, and I thought more and more about the story of the boy and his little red wagon. I asked my father to read it to me several times, and he told me how much he had loved his red wagon when he was my age. I became even more convinced that the story was right. The red wagon was clearly the key to the whole event, and definitely the best gift ever.

Mom noticed I was being very good, not complaining about bath or bedtimes, and not leaving clothes on the floor or pushing my horrid parsnips away. She even teased me about it a little, so I told her I wanted to be sure about the little red wagon. Her face seemed to change when she heard that. She didn't look as pleased with me, rather she looked almost worried.

"But I thought we talked about that," she said.

"We did! I told you how important it is." I laughed. "That's why I'm being so good!"

My mother sighed and walked away. I didn't understand what was wrong. It all made sense to me.

A week before the big day my parents always took me to see the special Christmas windows at the Toronto Eaton's store, at the corner of Yonge and Queen Streets. We went out for dinner, then walked along Queen Street and pressed our noses to the glass. Every year, the windows were better than the year before, and this year was no exception. There were dolls and baby buggies, toy trains, games and bicycles. And everything moved. But then I gasped—there it was: the little red wagon! It was so beautiful. It had bright shiny red paint with gold trim, a long black pull handle and black rubber wheels with little red hubs on them. No wonder the boy in the story wanted one!

"Mom, Dad, look! There it is! That's it! That's the little red wagon I want!"

They exchanged looks with each other, and then both looked

down at me. My heart was pounding, but they obviously didn't share my excitement. They didn't seem to understand.

"It doesn't say Canadian Tire on it, like in the story, but it does say The T. Eaton Company in gold paint and that's almost as good!" I was breathless with excitement.

"But you'll never play with it!" Mom insisted.

"If I don't get a little red wagon for Christmas everything will be horrible!" I exclaimed, bursting into tears. Then I felt a rush of shame. I hung my head. Dad took my hand and we went home.

As Mom put me to bed that night, she gently explained. "Julie, that story your teacher read to you has convinced you of something that just isn't true. What that boy wanted isn't what you want. It was just a story about hopes and dreams. And you should always dream of wonderful things. But even if you don't get what you wish for, you are still a very good girl, and we both love you more than anything!"

And with a kiss, she left the room. I knew what she was trying to explain, but I wasn't sure I believed her.

I never mentioned the story or the wagon again. I knew it was useless, and I resigned myself to the situation. A strange sense of calm settled over me, and I no longer worried or dreamed about what I would find under the tree. But I wasn't excited any more either. My parents asked me if I felt okay, and kept putting their hands on my forehead. As they tucked me into bed on Christmas Eve, I knew I would have no trouble sleeping.

Then a miracle happened. On Christmas morning when I went out to the living room the little red wagon was there! It was tucked under the sparkling tree, surrounded by gaily-wrapped parcels, and it was truly the most beautiful thing I had ever seen. The lights on the tree reflected like diamonds in the shiny red paint. I was afraid to touch it, as if it might vanish like a dream does when you wake up. When I turned to look at my parents, my mom was crying with a hanky clutched in her hand. Dad's smile was bigger than anything I'd ever seen.

We carefully moved it out into the room, and I ran my hands over every inch. The metal was smooth and cool, and the long black handle fit into my small hand perfectly. The slanted "T. Eaton Company" gold lettering on the side was perfect. The tires were rough and nubby, and made a deep satisfying rumble when I pulled the wagon along the floor. Although I am sixty years old now, I can still smell those rubber tires.

I never did play with the wagon—Mom was right about that. But I never stopped loving it. It hung from a hook in the garage for years, and sometimes I saw Mom using it to pull bags of garden soil to her flowerbeds. But I never once regretted owning it. It represented more than I could ever measure. Love, I guess—a tangible display of pure love.

~Julia Lucas
Aurora, Ontario

31

Without Words

Nobody can do for little children what grandparents do. Grandparents sort of
sprinkle stardust over the lives of little children.
~Alex Haley

Granddad was deaf. Not stone deaf but sufficiently hearing impaired to make communicating with him a chore. He stubbornly refused to wear the hearing aid the family had purchased. "More bother than it's worth," he'd mutter. Frustrated in his attempts to interpret what was being said, he became gruff, taciturn, and withdrawn.

Most of the family, equally frustrated, minimized their conversations with him. Left largely on his own, Granddad turned to the dogs and horses that had always been a big part of his life.

As a shy, introverted child who preferred the written to the spoken word, and an equally passionate canine and equine fancier, I fit hand in glove as Granddad's companion. Each Sunday afternoon when my parents and I visited his farm, he and I would slip away from the cacophony of the family gathering in the kitchen. Without a single word passing between us, we'd saunter out to the barn, Granddad's dog at our heels.

Once inside we'd stroll past the cow stalls filled with large-eyed Jerseys in winter, empty in summer, then sit down on a bench against the wall beside the horse stalls. Granddad's pair of Percherons, Smiler and Lou, would back up their great haunches until they could turn their heads and roll big brown eyes at their visitors. They'd whinny a welcome, then return to their hay-filled mangers.

Granddad would then pull a couple of oranges from his mackinaw pocket and hand one to me. In companionable silence we'd peel and eat.

When we'd finished, Granddad would go to the back door that accessed the pasture and throw it wide open. The horses, in anticipation, stopped eating and began to move restlessly. Slapping them on the rumps to get them to move aside he'd go into their stalls and release first one, then the other.

With eager snorts and dancing hooves, they'd back themselves free, whirl, and thunder out of the barn, their hooves pounding the plank floor.

From the doorway Granddad and I would watch them race away across the pasture, tails and manes streaming, over brilliant green grass in summer and glistening snow in winter. Glancing up into Granddad's bright blue eyes I knew he shared my joy in those perfect moments.

Sometimes we watched them for nearly an hour, not a single word passing between us. Then, as the time for me to go home grew near, Granddad would call out to them. No matter how far out across the field the team happened to be at that moment, they'd pause, turn, and prick their ears in his direction. He'd call again and they'd start toward him at a trot, thick necks arched, obedient out of love and respect for the man by my side.

I was thirteen that winter, totally enamoured with horses, and dependent on those Sunday afternoon visits to shore up my spirits for the week ahead at junior high school. To this day the scent of oranges still sends my spirit back to those wonderful afternoons with Granddad.

Glowing from my time with Granddad and the horses, I returned to the farmhouse late one November afternoon in time to catch my ride home with my parents. My heart and mind were occupied with flying manes and tails and sleek, powerful creatures of incredible beauty, so I paid little attention to the discussion between my uncle, who had now taken over the farm from my eighty-year-old Granddad, and my father.

"Horses cost a lot to keep over the winter. We won't be logging with them this year either. A tractor..."

I climbed into the back seat and closed the door on my uncle's words. I wasn't worried. Granddad and his horses were as much a part of the farm as the orchards and meadows.

Then came the Sunday just before Christmas. A hard frost gripped a still, grey morning when I awoke. As my parents and I drove toward Granddad's farm shortly after noon I gazed out the window at the brown, barren landscape of a winter's day lying in wait for the first snow to give it life and sparkle.

I hoped there'd be snow soon; snow deep enough and soft enough for Smiler and Lou to gallop through, sprays of white crystals flying from their pounding hooves. Maybe it would snow later that day.

At the farm I jumped out of the car and headed for the barn at a run.

"Tell Granddad I'm out here," I yelled back over my shoulder to my parents.

I unlatched the door and sped past the row of placidly munching Jerseys. And stopped short.

The horses' stall stood empty. And clean. Pristinely clean. Hosed and scrubbed clean. A horrible sense of unreality swept over me. My uncle's words resounded in my mind. I felt lightheaded, my stomach roiled. No! No! No!

"Smiler! Lou!" I dashed to the rear door and flung it open. The pasture with its frost-dead grass lay silent and empty... except for a shiny red tractor parked near the back of the barn.

"No!" My cry echoed its despair out across the field. "No!"

I heard the front door of the barn open. I turned to see Granddad coming inside. He seemed to have shrunken from his lofty six-foot four-inch height, his broad shoulders stooped as he came slowly down the length of the barn toward me. As he drew near, I saw that his blue eyes were faded, their sparkle gone.

When he reached our bench he sat down heavily and looked up at me. His eyes filled with tears and so did mine. Sinking down beside him, I scrubbed them away with the backs of my mittens. He dug into his mackinaw pocket, pulled out two oranges and handed one to me.

I took it. Holding the unpeeled fruit in our hands, we sat silently side by side and watched the first flakes of winter begin to obliterate the hoof prints churned into the earth outside the back door of the barn.

At that moment no one could have convinced me that anything good could ever come from what had happened. It wasn't until a Christmas many years later, long after Granddad had died, that one snowy evening on my way home I passed a child eating an orange. The smell of it rising in the frosty air sent me down a road of memories… memories filled with precious moments shared with my soulmate grandfather, and our beloved horses.

Smiler and Lou had probably long since gone to their rewards, I realized, but the wordless bond they'd established between one shy teenage girl and her grandfather would live forever.

~Gail MacMillan
Bathurst, New Brunswick

32

The Great Chicken Escape

Ever consider what pets must think of us? I mean, here we come back from a
grocery store with the most amazing haul—chicken, pork, half a cow. They
must think we're the greatest hunters on earth!
~Anne Tyler, The Accidental Tourist

"Just pick it up in your hands!"

"Me? Why do I have to do it?"

"You're good with animals. Besides, chickens aren't very smart."

"Yeah, but I've never picked up a chicken before."

Christmas 2002 was the Great Chicken Escape. We spent the holidays on Pender Island house-sitting, cat-sitting and chicken-sitting for our seriously organic friends. Our friends were especially concerned that their four prized Rhode Island Reds got the proper care and attention while they were away.

We read the typed Chicken Care Instruction List, we really did, but something went awry. Those chickens just didn't like us.

On day one, we let them out into the yard, as instructed. Just as the day was fading we went out to shoo them back into the coop but two were missing. I figured the gals had panicked at the sight of twilight. There they were huddled on the woodpile under the porch, silent as eggs, unwilling to budge.

Great. It was Christmas Eve and the chickens were rebelling. It came down to a twilight relocation operation, and I was elected chicken-picker-upper.

I tried to cultivate an inner calm, though my mind was full of visions of being pecked to death. I reminded myself that none of the crazed attackers in The Birds were chickens. No, these chickens weren't crazed, they were dazed. Shut down like feathered tea cozies.

I approached slowly. Thanks to my Tao of Fowl approach, I managed to wrap my hands around one bird and carry her back to the coop. She was eerily compliant. Back to get chicken number two. She made one gurgly objection but went as gently into the coop as her sister. All chickens now safely in their straw beds, with visions of chicken feed dancing in their heads, we retired to the house for our Christmas Eve dinner.

That was when it occurred to me. Roast chicken. They must have panicked at the whiff of their distant cousin cooking in the oven. (The house owners, being vegetarians, are not known to roast flesh of any kind.) We had traumatized them.

Christmas morning we awoke to the sounds of a happy chicken choir. "Buck-buck-a-bwuckagghhh!" It was my turn to open up the coop, let the "girls" out, and then pilfer their nests for breakfast eggs. Judging by their contented behaviour, it seemed they had already forgotten their little jail bust of the day before.

I groped around in the straw for a big warm egg. I groped again. But this morning there were none. They had not forgotten. Pure chicken spite. I was half glad anyway because I felt a bit guilty about stealing their unrealized progeny.

Despite the eggless manger, we managed to enjoy a lazy Christmas breakfast and a lazy Christmas lunch, which brought us to the proverbial afternoon stroll to work off just enough calories so we could stuff ourselves yet again on Christmas dinner. We put on our coats and stepped outside into a deep fog bank, so thick that the only sign the Swartz Bay ferry was passing by was a low rumble and fuzzy lights gliding past.

When we returned from our walk, our cheeks cool from the fog, something seemed off. The chickens. They weren't kibitzing around in the back yard. They had flown the coop! (During our stay I came to understand every chicken idiom ever coined by man.)

In a panic we phoned our friends.

"Uh, Pamela, your chickens seem to have disappeared."

"What? What do you mean?"

"They're not in the coop, not in the yard. They've escaped."

"They've never done that before! Why would they do that?"

We assured her that we had followed every painstaking detail on the Chicken Care Instruction List (but conveniently omitted mentioning the roast chicken dinner). She gave us a few neighbours' phone numbers and told us to call back when we found her Rhode Island Reds.

The search was launched. We spent the next two hours of Christmas Day in the dwindling light, already obscured by fog, on a chicken hunt in the forests and fields of North Pender Island. While people sat snugly in their living rooms, glowing in the coloured lights of their Christmas trees, sipping organic wine, basting turkeys and tofurkeys, we traipsed through pastures and meadows and sword fern groves clucking like idiots in search of birds that were supposed to be stupid but had somehow outsmarted us.

The neighbour's dog, eager for a little adventure, tagged along—behind us. This was no Foxhound. In fact, hailing from Pender it was likely he too was a vegetarian. Over hill and dale and stump and swamp we searched. An hour went by. Two hours. It was getting darker. We were starting to stumble. Just as we were ready to give up in defeat, I heard a crackle in the nearby bushes. Aha! There they were, the first two escapees, hiding in a bramble-covered ditch, muttering.

Soon after, the other two were spotted in separate locations, looking a little weary of the caper. In the end, we gave up trying to capture them in our hands and herded them. They took their sweet time, poking their beaks into this and that along the way just to irk us.

Applying the ideal chicken benevolence behaviour practises outlined in the Chicken Instructions, we prodded them back into their little wooden house with its old shoe for a door hinge and its crooked scrap lumber walls. Tired and broody ourselves, we retired to our little house and its wood stove, the fire now a feeble heap of embers.

Next time we chicken-sit, it's tofurkey for dinner.

~Barbara Black
Victoria, British Columbia

Angel in Waiting

A good teacher is like a candle — it consumes itself to light the way for others.
~Mustafa Kemal Atatürk

I only wanted to be an angel. Just once. It was always Esther, or Karen, or my sister, or all three, but never me. I understand now why I was overlooked each year. I wasn't really the angel type. Grade six girls were not exactly contenders for anything that involved good looks. Our teeth were still falling out and coming in, which in itself was laughable. I have only to look at school pictures from those years for a good belly laugh! Add the monster, puberty, looming on the horizon, and the package was far from fetching.

I am sure my mother's genes were defective during my embryonic formative stages. Throughout my life I have maintained that I should have been a boy. I was muscular where other girls were soft and feminine. I had a "pioneer" stockiness that in later life gave way to a constant battle with the scales. My face was long and horsey, not heart-shaped and appealing like my female peers. I was gangly, walked and played rough like the boys, and cussed like them. So how could I be a sweet little angel at a Christmas concert? There was nothing sweet about me, and I hadn't been little since babyhood. I was slated to be one of the shepherds forever in elementary school.

Midway through the year our Miss Fraser became Mrs. MacDonald and Mommy all in a matter of months. She left, and a new teacher arrived to teach this gaggle of farm kids. The new teacher, Mr. Fuller, was a hoot. He made learning fun, and there wasn't a kid there who didn't like him. He was young, had new ideas that worked, and after a few short weeks he had captured the interest of every student and every parent for miles around.

Kids who never answered a question in class were winning public speaking contests, and the morale in his classroom was higher than any experienced in that school. I didn't know it as morale then, but I knew I was suddenly anxious and eager to be on that bus every day, just to show him my new project or read my latest story. He is definitely the teacher who sparked my love of writing. Mr. Fuller saw a vision of the writer-to-be. He read all of my stories in class, pointing out what I did naturally as what writing was all about to my classmates.

Christmas was one month away. Mr. Fuller told us to be prepared the next day—he would be choosing class members for plays and singing, and other acts. Already knowing my fate, I dug out my towel and the piece of rope for my headgear and Grandpa's old striped robe for my costume. I still had my shepherd's crook that my mother had made from a willow branch, soaked and bent at just the right angle.

Class on "choosing day" was relaxed and fun. It was hard for Mr. Fuller to bring us to any kind of order.

"Class! Listen up," he announced. "We are doing something very different this year. I've talked to the other teachers, and no one else has used the entire class for their contribution to the concert. We are! Every one of you will be in this play. It is a musical rendition of the Nativity. That means it is all singing, so you better oil your vocal cords! Yes, we are doing the first musical ever at Warren Central School. I want your attention, and I need volunteers."

He had a long list in his hand. I didn't have to volunteer. I knew I would be appointed the shepherd, even if it was in a play in someone's living room. Everyone knew I had the outfit.

"Who wants to be Mary?" he asked.

Well, that wouldn't be my first choice. I wanted to be an angel. Karen put her hand up, and she was Mary. Joseph was next. Lance became Joseph. I wondered if Joseph had a crop of blond peach fuzz on his chin like Lance, but they would likely cover it with one of

Mrs. Reid's woollen beards. She made beards for everyone, including Santa, if we needed one.

Mr. Fuller told us he had auditioned his newborn baby at home last night, and the baby had passed the test at two in the morning. He said he knew how to sing just like the Baby Jesus did so long ago in that stable far away. So, we were also having a real baby in the manger! This was looking like great fun.

"Okay, good news for the rest of you," he continued. "Really easy costumes." Yep. Really easy. I had mine ready. I could see me now, kneeling in the background, with my shepherd's crook.

"The rest of the girls will be angels," he said, and that was all I heard. As far as I knew, I was one of "the rest of the girls" and I was finally going to be an angel! I would be the best angel they had ever had. I had been practicing for this role for years in my dreams.

I willed the bus to go faster that night. My mother had an angel costume to make, and for once it wasn't her usual darling who would wear it. I was the newest angel on the cloud.

I will likely never forget that Christmas concert, mostly because I was an angel. A halo-bedecked, white-gowned angel with coat-hanger wings covered in organdie filched from a discarded crinoline belonging to my aunt. I was "precious," my grandpa said, although my mother was much less effusive in her praise of my costume.

"It'll do," she muttered matter-of-factly as she pulled it from the sewing machine the morning of the concert.

It'll do? It was far better than "it'll do." It was the most breathtaking costume I had ever had on my body. I knew my songs inside out. They were old favourite carols we had grown up singing at home and at Sunday school.

We sang like angels, and Mr. Fuller's little baby boy, the Infant Holy, squalled like any newborn as we sang. The musical was an unrivalled success in the Christmas concert history of Warren Central School. And best of all? I was finally an angel.

~Gloria Jean Hansen
Elliott Lake, Ontario

The Holiday Diary

The only gift is a portion of thyself.
~Ralph Waldo Emerson

I t was difficult to leave the hospitality of Victoria. This port town on Vancouver Island has a special charm all its own. The pace is relaxed and the walks are well marked and so welcoming. My husband and I rented a car and headed out to the town of Tofino on the west side of the island. The five-hour drive through winding mountain roads and forests was simply breathtaking.

We arrived at our lodge, situated on a private beach located on the ocean. Our room consisted of a sitting room, a bathroom with a hot tub, a bedroom with a picture window overlooking the beach and ocean, and two fireplaces. There was also a small balcony. Here we would spend our Hanukkah together.

The romantic holiday atmosphere of this setting was close to perfection. Enjoying the cozy warmth inside, we rarely left our suite.

One morning as we were enjoying our breakfast in front of the picture window, I glanced at the fireplace and noticed a small book sitting on the mantle. I reached for it, and when I opened it I discovered it was a diary written by guests over the years who had stayed in this room. I began reading the first entry.

"My name is Jim. My wife and I are searching for the most beautiful places on earth to visit before I die. I have terminal cancer. We love this spot, this view and this room."

I started to cry. When my husband asked me if I was okay, I began to read the entries out loud to him.

The next writer began with the words, "Before I write about why I am here, I want to comment on what Jim wrote." By now I had a box of Kleenex next to me and soon needed a second one. Each story was more moving than the last. "We return here for each anniversary." "We are on our honeymoon." "He proposed to me in this room." "We come here to watch storms and to hold one another."

When I finished reading, my husband asked me, "Are you going to write in the diary?"

"Yes," I answered with a smile. I gazed at my wonderful husband for a long time. With this man I had found the love for which I had long searched. He was not only my husband but also my best friend with whom I shared everything in my life. Like the others who had come before, I was so happy on our special holiday, in this special place because I shared it with him. And that is what I wrote about.

The romantic intimacy of this room was ours at this moment in time, yet we were connected to all the couples who had been here before us and would come here after us. It felt to me like we were strangers who were all family, because this room and its memories belonged to each of us. Being able to read and share in the messages of this lovely diary could not have been a better holiday gift.

~Elynne Chaplik-Aleskow
Chicago, Illinois

A Last Gift

*He who has gone, so we but cherish his memory, abides with us,
more potent, nay, more present than the living man.*
~Antoine de Saint-Exupéry

On New Year's Eve, after almost two decades, we were about to view our wedding video for the first time. My children, Mia and Kieran, huddled beside me under soft blankets on the couch while my husband Michael dimmed the lights. The snow was piled high against the sliding doors on this cold, clear Northern Ontario night, but we were cozy cuddled together in our family room. I pressed "play" on the remote, waiting anxiously for the images to appear on the screen.

Before long we were transported back to December 30, 1995. Lights glowed on the towering Christmas tree beside the altar of St. Matthew's, our small Finnish Lutheran church. The pews, adorned with our homemade decorations of pine boughs, bells, and red ribbons, were filled with our family and friends, faces so familiar, but so much younger than I remembered. As I listened to the lovely strains of the string quartet playing Pachelbel's "Canon," I imagined the scent of red roses filling the air. I scanned the rows, realizing how many of these faces were no longer with us. I smiled to see my father-in-law so proud and healthy-looking, as he escorted my mother-in-law to their pew. Less than five years later he would pass away from cancer.

"There's Stephanie and Julia. Aw! They're so little," Kieran said, as he watched my two nieces walk down the aisle in their tiny ballerina flats. Six-year-old Julia's big brown eyes shone and her dark ringlets bounced, while five-year-old Stephanie, blonde and blue-eyed, smiled at her father, my brother John, behind the video camera. The girls wore nearly identical dresses fashioned from the silk of my gown and embellished with fabric roses. Rings of baby's breath encircled their heads like halos.

A flood of memories engulfed me as I watched myself walk down the aisle to Bach's "Jesu, Joy of Man's Desiring."

"Look at your hair, Mom." Mia giggled, as she pointed to my teased tresses. "And those poofy sleeves."

"Hey, those were in style then," I said. "Your mummu made me that dress from raw silk we found at a fabric warehouse in Toronto. She created the pattern herself after seeing the Laura Ashley dress I wanted."

"Look, Dad. You had hair!" Mia laughed. "And check out those big glasses."

"Yeah, I looked good," Michael said.

My eyes welled as our parents lit candles for us. I laughed as I saw myself discreetly wiping my nose. Some of my guests commented later on how touching my tears were during the ceremony; they didn't know the fragrant flowers were to blame.

My brother John had captured every moment. The family photographer, preserving precious moments on film, he was a natural choice for our videographer. He always ensured the lighting was perfect, the angle just right and everyone's eyes were open. Sometimes his subjects got irritated. "Take the photo, already," I'd groan, but I knew he'd take a flawless shot.

The day after the wedding ceremony, John's footage played in the living room of my parents' bungalow while we opened our wedding gifts. Assuming there would be plenty of time later to see the footage, I paid little attention, and focused instead on family and friends. Afterward, John took the film home to Sault Ste. Marie, promising to convert it from V8 to VHS for us. I left it in his capable hands.

I didn't see or hear about the videotape for several years. Sometimes, I asked about it during family gatherings, but it seemed to have vanished. I imagined it was in a dusty box somewhere with piles of others John had taken over the years. It will turn up eventually, I thought. But, after John and his family moved into their new home, I resigned myself to the fact that my wedding footage was gone for good.

One day, John arrived on my parents' doorstep, a small V8 cassette in hand.

"Guess what I found," he said. His eyes twinkled as he grinned broadly.

"It can't be." I turned the tape over in my hands.

"Well, it is, but look, there's just one problem. It's completely out-of-date. There is no way to play it now. You'll have to get it reformatted."

I frowned. "I'm not sure where to get that done."

"If you want, I'll take it back to the Soo (Sault Ste. Marie). I know a guy."

I hesitated. Finally, I agreed and reluctantly passed back the cassette.

Years passed—again. On January 1, 2004, our families assembled for a celebration at my parents' house. It was Stephanie's fourteenth birthday and my father had ploughed a rink on the lake as he had often done when we were children. We skated across the bumpy ice and raced around the curving tracks, the sun bouncing off the bright white snow. Camera in hand, John took several shots of our children skating together. Before the pale yellow sun settled in the late afternoon sky, he passed it to me. In a rare reversal, I was the one behind the camera capturing a special moment.

The four stood closely together, John's arms embracing his wife, Judith, and their children, Stephanie and Andrew. A thin blanket of snow stretched across the lake to the hills in the distance and a last show of light shone in the purpling sky. John beamed at the camera in complete peace and happiness. As I took the picture, I couldn't help but shudder. For just an instant, a flashbulb illuminated the sky. I didn't mention the strange sensation as I passed the camera back to my brother.

Two months later John was skiing on Red Lake when he was struck by a snowmobile, and killed instantly. The photograph was the last one taken of John with his family.

• • •

A few years later, I received a package in the mail from my sister-in-law. I ripped open the bubble wrap to find a small V8 cassette with faint pencil markings. My wedding video!

It sat on my kitchen table for many days before I finally placed it in a drawer. Once in a while, I would notice it as I rummaged for a pen or paper, a twinge of guilt passing through me. There was always something more important to do, a child needing my attention, chores to be done. I'd waited this long, I thought. Perhaps I wasn't ready to unleash the memories I knew it contained. Finally, I found a way to get it converted to DVD and gave it to my husband Michael as an anniversary gift.

Now, as we watched the film together, I realized it was eighteen years since my wedding and nearly ten years since my brother's tragic passing. When it came to a close, I wiped away the tears and hugged my children closer, thankful to share these precious moments with them, and even more grateful to see beloved faces from long ago.

When the screen turned to blue, I was about to press "stop" on the remote. But muffled voices caught my attention and then suddenly more images appeared on the screen. There was more footage. As we watched, little Stephanie twirled in her flowing nightdress with one of her cousins. I could hear John's voice chatting with the adults. Before long, everyone was wishing one another a "Happy New Year!" Then, with the camera safely on the tripod, John stepped briefly from behind and into the shot. There he was again, young and happy, full of life, capturing memories on film. I smiled through my tears at this unexpected, and absolutely perfect last gift.

~Liisa Kovala
Sudbury, Ontario

Chapter 4

Christmas in Canada

O Christmas Tree!

Perhaps the best Yuletide decoration is being wreathed in smiles.

~Author Unknown

Our Special Christmas Tree

Never worry about the size of your Christmas tree.
In the eyes of children, they are all thirty feet tall.
~Larry Wilde, The Merry Book of Christmas

December of 1982 marked the end of a year scarred by divorce, selling a house in a buyer's market, then finding and moving into an upper level, two-bedroom apartment on the Beach in Toronto. I was almost twenty-three and Ryan, my son, had just turned two. As a sole-support parent I barely eked out a living. Since we had moved on the first of December, I only had three weeks to get Christmas organized in our new home.

I bought the cheapest fake tree I could find and, as Ryan and I put it together, I accepted the fact that it wasn't much of a tree. But, the silver tinsel, cardboard angel and one string of lights I'd bought seemed magical. Every evening, after dinner and Ryan's bath, we would sit beside our tree and I would tell him how special it was. He was two and he believed me.

My parents wanted us to sleep at their house on Christmas Eve, but I was committed to starting our own traditions. I wanted Ryan to sleep in his own bed and wake up on Christmas morning in his own home with his presents under our tree. On Christmas morning, Ryan woke up so early and full of excitement that we were finished with opening presents and eating breakfast and on our way to my parents' house before they even woke up.

After Christmas that year I went shopping and bought cards,

a few more lights and some decorations at Boxing Day sales. Thus began my annual Christmas shopping habit. I didn't make enough money to pay for Christmas all at once so I bought gifts on sale when I found them throughout the year, and picked up decorations at garage sales during the summer. Even though I had little money, I wanted Ryan to grow up with happy memories of Christmas. So, our traditions grew. We put up our tree in late November and took our time decorating it.

Each Christmas Ryan discovered the new decorations I'd picked up the year before. We also began an annual practice of making our own decorations. When people we knew travelled they would bring us back unique tree decorations. It didn't take long before our scrawny tree looked full and stood proudly in our living room.

The side benefit of buying gifts all year was that my Christmas shopping was done by the end of October. This meant I could enjoy the holiday season without financial stress, and Ryan and I could have fun splurging on special treats and activities. We loved Christmas and our tree was at the heart of it. Over time, as my earnings increased, I bought a proper angel for the top of our tree, but the thought of buying a new tree never entered my mind. Even I believed that we had the best tree in the world.

When Ryan was eleven my father died, so we moved into my mother's house and had to put most of our stuff, including our precious tree, into storage. We celebrated at my mum's house for the next few years and Ryan really missed his tree. While her artificial tree was five times the size of ours, and actually looked real, it just wasn't special to him.

In 1994, my soon-to-be husband Dave and I bought a house in Richmond Hill, a suburb north of Toronto, and my mum bought a condo there. We all moved on the same day and her tree ended up in our garage. It was too big for her condo, and in any case, she no longer wanted it.

Ryan had recently turned fifteen and was overjoyed, as Christmas approached, to know he would finally have his own tree and decorations back. But when our little fourteen-dollar tree emerged in parts from its box, Ryan didn't quite know how to react. He'd grown a fair bit and was already close to six feet tall.

"It's not like I remembered," he said, his voice thick with disbelief. "It's not even half of what I thought it would be."

"It gets better and more special when we add all of our decorations," I reassured him. But even as I spoke those words, I too was shocked at how scrawny our little tree really was.

Dave happened upon us at that moment in the living room and saw the sad look in both of our eyes, and the even sadder sight of our little tree, which was dwarfed even more by the size of our new living room.

Dejectedly, Ryan waved his hand over our tree and said, "This, Dave, is the most amazing tree I have been talking about for years. Can you believe it? How can I have thought this was the most special tree in the world? And, yet how can it not be?"

And in that moment, Dave seemed to understand that the memory of our tree and the reality of our tree were two different things. "What if," he asked us, "we meld Nana's tree with yours? This way, your special tree will become a part of our new tree."

Dave was not enthusiastic about Christmas, so his suggestion surprised and thrilled us at the same time. He took our little tree to the garage and merged the poles from Nana's tree with one from ours, and then drilled new holes to accommodate most of the different branches. It took a while for Ryan and me to put all the mismatched branches onto our new tree, and we had some left over, but when we were finished it was truly an awesome tree.

And so, with Dave's help, we were content knowing that we hadn't abandoned our little tree that had meant so much to us, but simply helped it grow and be part of something bigger and better—much like we were now doing as a family.

The funny thing was that some of our Christmas spirit seemed to rub off on Dave. He took the remaining tree pole and, with the leftover branches, made himself a "Christmas Bush." He then set it up in his office and decorated it with old computer parts.

It felt so right that Christmas Eve to finally go to sleep in our own beds in our own home, once again with the best tree in the whole world still standing proudly in our living room — waiting for us on Christmas morning.

~Laura Snell
Wasaga Beach, Ontario

Answered Prayer

The message of Christmas is that the visible material world
is bound to the invisible spiritual world.
~Author Unknown

"Lord, what can I do now?" I asked, as I drove home without a Christmas tree for our family.

For weeks our nine-year-old daughter Janelle had been praying for a "real" Christmas tree. She thought the tiny hand-me-down silver tree we usually put up was simply not suitable anymore.

"Mom, our tree is so small — and you've said yourself that someone gave it to you, and some day you hope to buy a real one."

"A real one would be nice," I agreed, "but we don't have money for a real tree or the decorations we would need. What would a big beautiful tree look like without an angel to sit on top?"

I had usually put up the tree in late November. I loved the Christmas season and I felt decorating early was a great way to start the festivities — but not this year. Janelle was so sure that God would answer her prayer for a real tree, so we all had to wait.

The days went by and we were not any closer to getting a real tree. We'd had another poor year on the farm and simply could not afford to "waste" money on a real tree, especially since we did have this old one.

"Please help me to find a solution before this hurts Janelle's fragile faith," became my prayer. But as the weeks went by I began to wonder if maybe we should try to buy one.

About ten days before Christmas, I went into town to pick up our mail and a few groceries. I couldn't help stopping by the lumberyard where a local charity sold real Christmas trees. I just wanted to check out how much they were selling for. I gasped as I came around the corner and saw they only had three trees left. I walked briskly over to them, thinking they must be cheap or damaged to be the only ones left, but I was surprised to see three top-of-the-line trees and they had an out-of-reach price tag to go with them. I walked away knowing we could not afford one of those trees for sure.

That is why I was asking, "What can I do now Lord?"

I prayed as I drove and planned how I would break the news to Janelle. I knew she would be very disappointed and hurt, but we would have to go ahead and put up the little silver tree. Would it be better to have it up when she came home off the bus? Or should I wait, tell her what we needed to do, and let her help me put up the little tree?

Later that afternoon the phone rang. It was our neighbour Ted. We weren't close, so I figured he must be calling to talk farming with my husband Ken.

"No, you're just the lady I'm looking for," he said.

"Oh, really?" I replied.

"First, I'd better ask if you have put up your Christmas tree yet."

"No, as a matter of fact we haven't. I know it's getting late but…"

Ted cut me off with, "Now that my boys are married they wanted a tree for their own places so we went away up north this morning to get ourselves a tree. For some strange reason we ended up with an extra tree and, I wondered… could we give it to you?"

I was speechless. "For some strange reason," he had said. Could the reason have been a little girl's prayer?

I stammered as I tried to answer him. "Yes…Yes… sure… we'd love to have a real tree…." I was sure Ted would hear my heart pounding.

"You don't owe us a thing," he continued. "As I said, I don't know how we ended up with the extra tree, but you are welcome to have it. I'll drop it off in a bit."

I got off the phone shaking my head. How could Ted have possibly known? We hadn't told anyone, and we didn't know him well enough. He'd never been in our home to see our "little" tree. Only a God who truly cares about the little and big things in life could have arranged for Ted to get an extra tree, and then put it in his heart to call and offer it to us.

That day, as the bus pulled into the yard, there was one very excited little girl when she saw a "real tree" in our yard, ready to be pushed, pulled, and eventually cut down to fit into our house. It didn't matter that our decorations weren't the greatest, lights were nonexistent, and there was no angel for the top. After all, a "real Christmas tree" was what she had prayed for, and wasn't having a tree that had truly been delivered by angels better than having one at the top of the tree?

~Annie Riess
Unity, Saskatchewan

Waking the Tree

It comes every year and will go on forever. And along with Christmas
belong the keepsakes and the customs. Those humble, everyday
things a mother clings to, and ponders....
~Marjorie Holmes

Winter mornings in Canada are dark and chilly. We wake long before the sun has peeked over the horizon. It is early in the morning, a couple of weeks before Christmas. The hardwood floor is chilly and it creaks under my feet as I enter my daughter's room to wake her for school. Sometimes it's hard to get her out from under the warm covers. But during the month of December, my four-year-old wakes willingly. She knows she has an important job to do.

She must wake the Christmas tree.

Holding onto my hand, she walks with me into the living room. The scent of pine hangs in the air. One of our cats stretches and comes to wind around our legs, asking for breakfast. Not yet. We must wake the tree.

"Good morning, Christmas tree!" my daughter says, standing before the tall, dark tree. "It's time to wake up."

As she says this, I kneel down and plug in the lights. And the tree awakes.

Soft white lights glow among the branches. Stars, angels, and other ornaments twinkle in the light. My daughter's face reflects the glow. Her eyes sparkle.

The room no longer seems cold and dark. It has become warm and festive.

When I was a child Christmas was a magical time. I remember the soft light of Advent candles, the twinkle of the Christmas tree lights, hanging my stocking and wondering what Santa Claus would bring. Now, I realize that much of the Christmas magic is what we as parents create for our children. When my daughter wakes the tree, or when we set out cookies and milk for Santa or toss carrots on the front lawn for his reindeer to eat, we are the creators, the magicians. And for me, the joy of Christmas is seeing her delight. It is passing down the magic to her.

Perhaps one day she will be waking in the dark of winter, walking into a quiet bedroom to whisper in the ear of her own sleeping child, "Good morning, sweetheart. Let's go wake the tree."

~Anita Grace
Ottawa, Ontario

The Tree Trimming Party

When you look at your life, the greatest happinesses are family happinesses.
~Joyce Brothers

Although it was Wednesday and not an ideal night for a party, I still held out hope that our kids and their friends would make the drive home from university safely. Here, large snowflakes floated gently from the sky, but it was hard to know what the weather would be like between Owen Sound and Waterloo. It could be a clear starry night or a raging ice storm, as Highway 6 was famous for high winds and zero visibility during snowstorms.

Little scraps of material, piles of glitter, beads and buttons littered the entire dining room table, as I hurried to sew a Santa hat on the last snowman. "I hope they appreciate this," I groaned.

"Of course they will, sweetie," said Ed, my husband, as he stood by the patio door with the last empty gift box under his arm and a roll of wrapping paper in his hand.

"They've been wanting crazy Christmas sweaters for years. They're going to love them."

"I hope so. Don't tell them I've been working on them since Thanksgiving. They'll feel bad I wasted so much time on them... especially when they're only going to wear them for two minutes in a silly family picture."

"Your secret is safe with me," Ed replied. "Looks like our neighbours have stopped by for a visit."

"No way! Who is it?" I jumped off the chair and ran to the window.

He laughed and I smiled. Two deer had wandered into our back yard looking for something to nibble. Then, as quickly as they appeared, they bounded toward the woods, disappearing into the darkness. Something must have scared them.

"Oh no, the kids are here." Panic set in. I raced for the table, grabbed the sweater and threw it at Ed. He calmly folded it, placed it in the box and began wrapping. Car doors slammed and giggles became louder as they neared the house. The kids blew in the door, dropping their bags and backpacks in a large pile. There were six of them. Three were ours and three were tag-alongs. I reached out my arm and dragged everything on the table into a large bag, making my mess disappear.

"Is that pie I smell?" asked Ona, our oldest. "Lemon and pumpkin? Wow! This really is Christmas!" She started bouncing around the kitchen. By the way she acted, you'd never know she was turning twenty-two this year.

I looked up to see Nika, our middle child, as she kicked her shoes behind the door and ran toward me. She wrapped her arms around me and kissed me. "Missed you, Momma."

"Where are your boots?"

She dropped her head like a sad puppy. "I left them at school. We didn't have snow in the city... besides, who needs boots when you're spending Christmas in Cuba?" she sang.

How could I forget? Christmas in Cuba. What kid wouldn't love their father flying them to Cuba for ten days over the Christmas break?

"Well, we're in the middle of a Grey-Bruce blizzard here, so you probably should've brought your boots home anyway."

Ignoring me, she ran into the kitchen.

"Meatballs! My favourite! And is that shrimp?"

Our son, Foxton, dropped his huge hand on top of my head and gave it a twist, messing up my hair. He's the baby of the family, only sixteen, but towers over all of us at six feet four inches.

"How's my Mooo-der been this week without me?" he asked grinning. He's a cow lover and finds it important to be the funniest person in the room.

"Good, thanks, but I missed you, of course," I replied, flashing him a smile.

"Of course you did," he said. "That's because I'm your favourite child." He never missed a chance to use that line. "Come on Ben, I hear there's shrimp." He pulled his friend into the kitchen behind him.

After filling their bellies they all raced to the living room and circled around the naked artificial tree.

"Time to make our magic," announced Ona. "Jesse and I will put on the silver garland first. Foxton, you and Ben put on the Ottawa Senator and Toronto Maple Leaf Christmas balls, and Nika will do the blue and silver balls. Carlie, you hang the snowflakes. Special fragile ornaments go last, well not last, because the angel is last and that's my job... because I'm the oldest."

Everyone stood there making faces at her as she bossed them around, directing the tree trimming duties. It went like clockwork. Ed supervised, while I snapped pictures.

"Should we open one present tonight?" asked Ed, already knowing what their response would be. Our three kids dove under the tree and pulled out the gifts. Excitement filled the room as everyone pulled on their homemade sweaters and admired the unique Christmas themes.

"How cool is this?" Foxton asked, modeling his sweater, with his hands on his hips. "It's a camel in the desert with a Christmas palm tree. I love this!"

"Look! We have matching red sweaters," exclaimed Ona as she stood beside her boyfriend, Jesse, hers with Santa and his with reindeer peeking out from behind a giant Christmas tree.

"Mine is a cardigan with buttons... and a snowman. Did you make this? Are you sure you didn't buy this somewhere?" asked Nika.

"She spent about a week on each one, sewing until her fingers bled," responded Ed. "Oops! Sorry. I wasn't supposed to tell," he admitted, covering his mouth. He winked at me and smiled. I threw a candy cane at him.

I snapped the lid off of the last box. It was full of reindeer hats with antlers, elf hats with bells and fuzzy Santa hats. "Grab a hat and sit in front of the tree. It's time for the family picture," I said. I motioned for Jesse, Ben and Carlie to get in the picture. "Come on, you're our family too."

This had become our new family tradition: the tree trimming at our house before the kids flew south with their father. Not exactly fair, but it's what works best for the kids, and it's not like we could afford to take them south. Holidays can be a battlefield when dealing with blended families and quality time is hard to schedule, so we decided to celebrate with smiles, laughter and making memories with them, even if only for one night.

"Now it's rink time!" yelled Foxton. "Right, Ed?"

"Oh, it's definitely rink time." Ed grabbed the dozen hockey sticks leaning in the corner and hauled them outside to the truck. This was followed by hooting and hollering. Heading outside, the kids grabbed their ice skates, hockey gloves and helmets. Everyone sporting their new Christmas sweaters forgot their coats, as their heads and hearts were already in hockey mode. Renting the ice at the Keady arena for an hour of family hockey was always the evening's icing on the cake. It made the night complete. It was perfect. I grabbed my skates too, and I tried not to look at the clock, knowing soon they would be on a plane, leaving us behind.

~Lori Twining
Owen Sound, Ontario

Saved by the Tag

A person without a sense of humor is like a wagon without springs—jolted
by every pebble in the road.
~Henry Ward Beecher

"Hurry up Dad!" called Dana from the bed of our pickup truck. "I don't want to get left out of the tag making."

"Are the saw and rope on board?"

"Yes," replied her brother Rob. "I put them in myself."

I pointed to the cooler containing our contribution to the refreshments. "Add this to the load, Rob, and then climb in with it."

"Dana, get in up front with your mum."

Some of our family's fondest Yuletide memories involve acquiring our Christmas trees. This year in particular, getting our seasonal spruce would present us with an unexpected challenge and remarkable experience.

We were heading a bit north to see our friends, the Morleys, for their annual Christmas tree-cutting party. Once there, Carol and I would join the other adults and fortify ourselves with food and drink before venturing out. Meanwhile, the children would play outside in the snow or inside creating colourful, personalized "tree tags" to identify their family's selection. Eventually everyone would bundle up, grab saws and carpool to a nearby Christmas tree farm. Our host Larry would follow in a large cube van that would be used to transport the trees.

When we arrived, Carol, Rob, Dana, and I boarded the straw-covered cutter and enjoyed the thrill of having a team of high-stepping Clydesdales carry us to the trees. After the usual debate over which tree was best and responding to frequent calls of "look at this one!" and "there's a better one over here!" we cut a beautiful Fraser fir. Back in the parking lot Dana carefully affixed our tag, and our tree joined the others in the cube van for transport to the Morleys.

Back at the Morleys the older kids unloaded, placed the trees in, or on, the correct family's vehicle, and the party then moved into full swing. The eating, drinking, storytelling and seasonal singing lasted well into the evening.

Eventually it was time to leave, but we discovered our kids had opted to "crash" at the Morleys. So, looking very much forward to an unexpected "date night," Carol and I said our goodbyes. Before leaving I glanced into the open bed of our pickup to be sure our tree had been properly stowed and, opting to avoid the city streets, chose Highway 11 and headed south for home.

Upon arrival, the first order of business was to unload the tree and put it in the garage where it would defrost, ready to be erected and decorated on the morrow. I exited the truck and turned to remove the tree. That's when I discovered it was gone!

"Carol! Our Christmas tree is missing!" We looked at each other in dismay.

"Look." Carol pointed. "The rope's not tied off." While traveling home at highway speed, our unsecured tree must have flown out, and must now be lying somewhere back on Highway 11. We would have to retrace our route to find it.

Highway 11 has a centre divider so we had to travel north to an overpass before heading south again. Our fervent hope was that our tree had not ended up trunk first through some unsuspecting traveler's windshield or, failing that, been run over and ground into kindling by one of the numerous transport trucks that plied the busy highway.

We traveled slowly down the southbound lanes straining our vision, peering across into the northbound lanes, but did not spot our quarry. We reached our entry point and began to retrace our tracks northward. There were no streetlights, and a seasonal snow squall was now severely limiting our visibility.

Compounding our problem was the fact that this section of the highway had been planted with a significant number of evergreen trees as windbreaks. Also, we had no idea of the flight characteristics of a Fraser fir moving at 100 kilometres per hour. Ours could be lying in the ditch, or perhaps it had plunged trunk first into the snow and was standing straight and tall like one of the planted pines along the route. We spotted several possibilities and stopped to investigate but, alas, upon closer inspection, all were live. We were drawing nearer to home and hopes were dimming, when Carol finally spotted it off to the side and yelled, "There it is!"

Pulling onto the shoulder, I slid down the slope of a snow-filled ditch to the tree, where I confirmed its identity. Elated, I grabbed the trunk and began to drag it uphill to the truck. Carol came partway down to lend a hand, and between us we got it safely to the tailgate. While we were loading it a vehicle suddenly pulled in behind us, lighting the scene with its headlights.

A siren whooped, red, white and blue lights began flashing and a disembodied voice commanded, "Step away from the tree…!"

An Ontario Provincial Police officer exited the cruiser and approached, directing the beam of her flashlight into our startled faces. I had the urge to raise my hands in surrender.

"Good evening," she said.

"Good evening Officer," Carol and I replied, almost in unison.

"We're just getting our Christmas tree," I added.

The officer shone her light into the bed of our truck, noting the saw and rope and turned her gaze back to us.

"Yes, I can see that. But stealing one of Her Majesty's pines is definitely not in the spirit of Christmas."

"Oh no, Officer," said Carol. "You've got it all wrong!"

"That's what they usually say. License and registration please."

I presented the requested documents.

"Officer, it really is our tree." I began to explain. "We cut it earlier today and we were driving home and..."

"Mr. Forrest, please. You've been caught in the act. I will be issuing a summons and of course confiscating the tree as evidence."

"Please no, Officer, I can prove it is our tree," replied Carol. "Please bring your flashlight over here."

The policewoman followed and shone her light on our fir. Carol rolled it slightly to expose a piece of cardboard tied securely to one of the branches. It colourfully and clearly displayed our name: Forrest.

The officer nodded. "Okay, that's proof enough for me," she conceded. "Carry on, but please secure that tree properly this time. And Merry Christmas!"

Chastened, we headed for home with yet another Christmas adventure to add to the Forrest family archives. This time we had been... "saved by the tag"!

~John Forrest
Orillia, Ontario

Artificial Happiness

The perfect Christmas tree?
All Christmas trees are perfect!
~Charles N. Barnard

We had moved into our new home in the spring of 1994. Living on acreage just north of Cochrane, Alberta, we had spent the summer months enjoying our view of the Rockies and watching our two young children playing in the yard. We all seemed well suited to the country lifestyle. With the snow falling and blanketing our yard in early December, we were excited about spending a good old-fashioned country Christmas together. We decided that rather than put up an artificial tree we would go on an outing to find a grand tree to celebrate our first Christmas in our new home.

We signed up with our church to go on their annual trek to find Christmas trees in the designated areas just northwest of where we lived. When the day came for the great family outing, the temperature had plummeted to -30 degrees C with the wind chill, so I stayed home with the children while my husband braved the elements to find our "perfect" tree on his own.

Being one of only a handful of men who actually showed up for the event, my husband promised to load his pickup with extra trees for other families who weren't prepared to face the sub-Arctic temperatures. At home I prepared the front room for the arrival of what I knew would be the grandest tree we ever had!

It was mid-afternoon when my husband finally arrived home. By then I'd spent a frustrating day with two cranky children. I wasn't feeling well, my mood was poor and my morning excitement about putting up a grand tree was gone.

My husband stumbled in and, with much waving of arms and gnashing of teeth, told me of his "adventure" finding us our "perfect" tree. First, after driving for hours into the tree-harvesting area he became stuck several times and more than once had to resort to four-wheel-drive off-roading. Then he had to trek about a kilometre on foot in knee-deep snow into the wilderness to cut down not only our tree, but three more for church friends. He found the biggest tree that would fit into the box of his truck for us, and proceeded to topple it with his chain saw.

Unfortunately when he was only half done his chain saw locked up and died. He then trekked all the way back to his truck to collect his hand saw, then back again to fell the massive tree. Did I mention it was -30 degrees C with the wind chill? Did I mention it was a kilometre back and forth from truck to trees?

After felling the great tree he dragged it back to the truck. Then he went back and collected the other trees, dragging two behind him before going back for the third and final tree. Loading them up, he was finally on his way back, but only a couple of kilometres from Cochrane one of the trees shifted and toppled out onto the road. Undaunted, he stopped, collected the road-mangled tree and flipped it back into the truck before delivering the trees to the other families. He did apologize for the mangled state of the one tree, but made it clear that if they didn't like it, they'd have to live with it, or go next week to collect one for themselves.

Having relayed to me his adventure he then off-loaded the gigantic tree into our yard and assessed how to best manoeuvre it inside. Realizing it would not fit through the front door he began trimming away branches, and then discovered the trunk would never fit in the puny tree stand we had. So he headed into town to buy the biggest tree stand he could find.

I waited for my gallant knight to return, all the while feeling more and more queasy and moody, and more than a little impatient to start the decorating. I really wanted to call it a day. After visiting four different stores he finally found a stand large enough to accommodate our tree. When he returned an hour later, working on our back deck he battled the tree into the largest tree stand I had ever seen. The sun was beginning to set as my husband hoisted the massive tree… up, up, up… and stood proudly beside it—dwarfed in its mighty shadow.

Satisfied by his day's herculean efforts, he pounded on the back window for me to see it. His cheeks glowed red with pride and accomplishment, while icicles of spittle and snot stuck to his mouth and nose. He probably thought himself the conquering hero, but looking out the window I saw something totally different. Then, in what I can only be described as a fit of insanity on my part, said, "I hate it!"

"What?" he yelled through the glass at me.

"I hate it!" I yelled back.

The tree was tall, certainly, but after my husband's feverish "trimming" the big Albertan Jack Pine had perhaps four or five branches left, and very little foliage. It looked like a Charlie Brown tree, but ten times as big. I thought about the hundreds of ornaments I had collected over the years and realized I'd be lucky to put twenty of them on that tree.

"I hate it! Take it back!" I cried.

I have never experienced a mad grizzly bear charge, but I had a good idea what it might be like when my husband barrelled into the house and stood before me snarling, "What's wrong with it?"

I tried to explain, but a grizzly bear is hard to reason with… so I made no attempt to stop him from bringing the tree into the house, all the while snorting and huffing at how insanely insensitive I was.

When he was finally done, it stood like a huge pine stick in the middle of the living room. We both decided to leave it until the next morning to decorate.

To say the atmosphere between us that evening was a little tense would be a drastic understatement. It got even worse when during the night I awoke struggling to breathe! The pine scent had wafted throughout the house and I discovered, quite by accident, I was allergic to pine!

The next morning, with my eyes swollen nearly shut, I stumbled downstairs to find the tree dripping white sap all over my hardwood floor.

When my husband emerged he took one look at my face and then at the tree and, without a word, pulled his boots on over his PJs, dragged the giant pine out of the house and heaved it into the yard.

A week later, our new nine-foot artificial Blue Spruce tree stood majestically in our living room. The giant Charlie Brown tree was donated to the seminary's children's Christmas party. They were very grateful and the children loved it… well… like Charlie Brown would have.

As we snuggled together and watched the twinkling lights on the fake tree, my husband winked at me. He had forgiven my fit of "insanity" and chalked it up to hormones. Patting my tummy, he grinned. A wonderful miracle was growing inside of me. My sudden allergic reaction to pine had prompted a visit to the doctor, and we learned I was expecting. We joked together that despite how our first Christmas in our new home had started out a little shaky, it was going to be one of the most memorable for us. There was no need to put any presents under our new tree… God was giving us the best Christmas present we could ever have hoped for!

~Lynn Dove
Cochrane, Alberta

Chapter 5

Christmas in Canada

The Santa Files

Canada Post receives letters to Santa from all over the world in languages ranging from Albanian to Vietnamese. Postal code readers all over the world recognize the H0H 0H0 postal code as belonging to Canada.

~Malcolm French, Spokesman for Canada Post

Hospital Surprise

How beautiful a day can be when kindness touches it.
~George Elliston

It was December 3rd, 1963, and my mother and I had arrived at the Hospital For Sick Children in Toronto. I was there for a serious heart operation—but that was the least of my worries.

I was only six, miles away from my Newfoundland home, and Christmas was just around the corner. Prior to my hospital stay, like most six-year-old children, I had written my letter to Santa, stressing my address on the bottom of the page with a black Crayola crayon, as not to be overlooked. Now my Christmas dreams would be dashed, thanks to a blonde nurse with a strong Scottish accent who told me I would be spending Christmas at the hospital. I hated that nurse for telling me that.

I was sure my Christmas would be ruined as Santa would never find me there.

As I watched the fluffy snowflakes float to the ground the Scottish nurse came into the room and asked, "Are you waiting for the parade?"

"What parade?" I asked, deliberately staring at the floor.

"The Santa Claus parade," she answered. It was to start at 2:00. She then said, "If you want, I can come later and take you to the recreation room, where you can watch through the big window." She crossed the room and deposited two little pink pills in my hand and put a paper cup full of apple juice on the metal table next to my bed.

"And then," she said, "if you are feeling up to it, you can stay in the recreation room and meet Santa. He will be here after the parade."

"Meet Santa?" She now had my complete attention. "Santa is coming here?"

I agreed to go and watch the parade, and shortly before 2:00, the nurse reappeared and pushed my wheelchair to a large room that was filled with other patients, some of whom were attached to IV poles or in wheelchairs, and all trying to get the best spot to watch the parade. With the nurse's help we all found suitable places to watch from the window, and before long we saw the first sign of the parade. We all watched excitedly and waved to the clowns, the bumper cars, and the marching bands as they went by. I could only imagine the sound of the fine musical instruments as their sounds rang out in the cold Toronto air. Finally, at the end of the parade Santa appeared. He was waving and blowing kisses to the crowd.

As the parade went out of sight, the blonde nurse reappeared and announced that Santa would be arriving at the hospital an hour later, so if anyone wanted to get their letter ready, this was the time.

This was my chance! Immediately I wheeled myself to the table and snatched a pencil and a couple sheets of paper, and found a quiet corner of the room.

Dear Santa,

I need an Easy Bake Oven, a paint set and some colouring books, and don't bring it to my house, please bring it here to the Toronto hospital.

Thank you, Debby

Shortly after, the nurse came in and arranged us all in a semi-circle, and told us to listen for bells. Sure enough, within minutes the distinct sound of bells filled the hallway and spilled into the room. At that point, the room erupted in cheers and claps as Santa stepped inside.

He was plump, though not as plump as I had imagined him. His red suit fit perfectly, and his black boots matched his wide belt. His eyes were a twinkling blue and his white hair blended with the trim of his cap.

He laughed his famous "ho ho ho" and many of the children tried to imitate him.

One by one, the children had a chance to go up and drop their letters into the oversized mailbag he was carrying. Finally it was my turn. I wheeled myself to the center of the room and faced the big man.

He smiled and asked, "Who do we have here?"

"Debby Janes from Newfoundland," I answered proudly.

He leaned back on the chair and said, "Well, Debby Janes from Newfoundland, what brings you to the hospital?"

"Well, sir, I need to get my heart fixed," I replied.

"Oh, I see," said Santa.

"And here is my letter," I said, thrusting the folded paper toward him.

He laughed a loud "ho ho ho" and tucked the letter into the mailbag, promising to read it.

"Thank you," I answered, "and you and Mrs. Claus have a very Merry Christmas."

I wheeled myself back to my spot in the circle and watched as the rest of the children took their turn presenting Santa with their letters, but I have to admit, the remainder of the afternoon was a blur.

That night, as I lay tucked in my hospital bed, I refused to think of needles, operations, bad hearts, or anything else that would spoil my day. I couldn't wait to see my mother the next day and tell her what had happened. I slept soundly that night for the first time in a long time. I had met Santa—and he knew where to find me! Maybe Christmas wasn't going to be so bad after all.

~Deborah Janes Collins
Bolton, Ontario

43

Merry Christmas, Harry Hanukkah!

*Being considerate of others will take your children further in life
than any college degree.*
~Marian Wright Edelman

M y son Benjamin was eight years old when he announced that he hated Christmas, especially Santa Claus. "Why is that, Ben?" I asked. We're Jewish and have always taught our kids to respect other religions and holidays. Ben, being the most sensitive of my gang, had really taken this advice to heart, so to hear he hated Christmas was quite a shock.

"Well, it's the Santa thing. What about the kids like my friend, Adrien, who spend the whole year being good so Santa will bring them something? You know what he got for Christmas? Nothing! His dad said they were broke and Santa only visits rich kids. He's so bummed."

I could almost see the wheels in his young brain whirling. "And what else are you thinking?"

"I think kids who keep getting disappointed like that are gonna be so angry that by the time they're teenagers they'll do rotten things like stealing or maybe even murder somebody."

That was an interesting thought process that seemed to hold an element of truth. "So what do you think we should do about this?" I asked.

"Give agnominal gifts!"

My eyebrows rose. "Um, do you mean anonymous?"

Ben sighed in frustration. He loved big words and tried to use them whenever he could, but he hated it when he made a mistake in pronouncing the word.

"Yeah, anonymous, only we give them to kids like Adrien."

"How do you propose we do that?" I said.

"I'll think about it," muttered Ben. "I've got a year."

The next Christmas I met a single mother whose welfare had been cut off, which meant no money for food or Christmas for her three-year-old daughter, Marya. As we sat at the supper table that night I told my family about Marya. No one had anything to say. Or at least that's what I thought.

Ben called an emergency family meeting later that night. "Mom, we want you to use the money you would have spent on us and buy presents for Marya. And I figured out how we'll do it. We'll sign the card Harry Hanukkah! Eight presents from Harry."

"There's no such thing as Harry Hanukkah," said my husband, William.

"Well, there is now," said Ben.

A few days later, the kids and I knocked on Marya's door, eight gifts in hand—along with a brisket, a turkey, and a fruit basket.

My friend cried as she watched her daughter open her presents. Marya, on the other hand, was very suspicious.

"He's Harry Hanukkah?"

"That's right," said Ben.

"Why not Santa?"

"Because some children are so special that Santa asks Harry to give them presents," piped in Miriam. "Harry is Santa's cousin."

"Where does Harry live?"

"Jerusalem," said Ben. He was enjoying this. "And instead of a sled, he has a magic carpet with camels pulling it."

Miriam groaned and rolled her eyes.

Marya looked at Ben. "Does he have a red suit like Santa?"

"No," said Miriam. "It's blue with white fur."

"In Jerusalem?" I asked.

"Yeah," said Ben as he glared at me. "It gets cold once in a while in Jerusalem."

When Marya's inquisition ended we had discovered that Harry lived on a mountain in Jerusalem, Mount Scopus, where he taught students during the day so no one would know who he was. Kind of like Clark Kent and Superman, who just happened to be Ben's favourite hero that week.

Harry was more practical than Santa. He bought the toys and clothes from Sears and Toys "R" Us, just in case he misunderstood Santa on sizes and the gifts had to be exchanged.

Marya was satisfied with Ben's explanations—for the time being.

Harry visited Marya for four more years. Every year the questions about Harry and Israel became more intense, with more demands for "facts."

Ben had answers for every question.

There were twelve camels: Asher, Dan, Gad, Joseph, Benjamin, Issachar, Judah, Levi, Naphtali, Reuben, Simeon, Zebulah. Judah didn't really fly with Harry. Someone had to stay in Jerusalem and pick olives.

Apparently Rudolph the red-nosed reindeer was not needed to guide the flying carpet. Joseph and his brightly coloured saddle blanket led the camels when they flew. There was glow stick material in the blanket and the darn thing lit up like neon lights. Who knew? The camels preferred gefilte fish and falafel to hay, and a Bedouin family just south of Jerusalem tended to them during the year.

Harry preferred latkes and wine to cookies and milk. He was fatter than Santa. Much, much, much fatter. Sour cream and latkes put on a lot more weight than the average sugar cookie.

Since Marya, there have been others helped by Harry: six-year-old Jocelyn, who had to move in with her aunt because her single mother died of cancer at the age of forty; Andrea, whose mother was a drug addict and gave her to her father when Andrea was five. And then there were Adrien and his brother.

Fortunately, our city, Windsor, has been blessed with several charitable organizations that help out families slipping through the Social Services bureaucratic red tape. We are a city that truly has a huge heart. The Goodfellows organization alone gives out over 40,000 turkeys at Christmas. During the year they provide over 25,000 breakfasts to underprivileged school children. It is an amazing feat, considering Windsor only has a population of 200,000.

It's now very rare to hear of a child in Windsor being forgotten during the holidays, but Harry has not retired. My daughter has a friend working in a little village in Tanzania with a Canadian charitable organization. Harry has donated enough funds and books for all of those children to have at least one year of education. Something tells me he'll be doing that for a while. Harry has also donated books to one of the local grade schools where English is the second language. Arabic is the first.

Ben still plays piano for charities' fundraisers and Miriam recently ran in a marathon to raise money to clothe and improve the housing conditions of those children in Tanzania.

As for the kids we helped?

There's the true gift. Marya is studying to be a teacher and helps Aboriginal children. A certain First Nations Chief helps Santa, north of Ottawa, find kids who need special attention.

Adrien is a social worker in Vancouver, British Columbia. He created a "Papa Noel" who visits kids from broken homes. He figured out who Harry really was when he turned thirteen and thought it was an awesome idea.

Adrien's brother is studying to be a child psychologist and lives in Montreal. He and his buddies have developed a "Neiges Bonhomme," a snowman who leaves baskets filled with food, clothes, and toys on an underprivileged child's doorstep in the middle of the night. I look back on Harry's first visit to Marya and smile with fondness. Good old Harry.

Merry Christmas to Harry Hanukkah, Papa Noel, and Neiges Bonhomme.

~Pamela Goldstein
Amherstburg, Ontario

44

The Year Santa Came

I've seen and met angels wearing the disguise of
ordinary people living ordinary lives.
~Tracy Chapman

Christmas was never a particularly happy time for me as a child. In fact, I usually dreaded it—the lights, the preparations, my classmates' excited babble and anticipation of presents—even the decorations depressed me.

Gifts were not exchanged in our home. My family was poor, and even the bare necessities were hard to come by for my parents, immigrants to Canada from Europe, who had four young mouths to feed. We understood that from an early age and didn't resent it, but we did regret it, especially since there was never anything from Santa Claus himself to brighten our spirits. From time to time he would drop off a small gift for my brothers or me at a friend's house, but more often than not there was nothing to open on Christmas morning.

Each time I awoke on that special day, I hoped it would be different, but it never was. My parents would remind me of the true meaning of Christmas as they handed me a lone tangerine and a meagre handful of mixed nuts, traditional holiday delicacies in our home. If I were less than enthusiastic, they would point out to me how expensive those items were. They went on to emphasize how lucky I was to live in Canada, where food was plentiful and accessible if one worked hard to earn money to buy it.

I would peel the tangerine half-heartedly while I waited for my turn to use our only nutcracker. As I broke off the segments carefully so as not to lose any juice, I listened to my father tell me about the poverty and hunger he endured in the "Old Country" after the war. When I asked why Santa never came, my mother would urge me to forgive him, explaining that he probably had trouble finding our tiny rented flat because it was nestled among so many bigger buildings. Then she would go off to prepare the small ham or turkey she had saved her pennies to buy. I would swallow my disappointment and play with some castoff toys my friends gave me the year before after making room for the replacements they found under their trees. Our own small pathetic fir, decorated with homemade items, sat in a corner of our kitchen, the stand and skinny lower trunk glaringly visible since there were no presents surrounding it.

The only highlight during the holidays was Christmas Eve. Our family had settled in a predominantly Polish neighbourhood. Every year our church would hold a party for the children of parishioners, complete with Santa Claus. We got to sit on his knee and ask for things that we wanted. Sometimes he would tell the odd child that he just happened to have that gift with him, sift around in a large red sack at his feet and pull out the desired treasure, but it had never happened to me.

The year I was seven, I mechanically went through the ritual, asking for a doll I had wanted for a long time and some plastic farm figurines and pretty hair clips that the other girls had. I chanted out the items like a mantra. Even at that young age, I knew I was wasting my breath. I stared down at my chewed, ragged nails and held back tears, trying to be grateful for the candy cane and tiny bag of chocolates every child was given regardless of what they asked for.

"How long have you wanted your doll, sweetheart?" Santa asked, breaking through my sadness. "Three years," I mumbled.

"Were you a good girl?" he queried, placing his gloved hand under my chin, coaxing my eyes to meet his watery blue ones, so much like our pastor's.

"I-I tried," I responded. "But I get mad sometimes because my brothers tease me and the kids at school make fun of my clothes and boots," I confessed, holding up a rubber boot that had seen better days.

"That doesn't make you a bad girl," Santa assured me softly. "Sometimes big brothers can be mean. So can other kids. Just try harder next year, okay?"

"Okay," I agreed, preparing to slide off his knee.

"Wait," he told me, clasping my elbow gently to restrain me. "Where are you going?"

"It's someone else's turn," I answered, confused.

"But you didn't get your gifts yet," he chuckled, setting me down to dig through his bulging bag.

I held out my hand for the familiar sweets I'd almost forgotten, but instead he began to pull out several gaily-wrapped parcels. I looked past them, wondering why he was having so much trouble finding my candy, but he motioned for me to take the six packages he'd retrieved.

"For me?" I gasped, my eyes widening.

"Can you read your name?" he teased. "They all have your name on them."

Sure enough, they did! My hands shook as I reached for one.

"Let my elves help you carry them to that table over there so you can open them," Santa suggested.

"Oh, and here's your candy. I almost forgot. I guess Santa is getting old," he chuckled. "Merry Christmas, sweet child. Never stop believing in the magic of Christmas," he added as I walked away clutching the biggest box. An elf flanked me on either side with the rest of the parcels.

I opened the packages slowly, savouring the beautiful moment. The first one contained the doll I'd wanted for so long. I kissed her pudgy cheeks, and smoothed her beautiful blonde hair. The second was a brand new winter coat. Boots followed, along with a shiny pair of patent leather shoes. Another box contained several skirts and blouses and the coveted barrettes. Finally, I opened the barnyard set that had almost a hundred farm animals, including the horses I loved so much!

Tears streamed down my face and I heard a voice behind me. I turned to see my teacher, beaming at me.

"I see Santa got your letter," she grinned, and I remembered the wish list she had us write out in class earlier that month.

"Before I sent it," she explained, "I added what a good little girl you were all year, helping me clean blackboards after school. I also told Santa how nice and patient you've been to the new girl, Gina, since her first day of school in a new country. Her English is getting so much better since you started speaking to her at recess."

A shudder of emotion ripped through me as I swiped at the tears streaming down my cheeks. I was so overwhelmed, I was unable to speak.

"Don't cry, dear," she murmured softly, reaching out to wipe my face with a tissue from her pocket.

"You deserve all these pretty things." She pulled me close in a tight hug and then left me to enjoy my treasures.

Finally, Santa had found me! The disappointment of the prior years faded as I pushed my arms and feet into my new coat and footwear, all of which fit perfectly. The memory of that Christmas followed me for years to come—and I never doubted the magic of Christmas again.

~Marya Morin
St. Lin des Laurentides, Quebec

Christmas Coals

The little things? The little moments? They aren't little.
~Jon Kabat-Zinn

Growing up in China, the Christmas holiday seemed to me to be less meaningful than the extravagance of our Chinese New Year celebrations. I was only six when our family of five emigrated to Canada and my whole perception of Christmas changed.

Sitting in the back seat of our minivan with my two brothers I would stare out the windows to peer at the beautiful Christmas lights that adorned most of the houses in our neighbourhood. Occasionally I would catch a glimpse of a lighted Christmas tree dressed in lace and baubles, standing proudly in front of the windows we passed. I made my first gingerbread house at school, and smelled, for the first time in my life, the rich aromas of cinnamon and spice and gingerbread.

For our first Christmas Eve in Canada our family sat around the formal dining room table. We understood this Canadian tradition to be reserved only for the most special of occasions. While we ate, we admired the snow that fell silently outside our window and gathered thick and white on the fence around our home. I experienced for the first time a warm and golden feeling of family-togetherness that was not quite like any other. I would have felt full even if I never took a bite of dinner. I knew too, from my teacher, that later that night Santa would come and bring presents for the children. My friends had told me about him, but admitted that no one had ever actually seen him in action on Christmas Eve.

That night, as I went to bed, I swore to myself that I would catch this "Santa" whom none of my friends had ever caught. I put out some cookies and some baby carrots, hoping that Santa, or at least his reindeer, would be hungry enough to stay and eat. I knew I was going to be successful, and I dreamed of the flash of surprise that would light up Santa's face.

After what seemed like hours while I waited for the soft foot-steps of my parents to recede to their bedroom, I crept out of my room, careful not to let the hinges of my door squeak. I sat in the hallway overlooking the fireplace and watched through the railing of the staircase, relishing the fact that I would be able to boast to everyone if I caught Santa. As I waited and waited my eyelids grew heavy and my eyes felt sore. I told myself I would only close them for a few seconds. But as soon as my eyes shut, I couldn't open them. I fell asleep.

When I woke up the sun was already shining through the sky-lights and warming up my body. I sat up groggily, my back aching from sleeping on the hardwood floor. I was disappointed and very angry at myself for falling asleep. It was a once-in-a-year chance, and I had blown it.

But there—under the tree—was something glinting and shin-ing in the morning light… presents! Could it be? Did Santa actually come? I stared for a moment, and with the traces of disappointment vanishing with each passing second, I charged down the stairs and crashed into the presents resting under the tree. It was true, my teacher was right! You did receive presents in Canada! The din of pots and pans coming from the kitchen became silent, and my parents walked out. Laughing and screaming I cried, "Santa has brought us presents!"

My brothers soon ran downstairs as well. They dove in, argu-ing about whose present was whose. Once they had torn open the wrapping paper on their new toys, they went into the kitchen with my parents.

But I had this odd feeling that something was missing. The cookies! That's right! I quickly turned around and looked for the plate that held the snacks. Had Santa noticed them? Sure enough the plate was empty, except for a few crumbs. I grabbled the plate and raced toward the kitchen. And that's when something rough and sharp jabbed into my foot.

I looked toward the fireplace to see what I had stepped on, and that's when I saw them. Scattered on the floor were three little chunks of coal. I slowly picked one up and examined it. Had Santa perhaps hurried out in such a rush that he left behind a small mess? Without a second thought I raced into the kitchen, holding the coal above my head, screaming and yelling. My whole family then took turns examining the coal and theorizing how it had ended up on the floor outside the fireplace. But in my own mind I was too happy to argue with them. You see it didn't matter to me just how Santa had kicked out the coals. I only knew that on my first Christmas in Canada Santa had left me the most special gift of all—three oddly shaped coals proving he had been there.

Nine years later, I still have them sitting on my shelf. There is a certain spirit woven into each one. They remind me that miracles exist, and that Santa never forgot how much I wanted to catch him that Christmas Eve. He was far too busy, so instead, he left an autograph for me in three lumps of coal on the floor. Every Christmas Eve since then I've left out a plate of cookies and baby carrots for Santa just to say thanks.

I'm always the first person to wake up in my house every Christmas morning, and the first to find the small brass doors of the fireplace slightly ajar.

~Encina Roh
Surrey, British Columbia

On Guard

With my own kids grown to sophistication — and to sleeping in — I need
someone around me who believes in Santa Claus, and who thinks that
anyone still in bed at Christmas dawn has wasted half the day.
~Peter Gzowski

Some years ago my brother's two boys came to stay with us for Christmas. Despite the fact that his birthday was not until May, the older boy, Nick, was very happy to announce that he was almost six, and his younger brother, Chad, was almost four.

On the long wall of our living room was a large open fireplace with a pine mantle. On Christmas Eve, our family of two boys and a girl along with the extra two cousins gathered beside the hearth to participate in our Christmas traditions. The younger three children were piled on my husband's knee as he read *The Night Before Christmas*. The older two were taking turns jiggling the popcorn in the only-used-once-a-year vintage popper with the sliding lid, and trying valiantly not to let an errant flame leap from the fire into our treat.

The story over, the buttered popcorn eaten, and Santa's milk and cookies placed on a small table beside the tree, each of us hung one of my husband's socks from the pine mantle, and the five children headed for bed. Three steps out, however, Nicholas stopped.

"The fire!" he said in alarm. "When Santa comes down the chimney he'll burn up!"

"No," I said. "It'll go out. By the time he gets here, it'll be completely cold."

"Are you sure?"

"Absolutely, Nick, don't worry," I said and attempted to move him along to bed.

"But that little table in there," he said pointing to the grate upon which we had built the blaze. "How'll he get past that? There's no room. You need to take it out."

We had left milk and cookies for Santa, so why not accommodate him with the removal of the ash encrusted grate? It seemed obvious enough...

"Okay," we said. "But the fire needs to die down. I promise that later, before we go to bed, we'll get the oven gloves and lift it out then. There'll be plenty of room for Santa by the time he gets here."

"And now, off to bed with you guys," said my husband with a grin.

Now, when I was growing up, my parents insisted on following the truly horrible tradition of requiring the kids to stay in bed on Christmas morning until they themselves were up. This was followed by a mandatory sit-down breakfast before we could go into the living room to see what Santa had brought. Once this misery had been endured, the oldest family member then went first into the living room to see what was under the tree. After making the appropriate "oohs and aahs" he would get comfortably seated and then call in the next oldest person.

I love traditions, but not all of them, so I compromised by maintaining, but humanely modifying this particular ritual. Our kids were expected to wash their faces and brush their teeth while we prepared toast, coffee and juice, and then each of us could take our breakfast into the room with tree to minimize the torturous waiting.

On this particular Christmas, my husband, being the oldest, went in first, but instead of the regulation howls of delight, we heard his shocked voice call out, "Nick! What are you doing in there?"

Ever the traditionalist, I assured the kids it was best to stay in the hall awaiting their entry, while I hurried into the room. Well, it was my turn, anyway.

And there was Nick, arms and legs firmly crossed, sitting in the fireplace where the ash encrusted, Santa-blocking grate had been. He was posted among the debris left from the previous night, and obviously beginning to feel the cold. It is a bit chilly in an open, empty fireplace. And he was very, very dirty.

It seems that because of the time he had been required to wait, Nick, who was very energetic, had slipped unseen into the living room some time earlier. A quick peek wouldn't hurt anything, he figured. Impressed with the array of gifts, and seeing how many there were with his name on them, he had been stricken with the words from the popular Christmas song about Santa Claus coming to town and knowing "who's been naughty and nice." Nick suddenly realized that he had not been entirely nice all year and was, in fact, guilty of many naughty incidents. Fearful that should Santa decide to check his list again, he would discover that a grave error had occurred in the delivery of all these wonderful Christmas gifts to Nicholas Wyllie and return down the chimney to take them back. As a result he had placed himself in the fireplace to guard against such a possibility and fend off Santa.

~Robyn Gerland
Chemainus, British Columbia

Tracks

Sometimes the poorest man leaves his children the richest inheritance.
~Ruth E. Renkel

Nothing endures like memories from Christmases past. Like a magician, at any time, I can conjure up the sights, sounds and smells that permeated our house in the weeks before Christmas. All of these memories are held dearly in my heart, but it was only recently that I came to realize the true meaning of the "magic" of Christmas.

This "magic" that will stay with me forever began when I was only four years old, and still an only child, as my two siblings had not yet been born. It was a couple of days before Christmas when my father woke me early in the morning. He seemed quite excited about something, and for my dad, that was unusual. He did not excite easily. Dad provided the necessities of life for his family, and gave us the extras through his words and deeds. On this particularly cold winter's morning, after waking me up he told me to go quickly into his bedroom and look out the window. I was still in my flannel pyjamas and the floor was cold under my feet so I hastened into his room to see what had made him so excited.

As I peered out the frosted window of that upstairs bedroom, I looked down into our corner yard and then out beyond the side street, and across the neighbour's yard. Crossing all the properties I saw what appeared to be two long yet narrow lines in the snow in what could have been a set of tracks. Newly fallen snow remained undisturbed around these "tracks," with no evidence of human intervention anywhere. I didn't quite know what to make of this scene. After all, I was only four years old. But I could sense, even in my childhood innocence, that whatever I was looking at outside was something quite spectacular.

Leaning in close my dad began to explain it to me. In a lively and excited voice he said, "Ardy, those lines must have been made by the runners of Santa's sleigh! I think jolly old Santa himself must have been making a practice run during the night so he would know where to go on Christmas Eve."

Then he continued, "You see where the runner tracks stop, Ardy? That's where the reindeer took off from the ground to fly through the air with the sleigh back to the North Pole!"

Over the next couple of days I became even more excited as I waited impatiently for Christmas morning to arrive—especially now that I knew Santa Claus had made a practice run in my very own neighbourhood, and would find my house for sure on Christmas Eve.

Nothing in the world is more exciting to a four-year-old than Santa Claus and Christmas morning. So, as they say, I bought my dad's story about Santa making a practice run on my street hook, line and sinker!

Over the years during the Christmas season, my mind would often wander back to that time when I was four years old, looking out a frosty upstairs window, and seeing sleigh tracks in the snow several days before Christmas. I began to ask myself, "How did my dad achieve this wonder of wonders just for me?"

Many years later, when my dad was lying ill in a hospital bed with not many days left here on Earth, that I finally got my answer. During one of my visits we had been talking about the many good things we had shared over the years as father and daughter. I knew now was the right time to ask him that one burning, unanswered question. So I boldly asked, "Dad, how did you make those Santa sleigh tracks for me when I was four years old?" I simply had to know.

My dad, a kind and gentle man, looked me in the eyes from his hospital bed, and quietly answered, "Not me! Must have been Santa Claus!"

And so, that gift of "magic" from this very special Christmas, given to me long ago as a wide-eyed four-year-old, and the love of my father, will live in me forever.

~Ardy Barclay
Sarnia, Ontario

A Gift for Santa

Every child comes with the message that God is not yet discouraged of man.
~Rabindranath Tagore

W hen my five-year-old son opened his stocking gifts on Christmas morning, the toy he was most intrigued by was a Santa Claus Pez dispenser. He was enthralled by the red plastic chimney that offered little gift-shaped candies when he tilted back Santa's head. He handed the candies out to us all day, each one a tiny present, offered with solemn ceremony by my little guy. When Christmas Day was over, that little toy was still his most treasured item of the day. Imagine something so simple, so inexpensive. Santa hit the jackpot on that one.

As I tucked my two little sons into their beds on Christmas night, Joshua asked me, "Mama, does anybody give Santa presents at Christmas? Besides the cookies we leave him, does he get any gifts? I want to give this Pez toy to Santa next year as a present from me."

"How sweet," I said, patting his cheek as I pulled up the covers. "I am sure Santa will like that." Not really thinking anything of it, I turned off his bedroom light and closed the door.

All through the holidays Joshua played with his Santa toy. And then came the new year and life got busy. I never gave that toy another thought, although I must have seen it in his room from time to time.

In summer a friend and I decided to take our children on a camping trip to Santa's Village in Bracebridge, Ontario, a few hours north of our Toronto homes. We packed up the van with food and toys and diapers, camp stove, bug spray, sunscreen, all the things required on any trip with preschoolers. The journey was not without its challenges, and at least twice I questioned what we were thinking when we decided to take four preschool kids tent camping. But the weather was fine, it was summer, and we were nothing if not courageous.

Besides, as I sometimes said to my friend, "We make a good mom." Complementary parenting styles, and loving each other's kids as well as our own, we could figure out how to handle meltdowns, burned hotdogs, lost hats and whining.

Santa's Village is one of the places where Santa spends his summer while taking a break from making toys at the North Pole. It is also lots of fun. We enjoyed the train, the petting zoo, and the playground. But the highlight of our day was the visit with Santa and Mrs. Claus in their own little cottage. We stood in line with other parents and kids, and it seemed to take forever. Finally my two boys and I were ushered into the presence of the jolly old man himself.

I introduced my boys by name, just to remind him and Mrs. Claus, and they began to visit with my sons. Both the old folks focused completely and solely on my little boys, seeming to have all the time in the world for them. They asked Joshua about his interests, and held his baby brother on their laps. Santa was wearing the perfect Santa beard and red Santa suit. Mrs. Claus in a long red dress and apron had curly white hair peeking out from her cap. Santa's round belly really did jiggle when he laughed. The thing I noticed most was their kind eyes with little laugh wrinkles at the corners. They were magnetic, and my boys wanted to talk and cuddle and just be with this old couple. Wow, I thought. I am a grown woman, and I have finally met the real Santa. The feeling of magic in the air was palpable.

Just as we were about to be escorted out by a sweet teenaged elf, little Joshua reached into his pocket and pulled out the Santa Pez dispenser toy from the previous Christmas.

"Santa," he said, in his husky little boy voice. "This is for you. I have been saving it for you since you gave it to me last Christmas."

"Are you sure?" asked Santa. "Are you sure you want me to keep this?"

"Yes, Santa," said Joshua. "You give everybody presents. I want to give a present to you. I love you, Santa."

The two older folks exchanged a look and Santa said, "Mrs. Claus and I thank you, Joshua. We love you and little Noah, too."

There was so much love shining in their eyes as they gave each of my boys another hug. I shook hands with them with tears in my eyes, said thank you and we left the cottage.

Christmas in July. Santa is as real as Love.

I believe.

~Deborah J. Kinsinger
Newmarket, Ontario

Santa's Surprise

Santa loves to receive mail, and a very dedicated group of volunteer postal elves — more than 11,000 of them — are proud to help Santa with the task.
~Louise Chenier, Canada Post's Chief Postal Elf

"We don't have any carrots, Mom!" my four-year-old hollers from the kitchen.

From the opposite end of our mobile home I shout, "There's celery in the bottom crisper, Jeremy."

"Reindeer don't eat celery!"

Oh dear. Someone is very close to a pre-Christmas meltdown. I walk into the kitchen, open the fridge door further and bend down to help him search.

"Are you sure they don't like celery?" I shake a plastic produce bag. "We have lots."

Jeremy shakes his head hard till his hair flies straight out. "It has to be carrots!"

"Okay, don't panic." I grab the phone and call my dearest neighbour.

"Hey Sharon, Merry Christmas Eve."

I hear her laugh. Sharon's not big on all the fuss over Christmas but she has a soft spot for Jeremy.

"I'm having a carrot crisis. Apparently reindeer don't eat celery." I stretch the phone cord far enough to check the time on the cuckoo clock. "Do you have any carrots?"

I place my hand over the phone. "She's checking."

Jeremy stands in front of me with pudgy fingers on hips and his head tipped to one side. I bite down on my bottom lip so as not to grin at his stern expression.

"You're a life saver. Thanks a bunch." I hang up the phone. "She's got carrots. Now go get ready." I point to his room. "Your clothes are on your bed. We can't be late."

Jeremy runs to his room while I organize Santa's snack on the kitchen table: a glass of milk, three cookies on a napkin and a plate for the incoming carrot, which soon arrives. Crisis solved.

After we finally buckle into my Fiesta, I turn to Jeremy and smack the side of my face. "Oh no!" I exclaim. "I forgot my purse. You stay put. I'll just be a sec."

With keys in hand, I rush back wearing a huge I'm-so-sneaky grin. Once inside, a quick dash to the closet to pull out the hidden present and then I crouch down, scoot across the dark living room and tuck it under our tree. Perfect. I remember to grab my purse, lock the door and we're off.

"We don't have a chimney," Jeremy states as we pull onto the street. "How will Santa get in?"

Ever since missing the annual Santa Claus breakfast two weeks ago, Jeremy has been obsessing about the jolly man in red forgetting to stop at our house. Dealing with his chicken pox was easier than dealing with his disappointment about not being able to sit on Santa's knee. There were a few times I debated exposing everyone's child to his itchy spots.

I glance over and see Jeremy's way-too-serious expression.

"Don't you worry. Santa doesn't need a chimney. He has ways of getting in."

Jeremy sticks his chin out. "But that's how he gets in, down the chimney."

"Does Jillian's house have a chimney?"

No response. I bet he's trying to remember if they have a fireplace.

"Does Travis's house have a chimney?"

I shake my head. "They don't. And Santa still comes to their house."

"Are you sure?"

"Of course." I nod. "He came last year didn't he?"

"But last year I went to his party. I told Santa what I wanted."

"And this year we wrote a letter and mailed it."

Jeremy's ski jacket rustles as he crosses his arms over his chest. The wipers flip-flap and squeak the fresh snowflakes across the windshield.

The evening at my parents' is full of festivities that includes a full Christmas feast of delicious food, the family picture where it takes longer to figure out the camera than to organize the people, family gifts and, last but not least, the proper amount of sibling bantering reserved for just such occasions. A fun and exhausting evening for everyone.

It's a blizzard when we leave. Fresh powder for Christmas Day—how perfect is that? My nostrils stick together as I brush the snow off the car.

As we pass the last lights of Main Street, I stretch my neck out to peer into the white blur. A large, dark object approaches in the other lane. No headlights. Just one red light that flickers. As the shape gets closer I see it's four horses, a sleigh and Santa.

I smile at my son, and point. "Look."

Jeremy pushes against his seatbelt to see. "It's Santa!"

He waves and twists around to follow them as they move through the snowstorm on their way out of town.

"That's Santa!"

"It sure is." I nod. "Hey, maybe he's already been to our house!"

"Really? He did us first?"

"Maybe." I grin.

How perfect is that for timing? Almost like I planned it.

When we arrive home, Jeremy runs up the steps and jiggles the door handle.

"Slow down." I stick in the key. "I have to unlock it first."

Once inside I flick on the light as he makes snowy footprints across the rust-orange living room carpet.

"Boots," I remind him.

"He was here!" Jeremy rushes back to the mat, steps on the toe of one boot, yanks it off and almost falls over getting the other one off. "Santa came!"

Halfway through taking off my coat I stop and stare under the tree. Sitting right beside the present I put out earlier sits a fancy, red-foil, store-wrapped, large box with a giant gold bow. I glance into the shadows of the kitchen, then peer around the corner to check the hallway. Goosebumps make the hair on the back of my neck stand straight up.

"Can I open them?" Jeremy shrieks.

"If you open them now, there's nothing for the morning."

"That's okay." He nods with conviction. "Can I?"

"Open away."

I put my ski jacket in the closet and flick on the rest of the lights.

Jeremy tears through the shiny red paper to get at the box.

"My fireman hat!" He yanks and pulls till the plastic wrapped helmet tumbles out.

"A fireman hat?" I question.

"Just what I wanted."

Jeremy hits a button on top of the helmet. Red lights rotate across our wood panel walls. A piecing siren wails. I cover my ears. He plops it on his head, puts his hands in front to drive his imaginary fire truck and roars in circles around the room.

"I thought you wanted the..." I call out as he zooms past me.

With a huge grin, he tilts his shoulders and banks the corner into the kitchen. The light flashes faster; the siren screams louder.

"Oh Santa," I say through a clenched smile. "We will be chatting really soon."

~Barbara Wackerle Baker
Calgary, Alberta

Naughty Granny

There's nothing sadder in this world
than to awake Christmas morning and not be a child.
~Erma Bombeck

Winters were extremely chilly where I grew up in Saint-Jean-sur-Richelieu, Quebec, about fifty kilometres southeast of Montreal. My siblings and I relished the cold and snow when we were youngsters, and our Christmas holidays, with a week or more off from school, were eagerly anticipated. We'd have snowball fights, make snow angels, and play ice hockey on the icy street. When the snow reached the top of our house, which it often did, we'd shovel out snow forts and play in our creations.

One holiday season in particular stands out. It was the Christmas my maternal grandmother, Granny Whiting, spent with us. Actually, it was her very first Christmas in Canada. She and my grandfather lived in Bermuda. Neither one had experienced a Canadian winter. Play forts dug into the banks of snow and snow angels were foreign to my grandparents. But after my grandfather died, my grandmother made her first visit to Canada.

Christmas Eve, my father stayed home with us children while Mom and Granny attended the midnight church service. They didn't arrive home until after 1:00 a.m., so it was late by the time they climbed into bed.

We kids always rose early on Christmas mornings and snuck down to the Christmas tree. But that year things unfolded a little differently. At three in the morning, Granny woke up my younger brother Harry and me. Perhaps, after attending church at midnight, she had never fallen asleep.

Granny Whiting was a staunch Englishwoman. Prim and proper, she did no wrong, and truth be known, she never wanted to do wrong. I'm not really sure why Granny wanted to break the rules this time, but the three of us slithered down the stairs into the living room.

"We have to be quiet," Granny whispered. "Don't want to wake the others."

One of us plugged in the tree lights and the bountiful tree glowed, creating shadows in the room. Silver icicles, hanging from the spreading branches, sparkled like a kaleidoscope as they picked up the colours of the bulbs. Below the genuine pine branches was an expanse of gaily wrapped gifts of all shapes and sizes.

"Let's look," Granny whispered with excitement. Then, gathering her nightgown she leaned into the gifts. "Cathy, do you see one for you?"

"Not yet," I said.

"I can't find one for me either," she moaned. "Harry, do you?"

Like co-conspirators, the three of us began rooting through the gifts. We were careful to whisper, for Mom and Dad's bedroom was at the top of the stairs of our split-level house. We didn't want to wake our parents, nor did we want to wake our siblings who would be too little to remain silent.

We were soon fully involved in our escapade, searching for our names on gift tags. Once we found one of our gifts we proudly showed it to the others and tried to guess its contents. Sometimes, when curiosity overtook us, we tore off a bit of wrapping paper. Granny had as much fun as we did.

Suddenly, out of nowhere, a voice bellowed, "Get back to bed!" There was a pause. "And that means you, too, Mother!" The voice belonged to my mother, and she sounded angry.

Before Harry and I had a chance to move, Granny had dropped whatever gift she held, jumped up, and bolted away, her flowing, white nightgown ethereal like a ghost floating up the dark stairs. Harry and

I remained by the tree, staring at each other, wondering what had just transpired and how Granny had disappeared so quickly.

"Get back to bed," Mom bellowed again. Like Granny before us, Harry and I scrambled up the stairs and back into our beds, giggling as we went.

The next morning there was lots of laughter when, at a more presentable hour, our entire family gathered around the tree. Granny, Harry, and I giggled as we recalled our middle-of-the-night caper.

I'll never forget that episode and how in the middle of the night our straight-laced grandmother became a child, how she instigated an adventure, how our mother had scared her, and how she got all three of us into trouble. For Mom blamed her, of course. Granny was certainly old enough to know better!

~Catherine A. MacKenzie
Fall River, Nova Scotia

Extraordinary Magic

Those who don't believe in magic will never find it.
~Roald Dahl

My husband, sister Natalie, and I packed up the kids in the van and ventured off to our favourite tree-cutting farm. Jacob, who was turning four on Christmas Day, was up for the challenge and Bruce, who was just six months old, was happy to be along for the ride with his big brother.

We couldn't have picked a more perfect Sunday morning. A heavy snow had fallen the night before, covering everything with a clean white blanket. It was cold, but the sun shone so brightly it was almost blinding as it reflected off the sparkling white landscape. It was truly a winter wonderland.

Happily, we tromped through the deep stuff, trying not to fall. Baby Bruce, bulkily bundled in a snowsuit and blanket was pulled in his sled close behind. We could only see a tiny bit of his face, lightly glowing red cheeks and eyes filled with wonder.

Eerily, no one was around—I mean no one. It was only two weeks before Christmas, and this huge tree farm was completely empty: no one to be seen. There weren't even any tracks in the snow to indicate others had preceded us.

We forged ahead in search of the perfect tree when suddenly, off in the distance, we noticed a man riding a horse on top of a large hill. We all seemed to spot him at the same time, awed and transfixed; everyone but Bruce of course, who was now sound asleep.

Upon closer scrutiny, we realized the man had a white beard, yet oddly, because of the sun, his image wasn't totally clear. He had a glow about him, a somewhat mystical aura.

Mesmerized, we watched as the man and his horse slowly descended the hill and came toward us. Jacob became very excited and shouted, "Santa!" The man did not correct him. His horse was mostly white but dappled with a few black spots, while the gentle rider was cloaked in a red outfit… fit for working on a Christmas tree farm. It didn't matter to our boy that he was not wearing a traditional velvet coat or pants trimmed in ermine. He knew it was Santa.

The man carefully reined his horse in just short of Jacob, who was not the least bit frightened by the large animal. Remaining very high on his saddle, he leaned over and quietly asked him how he was and what he might like for Christmas. The man didn't acknowledge anyone else, but concentrated on our small boy. After the short exchange, he announced that he should be on his way, turned the horse around and slowly moved back up the ridge. We watched silently as he returned to the top, and then he turned and waved as he called out from the distance, "Merry Christmas, Jacob." In the glow of the sun, the figure became hazy once more as he disappeared over the ridge.

Jacob was thrilled and jumped up and down in the snow calling out, "It was Santa! It was Santa!" The three grown-ups just stared at each other, searching for an answer as to what had just transpired. Did we each see what we thought we saw? Could it be?

Christmas is a magical time for children… but what about for adults?

When children believe, it's magic.

When grown ups believe, it's extraordinary.

~Nancy Koruna McIntosh
Thorold, Ontario

Chapter 6

Christmas in Canada

A Winter Wonderland

Winter came down to our home one night
Quietly pirouetting in on silvery-toed slippers of snow,
And we, we were children once again.

~Bill Morgan, Jr.

A Snowmobile Christmas

Christmas is the season for kindling the fire of hospitality in the hall,
the genial flame of charity in the heart.
~Washington Irving

"Wow! Oh, wow!" my brother, Doug, exclaimed.

"What is it?" When he didn't answer, I rushed to join him at the window.

As I approached he turned, his eyes wide, his open mouth formed in a big O. In the next instant he was whooping and bouncing around like a little kid instead of a thirteen-year-old. Then I saw the cause.

Dad was exiting the pickup, back from a trip into Edmonton for parts, or so we thought. On the back of the truck was a brand new, fire engine red snowmobile! Dad had a huge grin on his face. We lost no time in yanking on boots, hats and coats as we ran outside.

"Merry Christmas!" Dad's voice boomed. "This is your present this year so there won't be anything else."

A snowmobile was an expensive toy, purely for fun, and we both understood that. It was a Massey Ferguson Ski-Whiz, small by some standards but built to outlast the others. Doug could hardly wait to go for a ride. Given that it was a bright sunny day, he and my dad had it unloaded, fuelled and fired up in no time. I was glad I had the hood of my winter coat firmly in place to block out some of the noise. My brother talked a mile-a-minute the entire time they were readying the machine.

"Now remember, we have to take it easy," Dad stressed. Then in the next instant he waved my brother on while he took up the front position for the initial ride.

"Your turn next!" they yelled in unison, as Dad eased the throttle from idle to give them power.

I watched as they rode over the packed, manure-clumped yard, and through the open gateway leading to a hayfield. It wasn't a warm wait but in no time they were back; this time my brother was driving.

"Come on!" Doug called and I wasted no time in replacing Dad.

Boy, was it cold! In the future I would wear a lot more clothes, but for the initiation ride, I didn't care. There was a mantle of snow over everything, just like on a Christmas card.

Over the course of the next couple of days, more snow fell but the novelty of the snow machine hadn't worn off yet. Then, on Christmas Eve, the wind started blowing, fiercely.

"I hope this doesn't keep up too long," Dad said with worry at the supper table. "The roads will be drifting."

"What'll happen if the grandpas and grandmas can't get through?" I wailed.

"Well, then I guess it will just be us for Christmas dinner," Mom said.

"What will they eat?" Doug added his concern.

"They won't starve," Mom replied. "They just won't have turkey."

For us, a turkey dinner was a rare treat reserved for Christmas and New Year's. Everyone looked forward to arguing over who would get the neck and the giblets, and the rich gravy made from turkey drippings was equally coveted, slathered on with total disregard for its fattening qualities. After all, we didn't get to indulge in the treat often.

We went to bed to the eerie howl of the wind. Christmas Day dawned still and bright; the snow sparkled. Huge drifts were now piled in our yard and on the driveway.

We could see that the two sets of grandparents would not be coming for Christmas dinner.

The turkey was thawed, the Christmas pudding made, and all the other food ready to cook. Mom had to proceed, with or without guests.

We hoped the roads would be cleared for Boxing Day. We would try then to get together for leftovers.

"The Crosswhites won't be able to get out either," Mom said with concern for our nearest neighbours, an elderly couple who planned to celebrate with their own family.

"Too bad they can't come," I said.

Not one to miss an opportunity to ride our newest toy, my brother announced brightly, "I can get them with the Ski-Whiz. It's only a mile to their place."

"You'll have to bring them over one at a time," Dad pointed out.

Over the phone, Mom was assuring Agnes that it was perfectly safe.

Doug set out at eleven o'clock. We had no snowmobile suits back then, so he wore long underwear, two pairs of pants, shirt, sweater and a heavy coat. His boots had felt liners. After donning a thick winter cap with earflaps, he tied a scarf around his face, pulled on leather chore mitts with another pair of knit mitts inside for liners, and he was off. It seemed like no time at all before he returned with Agnes, well bundled up and tucked in behind him. After reassurances at the Crosswhite home, she'd reluctantly climbed on, fearing for her life. Now, her cheeks were rosy and her eyes bright with excitement.

"Doug drove very nicely and it was kind of fun," she confided after my brother left to collect her husband. "We just rode along on top of the drifts, up and down, up and down," she said, giggling as she gave us a demonstration.

Her husband, Shorty, was equally impressed with the ride.

"It smells wonderful in here!" he declared of the aroma of roasting turkey wafting out the kitchen door and into the porch where he was pulling off his outer clothing. "I'm certainly glad you called because there wasn't a thing to eat in our place! We'd cleaned everything up thinking we'd be gone for a few days."

And so we sat down to a table heavily laden with the Christmas

Day feast. The visit was short since chore time came early in winter, and so did the end of daylight. The trips back were uneventful and no one got cold. Just getting in and out of all those clothes made for a warm start!

Because we milked cows, the snow plow was obliged to come down our road before the day was over. Dad cleared our driveway with the tractor, and the milk truck was able to get to us by ten that night. By dairy regulation, all producers must have a tank large enough to hold up to two extra milkings. We would have been pushing those limits so we were happy to hear the truck arrive in the night.

All four grandparents arrived on Boxing Day without incident and we had a repeat of Christmas. We opened gifts and pulled Chinese firecrackers, producing a bang of sound and a smell of sulphur. It was a memorable Christmas, and it turned out that our gift was way more useful than a toy!

~Lori M. Feldberg
Wetaskiwin, Alberta

Christmas at the Spit

There are some secret elves who decorate a standalone
Sitka spruce on Whiffin Spit each December
(and mysteriously undress the tree again in January).
~Editor, Sooke Voice News

Sunday morning was the start of another cool, breezy day with bits of sunshine lighting the hills surrounding the water near our home. The trails crisscrossing the woods would still be damp and muddy from the overnight rain. This is a winter on Vancouver Island. It rains a lot and it hardly ever snows.

"Where to this morning?" I asked my husband as I glanced over at Huey, our Cocker Spaniel.

"Well, Whiffin Spit, of course," Donny answered. "It's time for our Christmas pilgrimage."

"You're right. How could I forget?" I said as I attached Huey's leash.

Our twenty-minute drive to the trail took us on a series of circuitous, hilly roads around the Basin and through the town of Sooke before turning left onto Whiffin Spit Road. At that point Huey stood up, each of his front paws on an armrest while his back legs perched precariously on the back seat. He knew exactly where we were headed.

There on the water the wind was strong. The clouds moved quickly over the mountains in the distance. The air was filled with the briny smell of the ocean. We stopped occasionally on the winding trail to chat with familiar people and for the dogs to mingle and sniff. As we neared the breakwater, some water crashed onto the pathway in front of us.

We began walking more quickly, no longer ambling. We tugged on Huey's leash to keep him moving. As we rounded a deep bend in the trail we finally saw the small Christmas tree. It was fully dressed for the holidays and looked beautiful. This tree was the reason we'd gone to Whiffin Spit.

Seeing the tree in all its Christmas glory makes it easy to forget that this is normally a scruffy, under-sized Sitka spruce that has been beaten down by the winds over its lifetime. Each year, for about two weeks, it takes on an entirely different life, elevated to a new status by the people who frequent Whiffin Spit. We, along with the rest of the community, make this a destination at least once over the holiday season.

Every year, the tree stands before us laden with handmade decorations that include glittery pinecones, colour plastic prisms, old beach sandals, painted ping pong balls, stuffed animals wearing Santa hats plus a variety of store-bought ornaments. Some of the pieces have been crafted by schoolchildren. The tree has been transformed and is a testament to the people who live here. The little tree has been decorated with just what was available, nothing more. It is basic: not overdone, not fancy. It is a work of art, crafted by a community.

The metamorphosis of the pint-sized tree takes place literally overnight. I'm not certain who magically performs this feat. Long-time residents may know who secretly decorates it, but we don't. We just stand in admiration for a few minutes with several other people. The little tree wears its holiday plumage through New Year's Day, when other annual events such as the Polar Bear Swim take place. And with Whiffin Spit being a haven for dogs, it is no surprise that they are included on that day by way of a parade in which the requisite canine apparel is a Santa hat and a collar festooned with red bows and jingle bells.

After admiring the tree that Sunday, we moved up the trail

toward the lighthouse at the end, turned around and made our way back to the car. We'd managed to catch whatever sun peeked through the clouds that morning—an added bonus on our annual Christmas pilgrimage to Whiffin Spit.

~Janet Caplan
Sooke, British Columbia

54

Holiday on Ice

When I was young I admired clever people.
Now that I am old, I admire kind people.
~Abraham Heschel

I t was the Saturday before Christmas and the freezing rain was predicted to last for several days. We were facing an ice storm. No one who was in the Greater Toronto area over Christmas 2013 could imagine what it would bring.

As the rain fell the ice built up on power lines and trees. When they could no longer support the weight of the ice, huge branches came down, sometimes whole trees—taking the power lines with them. The electricity went off, and along with it every electrical device in our homes, and most importantly, our heat. Toronto and the surrounding area were brought to a total halt, devastated by the glittering, beautiful, and deadly ice.

For our three days without power we were lucky—a natural gas fireplace on each floor of our home created pockets of warmth, relieving us of worries about pipes freezing. But others were not so lucky and temperatures inside their homes quickly dropped to the low single digits—some for up to eight days.

On Christmas Eve, only twelve hours after our electricity was restored, we packed up our luggage, food and five boys into two cars and headed north to our cottage near Orillia for winter break. I left the house with my eldest son, Zak, thirty minutes before my husband Daniel left with the other four kids—including our two babies aged one and two years. We planned to start our holiday with a movie in Orillia and aimed for a 5:45 showing of *Frozen* (how apt). As Zak and I arrived at the cottage I knew Daniel was close to the theatre. He would buy the tickets; my job was to turn up the heat from its "away" setting of 13 degrees C to a more comfortable 21 degrees, then race into town and join them at the theatre. A perfect plan.

After three icy days of no electricity, no showers and no heat, I entered the cottage. The thermostat read -0.5 degrees C and the furnace was not coming on. Clearly we had a problem!

Our getaway from the angst of the ice storm in Toronto had suddenly morphed into a whole new trauma, so I shifted into emergency management gear. Quickly checking sinks, I discovered ice had already formed on the faucets and the water flow was impaired. After running all the taps to get the water moving and melt the ice, I had to think fast. With every fraction of a degree the temperature dropped the pipes were in greater danger. We had to heat up our cottage fast!

Now racing against time, Zak and I got back on the road. After dropping him off at the theatre to enjoy some heat, I headed to the local Walmart. I was after heaters. If Walmart was open, they might have some. I might still be able to save the pipes from freezing.

It seemed Orillia had also been without power for about twelve hours, and with all the beleaguered Torontonians heading to cottage country for their Christmas celebrations, management had decided to stay open as their Christmas gift to those in need. And there were many. As one of those in need, I was extremely grateful! After spending $800 and loading nine heaters into my overloaded Honda I was back on the road, and racing against the clock.

You might think this should now be a straightforward venture—plug the heaters in around the house as fast as possible and presto—heat. But as I did, the circuits became overloaded and I blew fuse after fuse. Thus I started the laborious task of juggling the fuse panel to identify as many different circuits as possible. Thank God I'm an electrical engineer!

So began the slow process of nudging the temperature above

zero. As I thanked God again for giving women the ability to multi-task, a corner of my brain started working on how we could keep the heat going, manage fire safety and juggle two babies unhappy with living in their snow suits. The three big kids could lump it, but what about the little ones? I considered sending Daniel home with all five boys and stoically braving the cold, but honestly, I wasn't keen on the idea of being alone at the cottage on Christmas Eve with this frigid indoor temperature!

My cottage neighbours two doors down were my next call. Maybe they had more heaters. "Ruth," they said, "why don't you and your family come and stay the night with us? You can easily monitor your heat from here, and keep the babies safely warm."

Overwhelmed with their kind offer I gratefully accepted, and later that evening our family of seven descended on their home of five! As my husband and I lugged in more firewood to further raise the heat with our wood burning stove, our neighbours kept our five kids entertained. Not only that—they sent over food and help! My heart swells with gratitude when I think of their kindness.

Having found ten distinct circuit breakers in the fuse panel the heat was slowly creeping up. When we finally hit +1 degrees C the panic was over. Now it was time to address the root of the problem. Suspecting the culprit was one of our propane tanks my next call was to the local propane company. Around 10:00 p.m. that Christmas Eve, the kindest guy arrived and headed out to examine the offending tank.

"No problem with your tanks, Mrs. Levenstein," he reported. "The problem must be in the furnace itself."

We made the call, but as it was now a safe and balmy +7 degrees C inside, the urgency had passed. It was 8:00 a.m. on Christmas morning when the emergency furnace guy arrived and managed to kick-start our delinquent furnace back into operation. Crisis solved, holiday vacation saved, skiing and snow-play now awaited this relieved family of seven.

During this entire event, I found the kindness that shone through from the hearts of those who lent a hand to others in serious need to be overwhelming! Thanks to the people at the Orillia Walmart, our amazing neighbours, the propane guy who came out on Christmas Eve to help us, and the furnace guy who left his family on Christmas morning to start our furnace, our 2013 "holiday on ice" turned out to be one of the best Christmas vacations ever!

~Ruth Levenstein
Thornhill, Ontario

55

The Backyard Rink

*You will find as you look back upon your life the moments when you have
really lived are the moments when you have done things in the spirit of love.*
~Henry Drummond

I believe it is a universal truth that every Canadian man, at some
point in his life, decides to build a skating rink in the back yard,
just like his dad did when he was a lad. This isn't much of a
problem in the city where he's perched on a piece of land appropri-
ately scaled for a three-bedroom bungalow and maybe a small shed
and swing set. He can quite easily flood the back yard during TV
commercials.

However, in Manitoba we learned that country back yards are a
whole different matter. When winter came, my husband Ross, the man
who laughed in such a condescending manner when I planted too
much zucchini in the summer, succumbed to Large-Yard-Syndrome
when building an ice rink.

Figuring there's no point in even bothering to build a rink if
an entire hockey league couldn't use it for practice games, Ross
spent ages planning and preparing the site. That was a mere blink of
the eye compared to how long it took to actually water the mighty
expanse with a standard garden hose, especially a ludicrously short
garden hose connected to a tap connected to a well with water pressure so inadequate that it only allows you to wet down the far side of
this putative Montreal Forum when the pump kicks in. As he stood
outside, icicles formed on his nose, the glove clutching the hose, and

the hose itself, until he had to come inside to thaw the nozzle so he could start the flow again.

Yet despite the amazing fact that I couldn't find another garden hose at Canadian Tire in Winnipeg in the middle of December when everyone else was doing their Christmas shopping, and I refused to take out a second mortgage to buy a Zamboni machine, Ross finally announced the rink "skateable."

That's when the real trouble began.

Up until this point my contribution had consisted mainly of waxing eloquent about how wonderful he was to go out there in that awful weather just to provide us with a venue for a little winter recreation. I plied him with mulled wine and hot toddies and commiserated with him on the treachery of a hose whose output slowed to a trickle as the ice built up, both inside the line and off the end of the nozzle, like a pack of crazed stalactites.

I kept a concerned expression on my face as he bemoaned the fact that after an hour or so the water would plop out of the hose viscously to form stalagmites on his increasingly bumpy stretch of ice. I even managed to keep up the sympathetic cooing as I watched the two of them (Ross and his hose) drip black slush all over the carpet as they thawed in front of the fire.

But when the rink was finally finished I was confronted with my greatest challenge — I actually had to go out and skate on it.

Ross belongs to the Conan the Barbarian school of skating, whose main tenet is that if you can still feel your feet after your skates have been done up then your laces are too loose. He also believes that figure skates are for sissies (as well as being bad for the ice) and real skaters (and their wives and daughters) wear hockey skates.

My outlook darkened rapidly the first time I actually tried to skate in the darn things. I was on a huge expanse of unsympathetic and deadly ice with no picks to either get me started or stop me when someone else gave me a shove. Wholly dependent on surface friction and my own vast capacity for inertia, I felt like a curling stone.

When, after about a minute and a half, I complained about the cramps in both my feet, Ross shook his head in a disappointed puppy kind of way and hurried me hard over to the bench, which I had, with stunning insight, ordered to be placed by the rink in anticipation of just such an emergency.

I thumped down, and then proceeded to break three fingernails and a tooth trying to get my laces untied.

It never ceases to amaze both Ross and our daughter, who now frequently and maliciously skates circles around me, that after this many months my skating has not improved in any way.

In the hopes of spurring me to skating competency, Ross promised me a cool NHL sweater as soon as I proved worthy of it. When it became woefully apparent this tactic was doomed to failure, a Montreal Canadiens sweater found its way under the Christmas tree anyway, while my husband lied sweetly about my "huge improvement." Yet despite wearing his number, I still can't come close to skating with anything like the panache of "Rocket" Richard. And he's been dead for years.

So, I've become that crazy woman in the Habs sweater slowly spinning on her butt mid-ice.

At least I'm blocking the path for the Zamboni machine.

~Denise Flint
St. Philips, Newfoundland and Labrador

56

Hockey for Beginners

People would say, "Girls don't play hockey. Girls don't skate."
I would say, "Watch this."
~Hailey Wickenheiser, Canadian Women's National Hockey Team,
Five-Time Olympian

Girls didn't play hockey when I was growing up. Most of us got white figure skates for Christmas and were signed up for figure-skating lessons before we knew what was happening.

In the decade separating my generation from my baby sister's, everything changed. Suddenly girls played hockey! My sister didn't happen to be one of them, not in her youth, but her best friend did and went on to score a hockey scholarship. Eventually she played for the illustrious Canadian Women's Team.

Her friend's success inspired my sister to give hockey a go. In university she joined a special league—a hockey club for absolute beginners. Some of the women didn't even know how to skate. In addition to being inexperienced players, the women spanned every age group over eighteen. My sister played alongside grandmothers and university students. Once they were on the ice they were all about the game.

At the start of the season, my mother and I watched one of my sister's games. The pace was slow, the shots on goal weren't all that accurate and there was a lot of falling, but those beginners had heart.

They lost big-time. When my sister got off the ice, I could sense her frustration behind the "good sport" mask.

"Did you have fun?" my mother asked—the same question she'd put to me after my childhood soccer games.

"Yeah," my sister grumbled.

"Well, that's all that matters," my mother assured her.

"But we just try so hard. You should see us at practice. We work our butts off! The last thing we want is for people to watch us play and say, 'See? Girls suck at hockey, and they're proof.' We want to be better."

"You'll get better," Mom and I both said.

And they did, by leaps and bounds. When my mother and I drove out to watch a game later in the season, the players who hadn't known how to skate before weren't falling anymore, and after learning the fundamentals of the game some had become star players.

The next year, my sister went out for house league with the more experienced players at her university.

On her visit home at Christmas, my sister proposed that we all go pleasure skating. I hadn't set foot on ice in almost twenty years. My mother hadn't skated in even longer.

But we went. Mom was not enthusiastic. Even as we drove to one of the few outdoor rinks open on a holiday, she kept saying, "I'm not doing this, girls. I'm not getting out on that ice."

"But you need more exercise, Mom." That was my sister's usual chastisement. "You should be more active, do something every week. Like curling! Or you could join a yoga class… anything."

My mother changed the subject, and I kept quiet. Most of my physical activity involved the path between my computer and refrigerator. Not the healthiest lifestyle.

The weather was beautiful for December. When we got to the rink Mom struggled to lace up a pair of old hockey skates. When she saw other people on the ice who were a little wobbly, she perked up.

"Maybe I can do this," she said.

I stepped on the ice first, and quickly discovered it was just like riding a bicycle. That feeling of early childhood freedom came zooming back, and I immediately remembered how much I loved skating.

As they stepped onto the rink, my sister held Mom's hand as she took her first few steps onto the ice. As soon as she was close enough, she grabbed my hand. My sister and I held her steady — like we were the parents and she was the child.

"Can you pull me along?" Mom asked.

Laughing, my sister and I did as she requested and skated across the outdoor rink. The ice was dinted and rough, badly in need of a date with the Zamboni. A respectable coat of snow had built up on top as well.

My mother was finally ready to go it alone and my sister and I let go of her hands. Off she went, stumbling a bit here and there. At times I was sure she would fall, but she always managed to recover before losing her balance completely.

We skated alone for a while, my sister, my mother and I, always half watching for each other, but taking space to enjoy the winter air. The round-and-round was mesmerizing, and before we knew it an hour had gone by.

On the way home, we stopped at Tim Horton's for hot chocolate. As we waited in line, my mother asked my sister about that beginners' hockey league for women.

"Why?" my sister asked. "Are you thinking of joining?"

My mother half-smiled, half-shrugged, half-nodded. "I'm thinking about it."

I was thinking about it too!

~Tanya Janke
Toronto, Ontario

57

The Christmas Toboggan

Canada may be cold between November and March
but that doesn't mean we Canadians stay indoors.
~Jane McLean

T
he toboggan had been a Christmas present to our children. Living in Canada usually guaranteed a good pile of snow in the parking lot of our family business, and the toboggan was just the thing to turn the monstrous mound into a fun playground. Each winter we hauled that toboggan out of storage and dragged it to the hill, or to the local golf course, or even just for a walk while our three little girls rode along buried in layers of snow wear.

As time passed and our girls grew, the toboggan's short length became a detriment. The three of them could no longer fit, and faster, plastic sleds had become more popular. Every time I stepped into our barn to feed our horses I would spy the toboggan propped against the wall—abandoned. Perhaps I could find some use for it.

I had begun training our horses to harness. My sister had lent me her antique buggy and I thought it would be fun to teach my saddle horses to become carriage horses. That summer was filled with fun buggy rides down backcountry roads with my family. As autumn approached, I wondered if I could adapt the toboggan to become our winter chariot.

The toboggan would need cleaning and modifying. Through the fall rains, I worked to attach a piece of two-by-four wood to the inside curve at the front of the toboggan. My plan was to fasten the traces to this piece and hopefully have some fun moments pulling our daughters around the fields on our new sleigh.

Snow settled over our country property, bringing with it all kinds of potential. I harnessed our small mare, Lady, and called out. "Giddup." She couldn't budge the toboggan. It was stuck in the snow.

No problem, I thought to myself. I'll just harness Jess beside her. The three-year-old gelding was her colt and they worked well together. But I forgot to put the strap that keeps their heads together onto their bridles. So when they tried going in opposite directions, resulting in a mad dash across the field, the toboggan ended up flapping in the wind like a rain-soaked kite.

I gathered the horses, installed the strap that kept their heads together, and went for the first ride around our field. I was elated that our short toboggan had transformed beautifully into a snow chariot. My children were quick to see the potential for fun, and a second toboggan was tied on behind. The horses settled into the task and the afternoon air was soon filled with laughter as we looped around the fields.

After that, each winter the toboggans and the harnesses were pulled out, and we aimed for at least one day of sledding old-fashioned style. Then our children became teens with agendas of their own and, one winter, after the toboggans went back into the barn with the harnesses, they stayed there.

The girls grew up and moved out. Marriage and grandchildren followed. Life happened. Cancer claimed my parents, and some of the laughter went out of our lives. Christmases came and went without the joy that had filled our home when our girls lived there and my parents shared the season with us. Christmas had stopped feeling like Christmas. I prayed for a solution.

I wasn't alone in feeling that something was missing. As we were preparing for Christmas 2013, my middle daughter asked about me harnessing up a horse and taking the kids for a ride.

"It would be a lot of fun for the kids to have a chance to experience what we did when we were kids," she explained.

Her words triggered an idea. Could this be the answer to my prayer? Why not get that smaller toboggan out again? Our latest horse, Doc, was more than able to handle the weight of a loaded toboggan. I searched the shed for the harness. I checked it for worn straps, cleaned and repaired it. I checked the toboggan, tightening the screws that held each board in place.

Our family Christmas was suddenly filled with laughter and anticipation. The skies had cooperated by dumping another couple of inches of snow across the landscape. I waded my way to the barn to groom Doc and harness him up. Throwing extra hay in his stall, I left him to enjoy a last snack while I hauled the toboggan out into the snow. Seven of our eight grandchildren wiggled into their snow-suits and waddled out to the driveway. I thought about their mothers doing the same thing, excitement on their rosy faces.

I led Doc from the barn and clipped the traces into place. Standing by his head, lead strap in hand, I called to my daughters. "Okay, one adult, the rest children." My oldest daughter settled onto the back of the sled and her four children piled on top of her. We laughed as Doc and I broke trail through the stands of spruce and pines. We wove around snowdrifts and across the cornfield. Snippets of childish laughter were caught by the slight breeze and carried to my ears. We rounded the last curve and came to a stop on the driveway where one load of happy passengers rolled off into the snow, and another load climbed aboard. Around and around we went and I couldn't help but think of my parents who had watched as their grandchildren had ridden this same toboggan behind a team of horses.

The afternoon drew to a close after all participating family members had a turn or two on the toboggan. Doc was returned to his stall and his hay. The toboggan was returned to its place against the barn wall. The harness was hung in the tack room. We all trundled back to the house for our traditional Christmas turkey dinner. The talk that evening was filled with the events of the day. I sat back, content, and listened as joy filled the room. What we had purchased, those many years ago, as a simple Christmas present for three little girls had now become a tool in God's hand to return joy to our house. The old, faded toboggan had become part of our family Christmas tradition.

~Donna Fawcett
St. Marys, Ontario

58

The Best Present Ever

...I shall smile when wreaths of snow
Blossom where the rose should grow...
~Emily Brontë

Children living in Victoria, British Columbia, all share one dream in December. They see the weather reports of snow in other regions of Canada and dream of a white Christmas for themselves too.

The Christmas I turned ten I was one of those kids yearning for a white Christmas. But as Christmas approached, the forecast was for rain and more rain, so I focused instead on my three older brothers, who I was told were plotting something extra special for me under the tree. "The Boys," as my mom referred to them, were whispering more, grinning more, and planning more than usual. Anytime I would enter a room a hush would come over the crew. Papers with drawings and sketches were quickly hidden away.

I pestered each of my brothers in the days leading up to Christmas. What was it to be? What could warrant all the extra intrigue and detailed preparation? Where were they keeping it? The Boys were at their best when they worked together. I could hardly wait for Christmas to come.

On Christmas Eve, after the gifts were spread under the boughs of our tree, I began to look for the gift of my dreams. There were many large boxes under the tree. Surely the best Christmas present ever would be big. I pretended to be admiring the lovely wrapping papers and pretty bows, all the while carrying out my reconnaissance. There were gifts with my name on the tag, but none from "The Boys."

My attempts to be subtle in my search were abandoned. Efforts to locate the long awaited present turned into an all-out treasure hunt. Finally I spied a small package wrapped in plain paper. It was tucked way back under the tree. I reached back and grabbed the box. *To Kyla, love The Boys.* This was it.

It was not a heavy box. It was not a big box. It didn't resemble anything I could imagine taking weeks to orchestrate. Whatever it was, it was now the object of my desire. I tucked it back again where I found it.

When Christmas morning finally arrived and everyone was awake, we were allowed to head down to the tree and begin opening our gifts. This year I led the way. I led the way straight to the back where my little box from The Boys was stashed. I paused for just a moment to take a breath. One has to prepare to open the best present ever.

I ripped off the paper and looked down at the box in my hands. I had anticipated this moment for weeks, and now here it was. All I could think about was how to keep my face from showing the depth of my disappointment.

In my hand I held a gift box of Life Savers candy. It was the kind of gift box that contained ten rolls of the treats in a case that looked like a book. It was the kind of present you got from your grandma when she came back from the airport in Brandon. It was not the best present ever.

"Thanks boys," I managed to muster. "This is really cool." My voice was so flat I almost didn't recognize it myself.

In my hurry to reach the Christmas tree, I had not noticed that our front drapes were pulled shut, which was unusual. And now, as I tried to hide my disappointment, my mother had decided that it was important for me to open the curtains. I stood up and started to pull back the window coverings. That was when the light first caught my eye. It was white outside. Glistening. Crested. Snow. Snow on Christmas morning! Snow in Victoria! I worked to finish opening the drapes completely and shouted, "It snowed! It snowed!" But had it?

Our front lawn was completely covered in a blanket of fresh white snow. But our neighbour's lawn was just as green as the day before. The treetops were still wet and green. The road had no sign of white. What was this miraculous weather pattern that had made ours the only home to get a snowfall?

Then I finally noticed the big paper sign in the middle of our yard. It was a handwritten banner with large lettering in red and green that said, "Merry Christmas, Kyla. Love, The Boys."

Instead of going to sleep on Christmas Eve, my brothers had put their plan into action. They had borrowed my dad's pickup truck and driven around the city to all the hockey arenas they could find. Out back of each rink, they worked with shovels to load up the ice and snow removed by the Zamboni in the process of cleaning the skating surfaces. They knew these large piles of icy snow, once relocated to our home, would work perfectly to deliver the desired effect as they were spread painstakingly, lovingly, across our huge front lawn. I can't even begin to imagine how many loads it took to do the job. Every inch of our yard was covered.

I donned a pair of boots and quickly headed outside. The boys came too and helped me make a snowman. Walkers passed by, enjoying the odd sight of snow. Kids from down the block heard the news and soon arrived to play with us too. We had snowball fights, made ice sculptures, took pictures and played until our fingers hurt. It was every West Coast kid's dream come true—a real white Christmas.

I have kids of my own now and they enjoy hearing me tell stories of growing up with "The Boys." Each December, as we decorate our Christmas tree, we recall some of the best presents we have received over the years. Some gifts stand out in my memory more than others. I always recall the Christmas I opened that small box of Life Savers—the year my dream came true. It remains the only white Christmas I've ever had. It was simply the best present ever. A gift of love—from The Boys.

~Kyla G. Ward
Victoria, British Columbia

A Magical Conversation

Unless we make Christmas an occasion to share our blessings,
all the snow in Alaska won't make it white.
~Bing Crosby

It was two weeks before Christmas and I was not ready. Not ready with food, not ready with gifts and decorations and, most of all, not ready in spirit. Outside, the grass was still green. This Christmas, of all Christmases, I needed snow to cheer me. I am Canadian after all.

It had been a tough year of financial loss from the stock market crash and a failing business that promised to drain us further still. We had been forced to move from a lovingly renovated home in the historic section of Oakville, Ontario, into a house that needed a lot of work. Worse still, we had to cram our business into what should have been the basement family room. I had put my interior design business on hold to help my husband with his company. I loved my design work; I did not love accounting or administration and, with each passing day, life was leaching from me.

This Christmas was not going to be the same as all the others. I had already scaled back on decorating and baking and there would be no entertaining, just our Christmas Eve fondue, and the potluck Christmas dinner with extended family. No Martha Stewart Christmas this year. Though their lists weren't long, our three teenaged daughters weren't going to get everything they'd asked for. There had been no time to make a Christmas playlist to put me in the mood. I had balance sheets and packing slips on my mind where there should have been visions of sugarplums dancing. And there was no white Christmas.

And then I was offered a last-minute free ticket to see the musical *Jesus Christ Superstar* with my friend who had worked on it as a scenic artist. With my husband out of town, I was free to go. It seemed an odd show for Christmastime, but I was determined to take this break and get my mind off my troubles.

Coincidentally, a fierce storm rolled in that evening. As I drove across the city through blinding snow, I reminded myself I had hoped for snow every day for the last two weeks. "Be careful what you wish for," I scolded myself as I gripped the steering wheel with both hands.

Once inside the theatre, it occurred to me how apt this musical actually was for Christmas, sort of like reading the last chapter of a book before you begin at the beginning. It was an outstanding performance, and I felt faint stirrings of the Christmas spirit. By the time we left the theatre the wind had died down, and snow fell softly in enormous flakes. My friend and I raised our faces to the sky and laughed as we welcomed the cool kiss on our cheeks.

Driving home, it struck me that the sky was almost as bright as day. The snow had stopped and now the ground was a blanket of white and the night sky seemed to be filled with an ethereal milky whiteness, and a silent stillness. When I pulled into our driveway it was after midnight, yet two of my daughters wanted to go for a walk in the magical glow they'd been viewing from their windows.

We piled on our coats and scarves and hats and mittens and walked for forty-five minutes with the pristine snow crunching under our feet. It was truly enchanting. Then, somehow, the conversation turned to our Christmas traditions and I felt the twinge of guilt and disappointment at how different this Christmas would be. But the list they were making wasn't about the material things I knew we would be lacking this year.

"Getting our tree at Drysdale's," recounted Whitney, the mist of her breath accompanying her words. We went every year with their cousins, the tractor-drawn wagon moving past rows of pines and spruces and balsams to the Fraser firs that we preferred. Those fine needles and thin boughs were the perfect backdrop for the hundreds of tiny white lights we would wrap around the trunk and branches before we hung the garlands and ornaments. We would choose the perfect tree together and cut it down ourselves.

"Baking chocolate peanut butter pinwheels," said Morgan.

"No, caramel treasures," rebutted her sister. I smiled. Each of my daughters had her favourite Christmas cookie, and that was the cookie she helped me bake. Though our baking endeavours had been reduced this year, we had still made these favourites.

The list went on—*It's a Wonderful Life, A Christmas Carol, White Christmas*. The trip to Niagara-on-the-Lake to see the Trisha Romance-style decorations. Warm apple cider from Chudleigh's Apple Farm. Gramma's "nuts and bolts."

The last one got us reminiscing about food, especially about our unique Christmas Eve tradition of fondue and Yorkshire pudding. For a long time, I made Christmas Eve dinner of roast beef and Yorkshires for just the five of us because, although we were all together at all the big family functions, the season seemed to pass without our little family sitting focused on each other in a truly significant way. When we got together with family, the kids would rush in the door to play with their cousins, the adults would catch up with each other, and I barely saw my own children. So I made Christmas Eve our time to steal away from the chaos that we all loved and share an intimate evening with each other. I chose roast beef and Yorkshire pudding because it was the furthest thing from the turkey we would consume on Christmas Day, but one year I switched it to fondue. The girls liked that even better, but they didn't want to give up the Yorkshire pudding, so an unlikely Christmas tradition was born.

I smiled again as they went on about those dinners. As they had grown older we had stopped going to Christmas Eve church service. Instead, somewhere over the course of the evening as we set our skewered cubes of meat into the hot oil, we took turns recounting how God had shown up in our lives since the Christmas before. We learned so much about each other from those conversations.

We walked on and they added to the list—opening one gift before bed, Whitney reading the Luke 2 passage before we opened our stockings and gifts on Christmas morning. These were our traditions, the ones they talked about with enthusiasm. There was no mention of the gifts they wanted, no mention of the things I didn't have time to do this year. What they cherished were the things I had tried to instill in them all along, little things that had nothing to do with money or all the Christmas "bells and whistles."

As we headed back home in the magic whiteness, Morgan announced, "This is better than a sleepover!" With that, my cares and concerns of the previous weeks melted into gratitude. The snow was here and my kids understood what was important—perhaps better than I had this year. And I knew we would be all right.

~Marie MacNeill
Toronto, Ontario

Chapter
7

Christmas in Canada

Taking Care of Each Other

The way you get meaning into your life is to devote yourself to loving others, devote yourself to your community around you, and devote yourself to creating something that gives you purpose and meaning.

~Mitch Albom

A Christmas Turkey
in Turkey

Christmas is a necessity. There has to be at least one day of the year to remind us that we're here for something else besides ourselves.
~Eric Sevareid

When you are in a foreign country, especially one predominantly Muslim, December 25th is a working day. I was working as a teacher in Istanbul, and all the English, American and Canadian teachers told our boss we'd be calling in sick if we didn't get the day off. We had to somehow convince him that this was serious, indeed. He reluctantly relented and gave us the day off—without pay!

There were Christmas decorations in some of the streets, but the hotels and restaurants weren't celebrating and no special banquets were prepared that I knew of. The only solution was to try and create a Canadian Christmas in Turkey. I polled my friends and colleagues to see who would be interested in chipping in and coming to my place for Christmas dinner. Many were, so the game was on. All I had to do was plan the event.

To put everyone in the Christmas mood I went searching for a tree. The best I could find was an artificial one that looked like it was on life support—a Charlie Brown Christmas tree. It went up in a few seconds, and I left it in the hands of a friend to decorate. I figured the right person could make my tree look good—and she did. Wanting to make sure everyone got a gift, I scurried around getting little trinkets I thought my guests could use.

With guests coming to dinner I wanted a turkey. Just in case you wondered, a turkey isn't called a turkey in Turkey. It's called a *hindi*, and finding one in Turkey was a bit of a challenge. I trundled off to the local supermarket to get my bird. It should be noted that I don't speak Turkish and the butcher didn't speak English, but I did know that a turkey is a *hindi*. I boldly walked up to the meat counter and said "*hindi.*" Like somebody getting his photo for a passport, the response was a blank, expressionless stare. Perhaps if I said it louder. "*HINDI!*" I bellowed, but got the same result. I paused. What was the next strategy? As the butcher turned to walk away from this foreigner, I decided to say the word over and over, each time varying the pitch, expression and pronunciation of the word. "*Hindi, hindi, hindi, hindi,*" I rattled off in succession. They all sounded the same to me, but one must have clicked. Like a motor starting on a cold morning, his eyes suddenly sparked and he nodded, "Ah, *hindi!*" To this day I swear he said it the same way I had, but at that moment, I didn't care. I was marched toward the appropriate aisle in the store and left to fend for myself.

There were three birds. Which one to choose? I hefted all three birds and listened for a voice from heaven, as if there might be some sign like the star in the east. I finally decided on one that was slightly over ten kilograms. Success!

But buying the turkey was just the beginning. When you rent an unfurnished apartment in Turkey it is totally empty. I had managed to buy a fridge and some burners, but there was no oven. A friend of mine, Izzy, mentioned that a bakery near him had cooked his Thanksgiving turkey for free. I could do the same. So I headed to the bakery where I usually bought my bread. My only previous conversation with the owner had been, "*Bir ekmek, lutfen,*" which means "one bread please." How was I to explain to him what I needed?

When you visit another culture, shyness doesn't work. So, digging deep into my charades background I did my best to convey my message. I don't know if he thought I was doing the Chicken Dance or what, but I got that blank look again. Other customers moved away from me. Giving up, I headed to another bakery where I had bought my birthday cake. When I started my Chicken Dance again the owner held up one finger, rushed out in the street and dragged a surprised young man into the store to see my act. More importantly, it turned out he spoke English. Once I explained my situation, the owner smiled and took me back to the first bakery. This owner smiled, too, nodded his head and said, "Hindi." My problem was solved. I could smell the succulent roasting meat already.

Christmas Day came. To celebrate and clean up for my guests, I decided to get my hair cut. I went to a hair stylist, put my thumb and finger a little apart, and told him to take "a little" off the top. The clippers swooped down on my head like a combine cutting hay and left "a little" stubble. When I remembered that he probably didn't understand English, I realized I had likely told him to cut my hair very short. "Oh well," I figured, "it will grow back."

The next step was to lug the turkey to the bakery. The hills in Istanbul are steep; however, the bakery wasn't far, only about a hundred metres, and carrying it home would be all downhill. When I entered the bakery the owner smiled as I slid the tray onto the counter. Then he frowned. I soon found out why. His oven was for making bread. My hindi wouldn't fit in the opening. He started twirling knives, suggesting he cut the bird so it would fit. For me, that was out of the question. Both of us stood there frozen, but for different reasons. He was trying to figure out what I was trying to say. I had ten guests coming in a few hours for a turkey dinner and I didn't know what to do.

His finger went up. I gasped! He had an idea! Soon he and one of the other employees started punching their cell phones and slamming them onto their ears. The owner had two going at once! Within minutes, he grabbed me by the arm and we charged outside. He had found another bakery that could cook my whole bird. Eureka!

There was one slight problem. The other place was half a kilometre farther from my apartment. It was all downhill to get there, but getting home would be all uphill. However, there wasn't any other option. I could always take a cab home.

We entered the bakery. The owner took one look at my turkey, laughed and held up four fingers. I was to return later that afternoon. Perfect! Or was it?

At four, I had my rendezvous with my fowl. It looked and smelled delicious! There was also a lot of grease in the pan. After draining most of it in the street, I tried hailing a taxi. I must have looked like a drunk stumbling around with that ten-kilogram bird. They whizzed by as if I didn't exist. My guests were due to arrive soon so I had no option but to walk my meal home. When I looked at the first hill I gulped. It reminded me of heading up a black diamond ski run, but I pressed on. Halfway up I started screaming! My arms were falling off. The local residents began appearing at their windows to look at this strange man bellowing and walking uphill with a *hindi*!

I did it! I finally arrived home. My shirt was soaked so I changed quickly and began preparing for the arrival of my guests. Like the Wise Men who arrived at the manger with gifts, I had lugged my turkey from a distant land. Few knew of the sacrifice I made that Christmas. All that mattered was that the apartment was filled with joy that day.

And so it was. Everyone pitched in to help. We ate and drank well. We opened the presents and played the silly games one plays at Christmas. When everyone left, I had a home still warm from the love that had been there, and enough leftover turkey to last me for a month.

Each holiday is unique and special, but last year in Turkey will go down in the books as one of the most memorable.

~John Stevens
St. Marys, Ontario

New Year's Eve Warmth

Just like there's always time for pain, there's always time for healing.
~*Jennifer Brown*, Hate List

I t was the morning of New Year's Eve and I had no intention of having a good time that evening. I was never a fan of New Year's Eve. I couldn't stand the crowds, dressing up, the countdown and the pressure to kiss at midnight. Especially this year. My boyfriend had broken up with me and I had spent the past few months preparing for a lifetime of spinsterhood. I was feeling far from celebratory and wasn't eager to usher in a bleak New Year.

My first resolution was to not get suckered into any kind of social activity, and instead spend the night sulking. Unfortunately, my friend Jay had other plans for me.

"You are not going to sit in your bathrobe alone on New Year's Eve," she insisted. "We'll hang out and have a sleepover, just you and me." I had grown to love my bathrobe with an almost obsessive ardor, but Jay wouldn't take no for an answer.

We met in the afternoon in Kensington Market, a Toronto institution of fruit stands, cheese shops and butchers, around the corner from the city's bustling Chinatown. As we wandered along the icy streets, Jay shouted out greetings to people she knew, which seemed to be everyone. Her final encounter was with her friend Casino Paul, a swaggering Al Pacino look-a-like in a thick toque who also didn't have plans for the evening.

"You can hang out with us!" Jay blurted, despite my widened

eyes, head shaking and attempts to discreetly kick her. Either her boots were too thick to feel my kicks or her skull was. Next thing I knew, Casino Paul was sauntering back to my place with us.

I gazed longingly at my bathrobe hanging on the back of my bedroom door. Casino Paul was cagey about his Casino moniker. Who calls himself Casino Paul and then won't offer an explanation? Was his name even Paul? I couldn't believe that I needed to make small talk rather than curl up with a box of Kleenex for when I would inevitably start crying at midnight. It was going to be a long evening and I was preparing to throttle Jay when we had a moment alone.

When the doorbell rang I was surprised to see Andrew, another friend of Jay's, whom she had introduced me to a couple of months ago. I had, in fact, been appalled by the introduction, because immediately after telling her about my break-up she had said, "Don't worry, I have the perfect man for you." I was shocked at her insensitivity.

"Maybe I can mourn a little first? Cry for a bit? Go for therapy? Find myself before you set me up on blind dates?" I had hissed angrily.

Andrew explained that Jay had invited him over for a quiet New Year's. He handed me a Pablo Neruda poem he had copied on a wrinkled piece of paper.

"I was thinking of how sad it is over the holidays when you are heartbroken," he said. "This poem helped me when I was going through something similar. Maybe it will help you too." I couldn't turn away anyone armed with a bottle of wine and a poem, despite my inclination for solitude, and promptly let him in.

A couple bottles of wine later I was feeling slightly more gracious. Andrew was sweet and had sexy, full lips. I kept stealing glances at him, forgetting for a moment about my vow of lifetime celibacy. I caught Casino Paul kissing my cat on the top of his head when he thought no one was looking, and found his bravado less irritating. Jay kept emerging from the kitchen with fresh snacks. Despite my firm resolve, I was almost forgetting to sulk.

An hour before midnight it began to snow. The wind howled as fluffy flakes dashed across the sky, covering everything with sparkling ice. "Let's go tobogganing!" Jay shouted, emboldened by the wine and the frosty landscape. We found an old pizza box in my recycling bin and grabbed garbage bags to make makeshift toboggans. We walked with our heads bent against the wind to Christie Pits, a park near Koreatown with sloping hills leading to baseball diamonds and rusty swing sets. It was deserted except for a group of South American exchange students who were also tobogganing. They had a real sled, a round blue disc that could fit two people at a time. Taking pity on us, with our pathetic pizza box sled, they offered us theirs. I positioned myself at the front until Jay pushed me and motioned for me to sit behind Casino Paul.

"Human windshield," she whispered. I sat behind him, sheltered against the snow that pummelled Casino Paul as we cut a path down the untouched hill. Our South American friends tirelessly shouted "Happy New Year" each time they sent us on our descent, until soaked and giddy, we trudged back toward my apartment.

I am not a fan of the cold and I hate winter, always insisting that I was born in the wrong country. That winter night, however, was magical. The snow sparkled like tiny diamonds and the sidewalk glimmered. The streetlights bathed everything in a blue glow. The blanket of snow left everything still and quiet. Despite the frigid air I felt warm. The kindness of those around me was stronger than the frosty temperatures: Jay's unwavering loyalty and fun, the generosity of the exchange students, and Andrew's attempt to mend a broken heart. Tipsy on snowflakes, cheeks rosy from tobogganing, I suddenly felt more positive than I had in a long time.

When we arrived back at my place I found warm clothes for everyone to change into. We were a motley crew of flannels sipping cheap brandy to keep warm in my drafty apartment. It felt more festive than any sophisticated cocktail party, and I had to admit, better than an evening alone in my bathrobe. I leaned against Andrew, who seemed to possess the ability to transform himself into a human furnace, and was charmed to see my cat cuddle up next to Casino Paul. Jay never ran out of snacks and stories to keep us entertained. We talked well into the morning and eventually fell asleep on the living room floor, a tangle of blankets and flannel, as the wind howled outside and people in their flashy party clothes struggled to find cabs in the snowstorm. I marvelled that my icy, broken heart could begin to thaw a little on the coldest night of the year.

~Kristine Groskaufmanis
Toronto, Ontario

Room at the Inn

Call it a clan, call it a network, call it a tribe, call it a family.
Whatever you call it, whoever you are, you need one.
~Jane Howard

Sitting in the Intensive Care Unit on December 23rd, I began to wonder if the entire world had forgotten about those in the hospital who were sick. It was almost Christmas, yet here we were, my brothers and sisters and I, along with our mom, gathered at the big city hospital in Saskatoon many miles from our home. Our dad was dying, and we'd all put our lives, and Christmas, on hold to be there for him, just as he'd always been for us. We'd been staying across the road in the accommodations that were available for those with family in the hospital. But it was crowded, and my sister and I were sharing a bed. The situation was less than comfortable.

While I was sitting beside Dad in the ICU the lady in the next bed passed away. She was alone. As the nurse pulled the sheet up over her head I took a few minutes to wonder about her loved ones, and to say a prayer for them. A shiver went up my spine as I realized that Dad could be next. We were grown up now, but we still needed him—or perhaps more accurately, we wanted him. We certainly weren't even close to being ready to let go of our father.

Christmas is such a family time, and I was torn between needing to be there with Dad and Mom, and wanting to be home with my husband and three small children. My sisters and brothers all felt the same. As the day wore on, the problem of how to do both was starting to cause us a lot of anxiety. Tomorrow was Christmas Eve and we were all very stressed. If we could not find room for our families, we all felt we would have to return to our homes for Christmas Eve. But we really did not want to leave Dad and Mom there alone.

My sister Robyn and I then went to the Hospitality Center to see where the nearest place to stay was, and if they might possibly have space for our families.

"There is room for two more, right across the street, for a reasonable fee," the kind volunteer told us.

"Yes," I said. "We've stayed there for the past few nights, but it is very crowded, and they definitely don't have room for our families," I explained. "Tomorrow is Christmas Eve and our husbands and children would like to join us so we can all be together."

"Well, I don't know," she said, shaking her head. Then her face lit up as she was struck by a thought: "Christmas Eve!" she said. "You know what? Some of the hotels in town offer free rooms to anyone with a critically ill family member in the hospital over Christmas."

I couldn't believe it. "Really? For free?" I asked incredulously.

"Yes, you just need proof that you have a loved one in the hospital, and I can easily provide you with that document."

"Wow! What a gift this is!" I said.

"Yes," exclaimed Robin. "Our families can now come and stay overnight with us so we can all spend Christmas together, but also be here with Dad."

The woman looked up the number for me, and I called the Saskatoon Inn.

"Do you have any rooms available tomorrow night—for Christmas Eve?" I asked hopefully, explaining the situation.

"We do have two rooms for you, here at the Inn," confirmed the front desk. "And, because it is Christmas, and your dad is in hospital, there will be no charge."

Grateful beyond words, we called our families, who immediately began packing up. When they arrived the next day, we all headed over to the Saskatoon Inn to check in.

The hotel had a big Christmas tree, it was beautifully decorated, and the Christmas atmosphere was everywhere. The children simply loved swimming in the pool and going down the waterslide. We noticed other families, who had come prepared, opening gifts. But we didn't need any gifts—being together and close to Dad was enough.

That year, we all "enjoyed" our Christmas as much as one possibly can when someone you love is dying. The children in particular thought it was a real adventure to stay in a big hotel with a pool, and they really loved the big Christmas tree. The following year, when Robyn's three-year-old twins heard Christmas was coming, they were quick to ask: "When are we going to the hotel?"

I am so thankful for the blessing that hotel room was to us. Because of our experiences that year, I am much more aware of sick and lonely people who need a little extra loving care at Christmas. And none of us will ever forget that Christmas Eve when the desk clerk said—"Yes, we have room at the Inn."

~Annie Riess
Unity, Saskatoon

One More Life to Love

There is a very real relationship, both quantitatively and qualitatively,
between what you contribute and what you get out of this world.
~Oscar Hammerstein II

My mother had seen her Yugoslavian homeland torn apart by war, but it gave her an incredibly open heart. At no time was this more evident than when, some years ago, she sponsored a Jamaican child in need of open-heart surgery to come live with us in Canada for two years.

Escorted by her father, Nirene arrived at our suburban Canadian home in late October. She was the size of an average three-year-old though she had just turned five. My brother and I were typical teenagers, naïve about Jamaica and its culture. Upon meeting Nirene and her charming dad, we all felt an instant connection and made friends quickly.

Nirene was an adorable little girl with an infectious personality. She was outgoing, smart and loved to laugh. Her smile lit up the room and one could not help but watch her with joy.

Once her dad returned to Jamaica, we decided as a family to focus entirely on Nirene for her first Christmas in Canada. We each carefully selected the gifts we thought would most thrill her. Every present was elegantly wrapped and placed under the tree on Christmas Eve while she slept.

Christmas morning, Nirene woke everyone up with enthusiasm, announcing that Santa had come. She'd already seen "a whole heap of gifts under the tree!" It was her excitement that fuelled us to get up so early. Bleary eyed, we headed downstairs.

When we were all in place in the family room, Mom gave Nirene a nod to start opening her gifts. They were, after all, mostly hers. In the blink of an eye, the first present was literally ripped open. Then the second and a third! She did not stop to ponder each gift. No, this little one was just having a ripping good time in which she pretty much disappeared after all her twenty-plus gifts had been opened!

Then, from inside the pile of torn gift-wrap, Nirene popped up, and to our astonishment asked, "Is there any more?"

"No," I said. We all started to laugh hysterically at that, so she dove into her pile to find something new to entertain herself with. It was the best Christmas ever for all of us as a family, and also for Nirene.

The following spring, Nirene was scheduled for surgery at The Hospital for Sick Children in Toronto to correct the "aortic stenosis" she'd had from birth, which was not allowing her enough oxygen. Not being from Canada, Nirene's medical expenses were not covered by OHIP, so my mother had set up the Herbie Fund to cover them. To this day that fund is dedicated to helping pay for surgeries for seriously ill children who come to "Sick Kids" from foreign countries.

Finally, the day came when Nirene entered the hospital in Toronto. Her dad flew back from Montego Bay to be present for her surgery, and we all waited for what seemed like an entire day for Nirene's surgery to finish. The doctor finally came out with the news we wanted to hear. The operation was a complete success! Now there was the difficult task of Nirene healing and being weaned off the life support machines. Slowly, one by one, each machine was removed.

Nirene was on the road to living a healthy life with a good future. She continued to live with my family for another year and a half so she could go to follow-up appointments at the hospital. Soon enough it was Christmas once again; however this time it was with a very different tone. Nirene was no longer our special little foreign visitor; this time she truly felt like a real sister, a member of our family.

Today Nirene is a successful businesswoman in Washington,

D.C., with an MBA. She is engaged to be married and will soon celebrate her fortieth birthday. She was a bridesmaid at my wedding, and I had her introduced as "Sister of the Bride."

Life has a way of presenting us with opportunities that can really stretch us way, way beyond our ordinary selves, that is, if you see these opportunities. That's what my mother did. From my mother I learned that extraordinary selflessness will bring more love to your life, and more lives to love.

~Luanne Beresford
Maple, Ontario

Get to Work, Santa

Love is the condition in which the happiness of another person
is essential to your own.
~Robert Heinlein

"Hold it right there!" I froze in mid-step, pinned to the wall by a brilliant beam of light. The voice behind the flashlight echoed in the emptiness of the dimly lit stairwell.

"Where do you think you're going?"

"Well you see, officer... ah, my wife is on the next floor and..."

It was Christmas Eve. Dressed in a Santa suit, I had been caught sneaking in to visit my wife Carol in the hospital's Surgical Ward. Carol's December 25th birthdate always made our Christmas extra special, but this year, on December 22nd, disaster had struck! Carol began complaining of severe stomach pain. We rushed to emergency where the diagnosis was acute appendicitis. The treatment was immediate emergency surgery, and the prognosis—Christmas in the hospital. We were stunned. Realizing she would have to spend her Christmas birthday in a sick bed in the hospital, away from home, just broke Carol's heart.

During my post-surgery visit she was groggy, but able to squeeze my hand in response to my words of love and support. My stay however was brief. The ward supervisor, Nurse Krause, arrived to settle in the new patient. Visiting hours were strictly enforced and Krause was diligent in her duties. My appeal for special treatment fell on deaf ears and she dismissed me from the room. I spent the next two days dodging Krause in an attempt to extend my visits; however, she invariably managed to thwart my efforts. Even our Christmas Eve visit was terminated promptly at 9:00 p.m. But, unbeknownst to Krause, I had a backup plan! Just after midnight, dressed in a Santa suit, I snuck back into the hospital using the stairs. I had almost made it when I found myself caught in that beam of light.

"So you see, Officer, I have just got to get to her." After considering my plea, the man delivered me to the nursing station, right back into the clutches of Nurse Krause. After eyeing me for a moment, she ordered me to stay put and then set off down the hallway. And then a Christmas miracle occurred.

She returned pushing a wheelchair, and when I recognized its smiling occupant my heart leaped with joy. Krause parked the chair and then, without saying a word, disappeared from sight again. Now was my chance! Leaning forward, I took Carol by the shoulders and...

"Okay you two, that's enough of that. You've got work to do!" barked Krause as she reappeared pushing a large laundry cart filled with wrapped presents and stuffed toys. It turned out that Nurse Krause had a special mission of her own that Christmas Eve. The pediatric ward was right next door and, so that no child would miss out on their visit from Santa, their parents had left gifts with Krause for delivery. Noting my Santa outfit, Krause had decided to recruit me!

With Carol accompanying us in the wheelchair, we quietly slipped into the children's ward, where most of the little ones were asleep. Krause selected the appropriate presents and I tiptoed from bed to bed placing the gifts inside the bed rails with their occupants. By the time we finished, we had left more than one sleepy-eyed young believer in our wake. In addition, Carol and I found our efforts had done wonders in restoring our own somewhat trampled Christmas spirit.

Back in her room I assisted Carol into bed and chose that moment to deliver a long delayed Christmas/birthday kiss. I swear

Krause smiled, but just for a moment. "Okay Santa, on your way. Your work here is done."

When I arrived on Christmas morning loaded with presents, Krause was still on duty. "Good morning Santa, I mean Mr. Forrest. She's anxious to see you."

When I entered Carol's room I was pleasantly surprised to find her wearing her robe, and seated on the edge of the bed. She looked great, considering she'd had serious surgery less than forty-eight hours ago. After I took off my coat Carol told me about the doctor's visit a half hour earlier, his order to remove the IV, and his noncommittal reply to her plea to be released. Just as we were about to begin opening the presents, Krause appeared at the door.

"Mr. Forrest, I'll have to ask you to excuse us."

"Aw Nurse Krause," I moaned, "can't it wait until…?"

"Now see here you!" she exclaimed. "Just because I felt sorry for you last night doesn't mean you can get away with anything today. I have to change her dressing before she goes home, and I can't do that with you here."

"What did you say?" blurted Carol. "Did you say home?" she cried. "I'm going home today, really?"

"That's right," replied Krause, "as soon as we can get you out the door. When the doctor stopped by after rounds he wanted to know how you were really doing. I think your tale of woe had him pretty well convinced, but when I told him about last night, and added that if he didn't let you out today I'd probably have to install a cot for your husband, he decided that home would be the best place for you both.

"So you, out!" she ordered. "Make yourself useful and go find a wheelchair."

When I returned with the chair I gathered up the unopened gifts and Carol's suitcase, while Krause got her seated in the chair. Our little entourage then made its way to the elevator. When the car arrived I held it for a moment, looked down at Carol and then we both looked to Krause.

"Merry Christmas!" we said.

"Merry Christmas to you too," replied Krause. "And... ah... thank you for your help last night," she added, with just a hint of a thin-lipped smile.

"It was you who helped us, Krause," said Carol softly.

The doors slid shut, and we were on our way home for Christmas.

~John Forrest
Orillia, Ontario

Christmas on the Prairie

What do we live for if not to make life less difficult for each other?
~George Elliot

I grew up on a farm and attended a one-room country school. Christmas meant hefting the axe and tramping through knee-deep snow into our woods to pick the best Christmas tree we could find. It meant celebrating at church, putting on Christmas concerts at school, and visiting family or friends. Times were tough, so Christmas did not mean lavish festivities or fancy gifts, but even though our house was small, there was always room for a few more at the table. My mother was adept at tossing more potatoes in the pot and cutting the meat, which was often venison or elk steaks, into smaller portions.

We lived on a road that led to one First Nations reservation if one traveled east, and to another if one went west. The two reservations were several miles apart, but we often had travelers, either single wagons of families or little groups traveling together, pass by our place. Occasionally they stopped to sell smoked fish or other goodies. Truth was, thanks to an older sister who loved to tell her own versions of "Indian lore," I was afraid of them and always kept well behind a protective parent.

The year I was eight the Christmas season began as usual. We were all looking forward to the school concert. Of course we kids all had parts to memorize and perform, but there would also be neighbourly visits over a potluck lunch, candy treats, and a visit from someone's father dressed as Santa. We couldn't wait. We traveled by horses and sleigh, sleigh-bells jingling "all the way." Snuggled down in the heavy bedding of warm straw covered by blankets, we sang carols and counted falling stars.

On this particular evening we had an unexpected addition to the usual program. A First Nation couple had been making the trek from one reserve to the other and had stopped and pitched their tent in our neighbourhood. I'm not sure who first discovered them, but they were invited to the concert and then joined in as part of the entertainment. They both played guitars, and he sang and chatted comfortably. We were enthralled. A real "Indian" at our concert!

A couple of days later, word came that a bad storm had blown down a tree that ripped a big hole in the couple's tent. They were friends now, so my mom soon had Dad hitching up the team and going to look for them. It was cold and stormy, and as a child watching my dad go I was more than a little concerned.

Well, Dad found them and brought them home, even as the storm continued, and so we came to have guests for Christmas. The man's name was Mr. Northwest. The woman was very shy, and I don't think she spoke much English, but he more than made up for that. He was a wonderful storyteller and could do little tricks, like whistling into his guitar and making it sound like the echo was coming from the ceiling. Dad and Mom gave up their bedroom and shuffled us kids around to make room in our limited space. I suppose some of us slept on the floor—but we were used to that when guests came. Mr. and Mrs. Northwest were with us for a few days until the storm abated, and during that time I lost my fear of Canada's native people.

When the weather cleared and they were once again able to be on their way, it was with a sense of sadness that we watched them go—trudging off into the whiteness, their packs on their backs. I guess it was one of those wonderful lessons that God teaches when we least expect it. Christmas—my favourite time of the year—was even better when it was shared.

~Janette Oke
Red Deer, Alberta

Battery Included

Gratitude is the music of the heart,
when its chords are swept by the breeze of kindness.
~Author Unknown

When we first moved into that little basement suite, I felt very at home. The family who owned the house lived on the main floor and I felt so connected to them. Years earlier my older sister had lived there with her husband and baby daughter. I'd also gone to school with the son of the couple who owned the house.

Things had been tough for that family because their son had been killed in a farming accident, and they never got to see him grow up and have a family of his own. He was such a fine person and when I think of his parents having to continue their lives without him it causes a sad ache in me. And it touches me even more as I remember what his parents did for us on our first Christmas in their basement suite.

It was hardly a suite, just a huge room divided by two sheets of plywood. The bathroom down the hall was shared with two other "suites." Our kitchen area, besides a fridge and stove, featured a table and four chairs, cupboards and a huge box that my dad had made—a kind of hope chest. I always figured that when we could afford it maybe we would buy a television and it would sit on the hope chest.

There really wasn't money to buy a car so when it was time for our first baby to be born I phoned my dad and asked him to take me to the hospital. It would have been nice to have had a car to bring her home in because, even though it was April, the day the baby arrived a blizzard hit!

By the time Christmas rolled around our new baby was eight months old and we'd acquired an old car. Now our strained budget included car payments. That left very little in the budget for much of anything else. Even fruit became a treat.

Early in December, that old car decided it needed a new battery. Unfortunately there was no way we could afford a new battery, so the car sat at the curb while snow piled up on it. This meant we wouldn't be traveling very far in any direction any time soon.

In the weeks before Christmas we could manage the two blocks to the grocery store, but walking long distances in the cold to visit with family was out of the question. We made the best of it.

I didn't drop hints about our "needs." I didn't complain about not being able to afford fruit, so I sure wasn't going to complain about not being able to buy a car battery. I never imagined for a moment that others were aware of our needs.

That Christmas week, the landlord sent his daughter downstairs with an early Christmas gift for our baby. It was not only her first doll but also her very first Christmas gift! Then we were directed to come out into the hall and look up at the top of the stairs. When we did we could see something square and black sitting at the top. We were told it was from the family (our landlord). We flew up those steps, excitedly hoping that it really was what it appeared to be. And indeed it was—a new car battery. We were soon racing back down the stairs, along the hallway and back up another flight of stairs to give the family an excited and heartfelt thank you!

When I was little, my mom and dad got me this doll that made a soft crying sound when I squeezed her tummy. I was so thrilled. I thought I was the luckiest girl in the world. Well when I saw that car battery I got the same "excited in the pit of my stomach" feeling.

Our landlord and his family must have cut back on their own Christmas spending just to help us. These were people who really took the meaning of "giving" seriously.

I will carry the memory of this with me forever, of this special Christmas gift, with battery included!

~Ellie Braun-Haley
Calgary, Alberta

67

Love and Loons

Love is what's in the room with you at Christmas if you stop
opening presents and listen.
~Author Unknown,
attributed to a seven-year-old named Bobby

I t was the end of a long, lean year. My eighty-three-year-old dad had died, leaving Mom alone after sixty-two years of marriage, far from family. With his passing my kids lost their only grandpa. In the same month, my marriage suddenly ended, which I was unprepared for and much shaken by. I was barely keeping my head above water as I struggled to single-parent my two young sons, prepare our home for sale, pack up our life for a move, and return to work after years at home. And now it was Christmas. I was grieving, tired, worried about money and feeling alone and overwhelmed. I had no family in Canada.

There would not be many presents under the tree, but that would be okay, as I wanted my boys to know the holidays were not just about gifts. Even so, the list in my head loomed large — get the Christmas tree, do shopping/wrapping, make cookies and decorations and cards from the boys, help the boys write letters to Santa. In spite of my low mood, I did want to make Christmas special for my kids. I just did not know how I could do it all. The division of labour I had been used to in my marriage was suddenly gone. Like Atlas holding up the world, I felt like it was all on my shoulders.

First things first. A phone call to Mom—"Will you come for Christmas?"

She was eighty years old and having her first Christmas without Dad in sixty-two years. And it was her first solo travel, not to mention across an international border. Daunting but doable.

"We need you. You need us. Will you come? I will organize all the flight details."

"Okay," she agreed.

Great relief. The kids and I wouldn't be alone. I knew my mother and I could muddle through our first Christmas if we did it together.

Mom arrived in early December and quickly shifted into high gear, making pies for our freezer. She got the boys involved choosing cookie recipes, rolling out dough and frosting cookies. She made casseroles for dinners. A huge weight lifted off my heart having her with us. She reminded me we can go on even when our hearts are sad.

Next—the tree. I wondered if I should buy an artificial tree. We lived in the country and had our own pine woods, but I simply didn't know if I could cut down a tree on my own, drag it home through the snow and then set it up. The phone rang, and it was close family friends on the line.

"We have an idea," they said. "Could we get our Christmas tree from your woods this year? We will take the boys out with us, cut one down for you all, too, and even help you put it up in the house."

"Oh yes," I agreed, with relief. "And please stay for supper."

One more thing taken care of, and a happy, noisy holiday tradition preserved.

In the next two weeks, other moms invited my boys over to play so Grandma and I could do a little shopping unhindered. The nursery school my younger son attended gave him the star role of Santa in their holiday play, which greatly cheered my little one, and offered a delightful surprise to me on the night of the performance. Another holiday gift.

The four of us watched Christmas specials cuddled up on the sofa, and gave in to tears while watching Grandpa's favourite, *White*

Christmas. It was a tender time for all of us. And one by one, the Christmas tasks were getting accomplished.

Several friends called to invite us to join their boisterous extended family celebrations on Christmas Day, but we opted to stay home and be a little family of four instead. I knew it would be a bittersweet day for us, and I wanted us to have time and space to just be.

We sent letters off to Santa, and were surprised and delighted when he replied, his letters bearing the postmark of the town where my sister lived in the States, 2,000 miles away. I smiled as I thought of all the tender love coming our way.

The butcher gave me another light-hearted moment. When I asked him for his smallest turkey, since we did not need a big one this year, he offered to cut a turkey in half for us and vacuum-seal the other half so we could freeze it for a later holiday. "Serve it with twice-baked potatoes and you'll be all set."

Did my sadness show so much? Did the entire world know we needed extra help that year? I was grateful.

It was Christmas Eve. Stockings were hung, cookies and milk waited on a tray for Santa, boys in pyjamas were tucked into bed. Mom and I cleaned up the kitchen, and I put out the gifts, adding in some old teddy bears under the tree to fill up the space. I was about to turn off the lights when I had an idea. Opening a package of balloons, I inflated them, and tumbled them in around the gifts. The effect was lovely, colourful, and festive. The bright colours seemed to multiply the number of gifts under the tree.

Christmas morning came early, as it always does. While it was still dark, my four-year-old came running into my bedroom.

"Mama!" he shouted. "Santa brought loons! Lots and lots of loons! Get up, Mama! It's Christmas!"

Loons? Did my mom do something Canadian for us? What could it be? It was winter. There are no loons in Canada in December.

Taking my hand, Noah led me down the stairs to the living room, where his eight-year-old brother Josh grinned up from the floor with a bulging Christmas stocking on his lap. Noah ran and picked up a bright red balloon and gave it to me.

"Look, Mama! Santa came and brought presents and loons!"

We played with the balloons; the boys drew faces on them and popped some. The cat chased them. We had a good Christmas. The boys were happy. My mother and I laughed at our roasted half-turkey, and again when we realized we had finished half a pie. The boys and I played in the snow. We all roasted apples in the woodstove and toasted marshmallows. We talked about Grandpa and how much we missed him. Our family phoned from the U.S. with warm wishes.

What stands out about that Christmastime was the tender, sweet love at every turn, from friends and family, teachers and shopkeepers reaching out to lift us through a difficult season. That is what Christmas is all about. Love. And that year, loons.

~Deborah K. Wood
Newmarket, Ontario

68

Baking on Christmas Eve

Give freely to the world these gifts of love and compassion.
Do not concern yourself with how much you receive in return,
just know in your heart it will be returned.
~*Steve Maraboli*, Life, the Truth, and Being Free

Every year I say I am not going to bake. But as Christmas grows closer, comforting childhood memories draw me to my cookbook. Christmas just isn't Christmas for me without star shaped sugar cookies and the family's famous rum balls. And baking with a snifter of something, or coffee laced with rum, makes it just that more Christmassy.

And so it was on that particular Christmas Eve, I was baking. I did not normally bake so last minute, but I had been working overtime. And there was a reason I wanted to do extra baking that Christmas: I was newly single for the second time, and my first ex and our adult children were coming for Christmas dinner. I wanted to make it special.

"Shortbread," I said to the dog, who was hanging out in the kitchen, "I will make shortbread, and those little cookies with a maraschino cherry on top. And I could make chocolate covered almond bark—I have chocolate left over and everyone loves almond bark."

I got to work. It was a strange Christmas Eve, being on my own, the first ever not sharing the usual rituals and last minute gift-wrapping with family. The baking made it feel more normal. I allowed myself just a splash of rum in my coffee, no more, as I was on call with the crisis line. There were two of us on call that night; I was second in line and didn't expect to receive a phone call. Even so I drank the rest of my coffee minus the rum.

I loved baking for other people. I recalled making fudge for my father and how much he enjoyed it. I remembered first learning to bake cookies and cake at age nine, and watching my dad make Christmas pudding. And I recalled that Christmas at my house, when our kids were little, the one when we knew it was my dad's last as he was dying of cancer, the one where we didn't know it was also my father-in-law's last Christmas. We had all the family in our little house, with the tables stretched from the living room out into the hall where the youngest children sat at a card table. Sixteen of us in all, and I had baked for days. I cooked the turkey and made the gravy the way my father always made it. He barely touched his dinner, but I knew he approved.

I was remembering all the Christmases past and wondering about my need to nurture with baking when the phone rang. It was eleven o'clock on the night before Christmas, and I had just removed the last tray of shortbread from the oven. It was Mara, my crisis line partner. We had a call to go to the R.C.M.P. station in the nearby town of Lake Cowichan to pick up a woman and her preschool children. The police had rescued her from a violent domestic scene and she needed to be escorted to the women's shelter immediately. At that time there was no shelter in our area; the nearest one was in Nanaimo, about a one-and-a-half-hour drive from where we were to pick her up.

While I waited for Mara to collect me, I placed cookies, short-bread and almond bark in a small box to give to the woman we were meeting. I wondered if she had time to grab her kids' Christmas gifts before leaving her house. What a horrible way to spend Christmas; my heart went out to her. Like my parents, I always had extra gifts on hand at Christmas. I rummaged through what I had: Scented soap and hand lotion should be all right for the mother. A puzzle, a children's book and those rolls of Life Savers, multi flavours all packaged together, would do for the kids. In spite of the seriousness of the occasion, I was humming Christmas carols as I wrapped the gifts for the little family.

The woman was young and already looked beaten down by life, and I gathered this wasn't a new occurrence. She flashed us a defiant glance, a "don't dare judge me look," as she shuffled her kids into the back seat of our car. Snow was threatening, and it was already past midnight and into Christmas Day when we left the police station in the small lakeside community.

We tried to draw out the girl. She talked a bit about what happened, and seemed resigned about her husband's violence and worried that she was ruining his Christmas. There wasn't much we could do except drive her to a safe place where she would receive counselling and nurturing, so we drove through the chilly winter night mostly in silence and let her and the two young ones sleep.

When we dropped them off in Nanaimo I gave her my bag of baked goods and wrapped gifts, and briefly saw the protective veneer of toughness leave her face as she thanked me, her voice breaking with emotion. We watched as the mother and two young children were received by a caring support worker in the wee hours of Christmas Day. I silently sent her love as we turned our car around and began the long drive home.

A few hours later when my children and former husband arrived for Christmas dinner, I hugged them with fierce love, squishing them tight in my need to keep them safe. And then I fed them until they couldn't move. It was all I could do.

~Liz Maxwell Forbes
Crofton, British Columbia

The Door

If you want others to be happy, practice compassion.
If you want to be happy, practice compassion.
~Dalai Lama

Weird old Mr. Fingolde was our reclusive and eccentric neighbour. His quirky, unpredictable behavior made every child on the block afraid of him. Not that he ever hurt us. Or even spoke to us for that matter. Old Man Fingolde (if he had a first name, we didn't know it) was my childhood fear. My boogieman under the bed. And so, like the other kids, I was unkind to him in that uniquely cruel way that children possess. Singing a nasty song about him to the tune of "Jingle Bells" was our way of "warding off the devil."

Actually, he seemed a pathetic creature, a grumpy, old man who talked angrily to himself while walking around in the shadows of his dark, overgrown yard. Dandelions sprouted everywhere, the only element of colour in a primordial tangle of weeds. Winter was kinder to the Fingolde property, allowing it to look pristine and manicured under the undulating drifts of snow. During this season, neighbours found it less of an eyesore.

At school, my Grade Two teacher was pulling out the dog-eared bundles of Christmas carol song-sheets provided free to all Winnipeg public schools, compliments of the then thriving T. Eaton Company. Choirs were organized according to grade, and by the first week in December we were all gaily singing without even looking at the words. However, more often than not they were the "misheard" words, the phonetic words that sounded perfect to our seven-year-old ears. Phrases like "We three kings of porridge and tar" or "Oh come, froggy faithful," and of course, "Olive, the other reindeer." What we lacked in musical ability, we made up for in enthusiasm, including our twisted words.

As Christmas drew near, and with it, the school concert and the holidays, the excitement increased. Christmas parties in every classroom were planned, and inexpensive gifts were bought at Woolworth's. The wrapped gifts were then arranged under the class-room tree, which we'd all decorated.

But oddly, I wondered, why wasn't a Christmas tree also being put up at my house? Why wasn't my mother baking cookies with sug-ary designs of Santa and snowmen on them? Why wasn't my father stringing sparkling lights on our house, like nice Mrs. Carruthers next door, who smilingly invited all the kids on the block in for frothy cups of eggnog and gingerbread bells? In contrast, there was crazy Mr. Fingolde, a scary galoot who crept around in the neglected house and overgrown yard across the street, and that's when I learned he was something called Jewish. And then I learned the fact that altered my life forever: I was Jewish too!

"What's Jewish?" I naively queried my mother.

"Jewish people don't celebrate Christmas because that is Jesus's birthday," Mom explained.

"Well, what do we celebrate then?" I asked.

Here came the second fact to inextricably alter my life: Jewish people celebrated something unpronounceable called Hanukkah. To me, the word sounded like a sneeze.

Then one day, while visiting Mrs. Carruthers, she revealed a story to me while I sipped on a cup of her chocolaty hot cocoa: Mr. Fingolde was really a lonely old man whose wife of fifty-one years had died suddenly of a heart attack, leaving him heartbroken. After that there was no one to take care of him, and his mind was never the same. He and his wife had never been able to have children, which had deeply saddened them both. "Mr. Fingolde is just a little mixed up and angry sometimes, because he's so sad," explained Mrs. Carruthers.

Then Mrs. Carruthers revealed something else. It turned out that Mr. Fingolde had a first name. It was Bernard. His wife's name was Pearl. And in the years before she died, Mr. and Mrs. Fingolde had been as nice as Mrs. Carruthers. When the Christmas sugar-cookies and eggnog she served to the neighbourhood kids began to pall, there were crispy, golden "latkes" with honey-sweetened applesauce being served right across the street. All you had to do was knock on the Fingoldes' front door.

Clad in a white apron, her round face beaming in welcome, Mrs. Fingolde would half-yank, half-carry the rosy-faced kids out of the frigid cold. Mr. Fingolde would shyly hover behind her, murmuring his quiet "hellos." One by one, he would make his way through the parade of little visitors, peeling off parkas and unlacing heavy, wet boots. Then the couple would usher the children into their warm, fragrant kitchen to the table, which was already set with fine china plates, heavy, filigreed silverware and linen napkins. A crystal bowl, full to the top with Mrs. Fingolde's special applesauce, sat in the center of the large table. Mrs. Fingolde would then drop a half-a-dozen sizzling "latkes" onto each plate the minute her "guests" sat down, then stand back, smiling with anticipation, as the hungry children dove into the stacks. There were always more to come when a plate became empty. By the time the children went back into the cold and snow, hearts, as well as stomachs, were lovingly content and full.

Yes, Mr. Fingolde had been my boogieman under the bed. But the more I learned about him, the more I came to heartbreakingly regret my childish spiteful behavior. The epiphany came for me in a sudden flash as Mrs. Carruthers described the couple as they had been before life and its inexplicable losses had laid its burdens on them. And in that moment, I felt the searing shame of my thoughtless and childish behavior, both cruel and ignorant, and for the first time in my young life I knew compassion. With tears in my eyes I buried my head in Mrs. Carruthers' lap, repeating, "I'm sorry, I'm so sorry" into her apron. Oh, how remorseful and ashamed I was! She let me cry until there was nothing left but dry muffled sobs, then gently lifted my head and looked into my sorrowful eyes.

"Do you think you can look at Mr. Fingolde with more sympathy and understanding now that you know why he acts as he does? Do you see why he is so sad and confused some of the time, now that you know what has happened to him?" Mrs. Carruthers asked softly.

"Yes, yes I can. I promise! I'll learn to be as nice as you."

Graham Greene tells us "there is always one moment in childhood when a door opens and lets the future in." This was my moment… my door. It was the door that opened to compassion, the door that opened the way to my heart, the door to growing up.

~Sharon Melnicer
Winnipeg, Manitoba

Two Bits for Christmas

One can never pay in gratitude; one can only pay "in kind"
somewhere else in life.
~Anne Morrow Lindbergh

It was a few weeks before my first Charlottetown Christmas when I heard my mother-in-law Nanette say, "Well, fifty cents don't mean nothin' to me! It doesn't now and it didn't then!"

When I asked her to explain, she told me a story that helped me get to know her.

For Nan, it had always been easier to give than receive. "Not knowing how to receive is even harder when you don't have a gift in hand to return," she explained.

It was 1966 and Christmas was approaching. For Archie Reardon, not knowing how to give, and for Nanette MacLeod, not knowing how to receive, was a way of life. They both worked at the Oakville GE Electric Plant, just west of Toronto. The plant employed about a thousand people. Archie was the foreman on the factory floor where Nan inspected the incandescent light bulbs before they went for packaging. The eighty-seven dollars a week she earned paid the rent, and part-time house cleaning jobs bought food and clothes for her three kids.

Nan was thirty-one, and she and her husband Ed came from the kind of sturdy, working class, Irish/Scottish backgrounds so predominant in the red dirt of Prince Edward Island. But like so many

Maritimers, they had left the "have not," smallest region in Canada for one of the biggest and richest, simply for its steady paychecks.

Life was not easy, and for some, the strains of life are harder than for others. Married now for fourteen years, over the past few years Ed had gradually become a full-blown alcoholic. By 1966 his erratic behaviour and drunken depressions had spun out of control, and in September that year he ended his own life.

Between the police, the funeral and the unforeseen bills that were quickly mounting, Nan's already tough life had become unbearable. Now it was December, and with the constant grind of working two jobs she was worried about her children. They had all huddled together and found ways to survive the terror of that September night. But how were they really dealing with their father's death? Who was there to help a single mother now carrying the weight of the world?

Many people pitched in and many more offered, but with her natural defiance and self-sufficiency Nan was not given to accepting charity. Her strong work ethic demanded she double her efforts and rely on herself. But despite her steadfast determination she was burnt out and at wit's end. By December the company nurse had sent her home to rest several times. Nan's tough determination had staved off a formal breakdown, but the truth was she had hit rock bottom.

After three years Nan was known as a hard and dependable worker. But since September she'd made more "on the job" mistakes than in all the previous years. She had trouble focusing and frequently felt like she was asleep on her feet. Aware of her situation, the foreman did his best to ignore these issues. This was hard given the state of the business, but it was Archie's attempt to give someone a break.

Now there were rumours of plant layoffs expected in the New Year. Nan knew her lack of seniority would automatically put her job in jeopardy, and now, with her recent mistakes and the state she was in having drawn the attention of the company nurse, she was in trouble. When the layoffs came she'd be amongst the first to go. Job or not, there'd be no Christmas this year for the MacLeod family.

Just two days before Christmas, she had no presents and no plans. She'd done her best to prepare her kids. Even buying a turkey seemed unlikely. There was no money and no joy. There was only work and worry.

That day, two fellow workers were selling fifty-cent raffle tickets for a small prize to raise money for a good cause. Even in 1966 fifty cents wasn't that much. But they hadn't asked her. Approaching them at break Nan pulled two quarters from her purse.

"I seen you fellas sellin' tickets earlier. Why didn't you just ask?" she grumbled, dropping her coins into the hat.

As the two women handed over the fifty-cent ticket they glanced at each other, and then said, "We know things have been hard for you, and we didn't want to bother you... money being tight and all."

"Well, fifty cents don't mean nothin' to me," said Nan pridefully. And for her, that statement was enough. An opportunity to feel good on a bad day had presented itself, and she took it. It was the right thing to do, and besides, it's always better to give than receive.

Soon after that Nan was told to report to Archie Reardon's office at the end of her shift. This could not be a good thing, and a knot formed in her stomach. The rest of the day dragged on as the anger, fear, resentment and defiance that had shaped her life twisted in her belly. When she finally stood at Archie's door it felt like she was moving in slow motion. Like an aging fighter entering the ring her senses were on high alert. Now focussed solely on survival, she swore she'd maintain her defiant dignity.

In his mid-forties, Archie was a stern, somewhat unemotional man. As Nan entered he was looking out over the plant floor, his back to the door. She knew he'd watched her make her way up, so his not looking at her straight away couldn't be good. As he turned toward her, eyes down, she seemed to notice everything at once. The sounds from the production floor had disappeared. She noticed papers on the desk, the old wood smell of the office, the tired, greenish-yellow battleship linoleum floor, and Mr. Reardon's coat and boots set neatly behind the door. Now, as his eyes rose to meet hers, she noticed the tired wrinkles and furrowed brow on his worried face. She glanced down, and at that moment both sets of eyes went to a hat on the desk.

Her mind was suddenly filled with many questions, but they were all shattered as he prepared to speak.

Before he could begin she heard herself, in complete submission with not a trace of defiance, pleading for another chance. She was begging for her children. But the screaming was only in her mind. Toughness and pride kept her silent as she braced for the coming blow.

"Nan," he said, "we here at the plant know what you've been going through." Pointing to the hat he continued. "You know I'm not very good at this kind of thing, but we took up a collection and we hope it helps. It's about five hundred dollars."

If he said anything else, she didn't hear it. If she spoke, she didn't know it. As they both stepped toward the hat she froze, as if uncertain this was all real. Then, the awkward moment passed and her fearful anticipation ended. In 1966, five hundred dollars was a lot of money. Almost six weeks' pay. Almost five months' rent.

The sudden relief, the joy and the embarrassment all flowed in tears down her face. In an instant, she felt the love of almost a thousand souls who, at fifty cents apiece, had shown their compassion. Nan had nothing to give back except her tears, and she was too overwhelmed, too tired and far too shocked to be defiant, so she accepted the gift the only way should could, with relief.

Archie Reardon, uncomfortable with giving, was happy that Nan MacLeod, uncomfortable with receiving, did not overstate her obvious thanks and gratitude. Although brief, and awkward for both, the moment fulfilled the needs of an entire company of people.

For Nan, being a giver was always easier, but her gratitude was genuine and she was truly humbled by this kindness. It was a kindness, and an eternal moment that she remembers with great emotion to this day.

The gift for us all resides in the beauty that can be expressed in the simplest of terms. "Well, fifty cents don't mean nothin' to me," but for Nan, two bits for Christmas really meant everything.

~Bob Mueller
Summerside, Prince Edward Island

Not So Fancy

May you have the gladness of Christmas which is hope;
The spirit of Christmas which is peace;
The heart of Christmas which is love.
~Ada V. Hendricks

I'd always dressed up fancy on Christmas Day. By fancy, I mean a red sweater and flashy earrings shaped like Christmas ornaments. That all changed two years ago.

On my lunch break I phoned my seventy-four-year-old mother, Gerrie. After only a minute I realized something was wrong. Mom sounded off, and reported that while doing paperwork, her arms began flailing in all directions; when they stopped, she felt nauseous and cold. She had gone back to bed to warm up.

"Can you get a thermometer and take your temperature?" I asked.

"No need. I'll be fine. I just need rest," she said.

"Arms don't fly around without reason. Will you please find it?"

"Oh, I suppose there's one in my bedside table."

"Good. Push the button and put it under your tongue."

"Sure, dear."

Moments later, the thermometer displayed Mom had a fever.

My heart raced. "I'm coming to get you. We'll head straight to the hospital. Are you dressed?"

"Yes, but I don't need to go anywhere. I'm okay." She resisted but her voice was sluggish, and I knew my mother was far from okay.

"If you have a fever, we're to go to the emergency department. That's what your surgeon told us, remember?" I said.

Mom sighed. "Well, I guess it won't hurt."

I noticed the sickly yellow hue in the whites of my mother's blue eyes as I escorted her to my van. I swiftly drove to the hospital in Markham, Ontario, the home base of her surgeon.

"I hope they don't keep me overnight," she mused. "I planned to go to the mall tomorrow. You know I love Christmas shopping."

"Getting better is the priority now," I responded.

I knew Mom had already exceeded the life expectancy for a person with her health challenges. I knew she was in danger. And I knew she would fight like a warrior to get well. I remembered her family physician saying to me, "Your mom's tough. Most people don't survive an attack like she did, but her condition is unpredictable. You need to watch for signs of trouble."

"I'll drop you at the entrance and go park," I said.

"No, I'll walk with you, dear," said Mom.

I frowned. "I don't think that's smart."

"I'll walk while I still can," she countered.

"Okay," I said. She was, after all, still the boss.

We parked and started toward the door. Mom was unsteady. I took her arm.

"Why don't you sit on the curb while I get a wheelchair?" I suggested.

"No. We're close," came the reply.

We made it to the door. A short time later Mom saw the emergency room doctor and was put through a slew of tests... tests that showed big problems. She was admitted, medical professionals took over and she was given medications by IV. Exhausted, I went home and slept.

The next day, Mom's surgeon visited her room and explained that her liver bile duct was infected; she would be in the hospital for days. Once the infection cleared, he would do a procedure.

"I need to get that duct unblocked, one way or another," he said. I could tell by his expression that my mother's life depended on it.

By Friday, the infection had improved, and the surgeon was ready. As we headed to the operating room, I whispered in Mom's ear, "I love you. You'll be fine. There's shopping to do when this is over."

My mother smiled at me—a reassuring and tender smile. In that instant, I melted. It was the same smile she flashed to make me feel better when I skinned my toe on my bike pedal at age nine, when a boy broke my heart at age seventeen, and when I was about to give birth to my first child at age thirty-two.

"I love you and your whole family. You're the world's best daughter," she said.

We kissed as the surgeon arrived, and then she was whisked away.

I sat in the waiting room. Passing the time was agony. I stared at a TV. Finally, the surgeon dressed in his greens hurried into the room.

"Come with me," he said. His face looked drawn. I couldn't tell if the procedure had gone well or not. We entered a curtained cubicle in the recovery area, but Mom wasn't there. Deep inside, my heart dropped.

"It wasn't easy," he began, "but I got through the blocked duct. It's open."

My eyes suddenly welled with tears. Every pore of my body relaxed. "You saved her. I don't know how to thank you. I want you to know we both think you're amazing."

The surgeon grinned. His tired, gentle eyes danced. He nodded his head several times in silence. Then, he said humbly, "Mmm, yes. I'm glad it was a success. Look, here she comes."

An orderly wheeled a gurney toward us. Mom was asleep, looking small and peaceful under the sheets.

"I have another procedure now. See you soon," the surgeon said as he left.

My mom stirred. Her eyes opened.

"He did it," I said.

"He's incredible," Mom said.

"I told him so. I thanked him, too," I said.

"Good girl," she said.

After a few hours, Mom was wheeled to a room on another unit. Two days later, on December 23rd, the surgeon dropped by. He looked less tired and bore good news: I could take Mom to my home in Bradford, Ontario.

Upon our arrival, my husband Ian served up chicken broth. I spent the evening spoiling my mother. At bedtime, reality set in. I had a long gift-giving list, including toys for our two young children. My mother was weak, and not fit to shop. I had tons to do and little time.

The next morning after breakfast, I said to Mom, "You need to recover. Today's Christmas Eve day. I'll shop."

Mom nodded. "Thanks, dear."

I ran like mad around town. I cut my shopping list in half. I bought two toys, candy, turkey, and boxed stuffing. I returned home with a couple of bags.

"I got the essentials, the last dregs on the shelves. It's going to be a sparse Christmas," I said to my husband.

"Who cares? Your mom's here," he said.

"You're right," I agreed.

On December 25th, our family stayed in pyjamas all day. We watched the kids open their stockings, exchanged the few gifts under the tree, and played board games. My mom napped. We ate a yummy turkey dinner and watched a holiday movie. We never got dressed.

"What a lovely Christmas," Mom said as I kissed her goodnight. "We should do the exact same thing next year."

"Only minus the hospital part," I added.

Mom smiled that smile again.

The next Christmas, that's exactly what we did. And I may never dress fancy again!

~Patricia Miller
Bradford, Ontario

Gift of the Ages

Having a place to go—is a home. Having someone to love—is a family.
Having both—is a blessing.
~Donna Hedges

For five years my wife Teresa and I had been waiting, hoping, and praying to adopt a child. Our international adoption from China kept getting pushed back so we registered with two private adoption agencies in Ontario. When nothing happened, we applied to Children's Aid knowing we had a lot to offer an older child.

Three months earlier we had acquired a dog, at a time when we figured nothing would likely happen on the adoption front. We thought we'd at least have fun with a pup. We knew she'd be fun ripping open her gifts at Christmas.

A week later, we replied to an e-mail from a social worker asking for our full profile, a sixteen-page peek at our life. The full profile is only required when a prospective birth mom narrows her choice of adoptive parents to three couples from the twenty or more she reads about. We had provided our full profile a few times before but because we were the oldest couple of hundreds trying to adopt nothing had ever come of it. It was mainly couples in their thirties who were selected and at the time I was fifty-four and Teresa was forty-five.

The next evening we received a call from a social worker in Sault Ste. Marie, Ontario, who said, "I hope you're sitting down because you're going to get an early Christmas gift. A young woman gave birth yesterday to a healthy girl and she chose you and Teresa to be the baby's adoptive parents! We need you to come to the Sault on Wednesday to pick up your baby. Congratulations!"

We were both in shock. Suddenly we were going to be parents. Older parents. We had nothing ready. We didn't even know what we needed. A flurry of phone calls to relatives and friends kept Teresa busy writing down suggestions while I went to my pick-up hockey game to calm down. Her sister would get a "care bundle" of items to us. We needed an infant carrier/bed. Teresa had to put her job on hold for instant maternity leave. We had to quickly prepare a baby room.

The night of "the call" the social worker told us she had had to press the birth mom about the couple she was choosing, only to be told she was "going with the elderly couple." Great, no longer "older", now we were elderly!

So three nights later as we were to meet the social worker and birth mom for dinner in Sault Ste. Marie I entered the restaurant dressed as an old man with white hair, white beard, cane and slow limp. The two of them began laughing when I introduced us and with the ice broken, we had a great time learning about each other.

Shortly after we all arrived at the hospital to meet the baby. It was surreal picking up and cuddling this tiny child whom we had waited so long for. No Christmas present had ever, will ever, match the emotional bliss we both felt at that moment.

For the next two days we changed Brigitte's diapers, fed her, bathed her, hugged her, and finally, after red tape delayed our departure, we left on the seven-hour drive back to Toronto. We took turns in the back seat with Brigitte, both Teresa and I guilty of shining a little flashlight on her every fifteen minutes to ensure she was breathing! Such rookie parents.

Brigitte's first visits to Tim Horton restaurants were during that trip home (and she still loves going). We were tempted to tell everyone there our story! Arriving home late and exhausted, we were almost in tears as our neighbours and Teresa's sister surprised us with a little bed they'd assembled.

New parents we were but it wasn't a done deal. Every adoption has a thirty-day cooling off period during which the birth mother can choose to take her child back. We were mostly confident that Brigitte was staying but there was always that little doubt that haunted us right up to the final minute. Fortunately it was confirmed in our favour in mid-December and needless to say it was an unbelievable Christmas for us and our families, the "new" aunts, uncles, cousins and grandparents.

In between diaper changes and feeding frenzies that Christmas I pulled out my guitar and Christmas music to sing a few things to Brigitte. I must admit that John Denver's beautiful song, "A Baby Just Like You", hit home very eloquently and I sang the chorus to her the first time through tears....

"O little angel, shining light, you've set my soul to dreaming. You've given back my joy in life, and filled me with new meaning."

And now more than five years later Teresa and I are an even more "elderly couple" but really we're years younger because of a gift named Brigitte.

~Michael Brennan
Toronto, Ontario

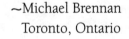

Chapter
8

Christmas in Canada

Angels in Our Midst

The Angels… regard our safety, undertake our defense, direct our ways, and exercise a constant solicitude that no evil befall us.

~John Calvin

Mysterious Visitors

Millions of spiritual creatures walk the earth unseen,
both when we sleep and when we wake.
~John Milton

For many years now we have hosted Christmas at our home. We invite close friends and family to take a chair at our table and share in the good cheer of the holidays. Before we eat, I am usually called upon to make a toast, and often raise a glass to absent friends and family. An old custom suggests you set one more place at the table with an extra chair in the event of an unexpected visitor at your door. It also serves to remind us of those who can only be with us in spirit.

For as long as I can remember, our front door opens by itself on Christmas Day. There is no set time, but I can usually count on it around the time of the opening of presents. You might think there is an explanation behind the mystery of this strange occurrence—a gust of wind, a guest not pushing the door closed. However, I believe it is a visitor. The door is not left ajar in order for this to happen. By the time we are aware of this presence the door is already beginning to open of its own accord. Our conversation stops and we all take a breath as we watch the door slowly open inward. There is no sound of footsteps and one of us usually gets up to close it. We have no clear explanation as to why this happens, but it does not seem menacing.

The first time we had one of these visits was not at Christmas, though.

It was an early summer's evening in the first few weeks following our daughter Christina's birth. She was in the crib in her room, asleep, and my wife and I were settled in for the evening in front of the TV. Suddenly, I saw a featureless, grey form move quickly in the periphery of my vision. It took a moment for it to fully register, but the figure was clearly headed toward the stairs to my daughter's bedroom.

"What was that?" Lydia asked. My heart skipped a beat when I realized we had both witnessed the same thing. I jumped up and ran quickly to the stairs. My first stop was the baby's room, but our daughter was sleeping soundly. There was no intruder there. I closed her door and tore through the rest of the rooms on that floor. I even raced into the bathroom and threw back the shower curtain. I looked inside every closet. The entire top floor was as it should be. There was no one there.

I was visibly shaken when I went back downstairs, where Lydia anxiously awaited my return. I told her I had found nothing. We sat together then, and thought about what had just happened. We were still emotionally raw from all the events that had led up to Christina's birth. You see, my father had died only a few days before she was born. I buried him in the middle of my wife's labour. I needed some time to say my final goodbye at the funeral, but Lydia's labour had begun earlier that day. We can't explain why, but her labour stopped and did not start up again until I returned to her. I was thankful for the time to say goodbye to my dad, but what happened with my wife's labour was strange.

During the birth we were on a roller coaster of emotion, overjoyed for the new life about to take a first breath, and at the same time saddened by my father's passing. I knew he tried to hang on in order to meet his new granddaughter, but his illness had run through his body like wildfire. This birth was a powerful reminder of the old wisdom that one life sometimes has to make way for a new life to begin. We were witnessing the great circle of life firsthand.

As Lydia and I discussed the shadow we both saw, we considered my father's passing and wondered aloud if something of his essence might have returned for a brief visit. I won't say it was a ghost, but similar stories have been told by others. We did not realize what a strange turn of events was in store for us until Christina's first Christmas.

The baby was resplendent in a beautiful, red Christmas outfit. A first Christmas Day in a new house is magical for so many reasons, but it is even more so when celebrated with your first child. Our daughter was mesmerized by all the twinkling lights on the tree as we began to place her presents around her day cradle.

Something wasn't quite right, though. I could not quite determine what was happening, but the atmosphere in the house changed. I looked up from the sunken living room and noticed the front door slowly opening as if a hand was gently pushing it from the outside. My wife was busy with opening Christina's presents and had yet to see what kept me from joining in. I walked over to the door, and Lydia looked up and asked if I had opened it. I told her it must have been a breeze, the only excuse I could think of at the moment. It took me a moment to close the door, but once I had the room began to feel normal again. The baby was looking in my direction, with just a hint of a radiant smile on her face. We have no clear explanation as to what this was, or why this happened.

Two years later our son Donny was born, and soon again it was Christmas Day. I was on the floor setting up a toy train set when, again, the door opened as quietly as before. This time, we were not as disturbed. In fact, it has happened now like this on this special day for so many years we would be more concerned if it didn't happen.

Now at Christmas when our front door seems to open of its own accord, my family stops for a moment to consider if it might be the essence of a loved one who has returned for a brief visit. We have come to believe it is a visitor from our past. I like to think it is my dad. This may be an unsettling prospect to some, but not to Lydia and me.

Unlike Scrooge's hasty denial of what he was witnessing and George Bailey's unwillingness to see the truth, my family has an open mind to our intimate connections to the universe, and beyond. And if, perchance, your door should open of its own accord on Christmas Day, you might say a silent prayer for a loved one you would give anything to see at Christmas again.

~Don Jackson
Whitby, Ontario

Our Christmas Miracle

The most incredible thing about miracles is that they happen.
~G. K. Chesterton

It was a perfect, peaceful Christmas Eve. A light snow was falling all around our century-old home in Orillia, Ontario. Friends and family had gathered for the traditional Christmas Eve dinner before heading to church. Our Christmas tree was sparkling with tiny lights, a warm fire burned in the living room hearth and candles danced their special magic in candelabra and stands throughout our home.

We got to talking about the best Christmas present we had ever received. For me it was my GPS, which had changed the way I drove, removing the frustration of wrong turns and misdirection. One of the grandchildren cooed endlessly about a particular teddy bear, the one with the squeaky nose. Another described a big dump truck in detail, complete with sound effects.

Daughter Sarah put the finishing touches on her Christmas tradition—ham and chicken dishes along with scalloped potatoes, beans with almonds and her special turnip and carrot medley. Ashley brought her famous berry salad, Maggie supplied the well-aged wine and Aaron brought one of his extraordinary chocolate pecan pies.

We gathered around the table that had been beautifully set by my wife Jennifer and held hands while I thanked God for our family and friends, for living in a peaceful country, for God's loving, protecting hand upon us and for Jesus, the gift of the first Christmas.

After the amazing meal we demolished an English trifle for dessert. Then, we were off to church. The grandchildren blew out the candles on the table while the adults snuffed other candles and ensured the fire in the fireplace was safe to leave. Our gang gathered in their vehicles and drove off to St. Mark's church for the Christmas Eve service.

Peace and love surrounded me in the church, surrounded by family and friends, well fed, the choir singing "Silent Night" in the light of the battery operated candles we use these days. I wished we could still use real candles, since I had never seen a problem with them.

As we left the church, I looked forward to a relaxing night. Taking off my shoes and loosening my belt would be my first acts upon my return home. I was wrong.

When we opened the door to the house my smile instantly faded. I felt a surge of fear and anxiety. The house was filled with smoke!

I ran to check the fireplace, but it was quiet. My wife checked the kitchen. The stove was off and nothing was in the oven. I opened a couple of windows, despite the cold wind. We walked around the house but could not find a source. Still, the smoke was very strong.

Then our daughter Maggie called out from the dining room. There was no fire, but about three square feet of wallpaper had burned black and crisp. Underneath, a small tabletop was badly scorched, the brass dish on it partially melted. The floor around the table was black, not with soot, but with scorching. There had been a real fire!

Reconstructing the scene afterwards, we realized we had missed snuffing out one candle in a five-foot candelabrum. The candle must have fallen onto the dried hydrangea arrangement sitting on the table, and started a fire that was so hot it had melted that brass dish, and burned that section of wallpaper. Our old house was full of drafts providing lots of air to fuel the fire. Why was there only a small section of destruction? What had stopped it?

We each had a theory, expressed in excruciating detail. In the end, we each came to the same, wonderful conclusion. The only reason we didn't turn the corner of our street to find the fire department fighting to save our house from total destruction was because the hand of God had reached out and, in that brief moment, overrode the rules of physics.

We let out a collective sigh of relief—and heartfelt thanks. Later, after the company had left, Jennifer and I sat down and held hands. The Christmas tree and all the presents under it stood to our left.

On the right sat the burnt reminder of our Christmas Eve miracle. In that moment we knew for sure that the best Christmas present we ever had was given to us that night by the One who gave the very first Christmas present.

~Ross Greenwood
Orillia, Ontario

A Miraculous Eve

Pay attention to your dreams — God's angels often speak directly to our hearts when we are asleep.

~Eileen Elias Freeman, The Angels' Little Instruction Book

I had a vivid dream on Christmas Eve. It was one of those dreams that you think about all day, that sticks with you upon waking because of its clarity. In this frightening dream, police marched by me with batons and shields. They shouted at people to take cover from an oncoming disaster, and people scrambled to hide inside a nearby mountain. I noticed a door going into the mountain and ran for it. As I got inside, grabbing the door to close it, my foot got in the way. It closed hard on my ankle. The dream then changed. The door was now made of foam and I was not actually hurt. I pulled my leg back inside, and I was safe.

On Christmas Day, I considered the strange dream. Was my guardian angel trying to warn me about something? And if so, what was it and when? I wasn't sure, and in the holiday excitement, I soon forgot about it — until one miraculous night a week later.

It was New Year's Eve 1999. I'd made some exciting plans with my friend Katarina, her younger sister Kristina and their friend Michaela to hang out at Katarina's condominium. We would enjoy some champagne and then head out before midnight to watch fireworks.

I got ready, putting on a sparkly top and some pretty lipstick. I made a kissy face in the mirror, and yelled "Bye! Happy Y2K!" to my mom as I left.

I took the TTC bus to Warden Subway, noticing the nervous excitement in other people's conversations. "Do you think the computers will all crash?" someone asked.

"No one really knows what's going to happen," I replied. I heard similar conversations on the subway ride downtown.

Walking to Katarina's from Bay Station, I kept wondering what would become of the millennium bug. I shrugged, thinking at least I'd be with friends if pandemonium erupted!

At Katarina's, I giggled when I saw her big cactus plant decorated in blinking Christmas lights. Prince was singing "I'm gonna party like it's 1999!" on the stereo as she poured the champagne. As the evening progressed, we turned on the TV and watched New Year's revellers getting pumped up.

"I don't think anything's going to happen with this Y2K bug, do you?" Michaela asked.

"We won't know until midnight when the computers roll over from '99 to '00!" replied Kristina. "The computers will think we're in 1900 not 2000."

At 11 p.m. we donned our "Year 2000" party hats and headed out for the celebrations at Nathan Phillips Square. It was cold as we walked down Bay Street, singing and laughing. Suddenly I heard a familiar sound. Glancing over my shoulder, I saw twelve riot police marching together down the middle of the street. A knot formed in the pit of my stomach as I instantly recognized this from my dream, and I stopped walking.

"Are you okay?" Katarina asked. I tried to look like it was nothing but I shuddered internally. Was something going to happen to me? But I quickly forgot about it as I got lost in the happiness of the throngs of people.

The crowd started chanting, "5, 4, 3, 2, 1…" Then all around us, it was "Happy New Year!" The fireworks began to explode, lighting up the night. Laughter was all around, and so were the lights! They continued to shine, so we knew the computers must have still been working. I was happy to think maybe this Y2K bug was just a myth after all!

After the celebration we began walking briskly back to the condo, still giddy from our earlier champagne. Linked arm in arm, we merrily sang along with the rest of the crowd to "Auld Lang Syne." What happened next was very quick.

The roads had been re-opened. At a stoplight we waited for the light to change. Someone was arguing in the car right next to us, and then a woman got out and started yelling at the driver. He yelled back and then blindly turned the corner, making a sharp right turn just as the light turned green. The four of us, arms still linked, didn't notice as we started across the street.

Michaela and I were the first to step off the curb. The car hit Michaela first and she rolled over the hood out into the road, quickly jumping back up onto her feet. I felt a huge pull from Katarina and Kristina as they yanked me back toward the curb, but I fell sideways and the front wheel ran over my left foot and ankle. The driver stopped the car. Kristina was still holding my arm, and she and Katarina quickly helped me up.

In the middle of the road, where she landed, Michaela was pounding on the driver's side window yelling at the driver. We stared at each other; glad to see she was okay. Katarina and Kristina looked at me. "Your foot...!" they yelled.

I was visibly shaken. Other people nearby asked if we were okay. The driver of the car said nothing and took off. A man pushing a stroller told us we should have taken down the license plate number, but it was too late.

I noticed a pounding sensation in my foot. When I stood on it, it was a little tender, but it took my weight, so we started walking back to the condo. I kept saying, "I can't believe this happened."

Kristina said, "I can't believe you can walk on it. Are you sure it's okay?"

I was stunned by what had just occurred, and couldn't really think straight. The warning had been there, it was so much like my dream. I tried not to think about it as we headed back to the condo.

Back at their place we examined my pounding foot and put some ice packs on it. We were all tired, and I was soon fast asleep in the living room. In the morning, I awoke to the smell of coffee brewing. When I remembered the evening, I peeled back the covers and wiggled my toes. I moved my ankle back and forth and felt all around my sore foot. When I realized it wasn't sore at all, I just sat there in disbelief. There were no visible marks, nothing was broken, and the swelling was gone.

Katarina came in then with a steaming cup of coffee. "For you," she smiled.

I looked at her and said, "My foot got run over by a car last night, right?"

She nodded, "Yes, how is it?"

When I showed her, we were both amazed. Then I told her about my dream from Christmas Eve—how I had dreamt about a door closing on my foot but then it turned into foam. In that moment I suddenly saw that my friends were the foam that saved my foot. That night could have easily ended at the hospital with one of us badly hurt. But it didn't. If ever I questioned miracles before, I can't any longer. I know I received a special message, and my friends had saved my life.

With a sudden burst of intense gratitude, I hugged my friend hard. Looking upwards, I then silently thanked our real hero with a prayer.

~Rachel Lajunen Harnett
Toronto, Ontario

Ice Angel

He shall give His angels charge over thee, to keep thee in all thy ways.
~Psalm 91:11

With Christmas just a few days away, we were in the middle of a vast wilderness in northern British Columbia in a helicopter, and trying to reach three people on the radio. The call was part of our safety routine. We didn't expect to get an answer because the trio was scheduled to have been picked up earlier by another helicopter. Suddenly we received an unexpected response on our radio, "This is Rob. We are all done and waiting to be picked up."

Hearing this I drew a quick startled breath. I knew the exhausted people below us somewhere were now stranded, and in serious trouble.

My husband was an archaeologist, and he and I had a consulting firm. We were under contract to a major oil and gas company to ensure government regulations were met whenever a new well or support facility was built. This required us to physically inspect the location of the proposed site to ensure the new well would not disturb any archaeological or historical sites. We usually did this by helicopter because there are very few roads, and much of the terrain is impassable thick bush. This was to be our last trip before stopping for Christmas.

I was along to assist my husband with the preliminary assessments, as well as take notes and photographs. Earlier that day, a ground crew had been dropped off by a second Bell helicopter to physically inspect and test a site for archaeological impact, tough work when the snow was up to their knees. They would be picked up later in the afternoon by a second helicopter.

It was already winter in northern Canada. The temperature was dropping quickly and we knew that in addition to the group below us being nearly exhausted, they were not equipped for overnight. For some unknown reason, that second helicopter had not arrived to pick them up. (We later learned a storm had blocked its departure from Calgary.) It was -20 degrees C and getting colder.

The problem was, with only two empty seats, we could not fit three more people safely into our helicopter. On this late December afternoon we had enough daylight hours to get ourselves back to base, but not enough for the pilot to fly out again to pick up the stranded group. We had to do something. But what?

"Okay, we have a slight problem here and we'll get right back to you," responded our pilot, Dawn. There was no sense in letting them know the situation was considerably worse than a "slight problem." Finding help in the short time we had would take nothing less than a miracle. In this part of northeast British Columbia the beaver, caribou, moose, wolves, bears and other animals far outnumbered the human inhabitants. I'd been on over fifty flights, crisscrossing this isolated, desolate area, and I knew from experience that spotting other people just didn't happen. We could fly for hours and not see another human being so the chances of getting help from anyone on the frozen land below were less than slim. In fact, we had been in the air all day and not spotted another vehicle. The team on the ground was more than a hundred kilometres from the nearest post of any kind. I knew they were in big trouble.

Our pilot must have felt the weight of the world on her shoulders as she realized that without the second helicopter we were now in a possibly tragic situation. We were running out of time. Our helicopter would soon have to pull out and head for base in order to beat the rapidly approaching darkness, yet below us, about three miles away, were three young people who would not survive the night in the bush. It seemed we truly needed some heavenly intervention.

Suddenly and unbelievably, out of nowhere a tanker truck appeared below us. What? Where did he come from? We were all stunned! If our pilot could get his attention, he could be the answer to our prayers and our dilemma!

Dawn flashed her lights a few times, and the truck stopped. I let out my breath in relief, but the feeling was short lived, as the driver began pulling away again. This time Dawn pulled up the helicopter and came around the front of the truck, fully intending to come down directly in his path so he'd have to stop. He stopped. Only instead of acknowledging our presence, the trucker began backing up. It turned out he was actually preparing to position his truck to take on some water, as he was out working on an ice road.

Once we were landed, my husband, as the archaeologist in charge, hopped out and, ducking under the still rotating blades, ran over to the trucker to give him a quick rundown of the situation. Next he ran back to our copter and instructed our pilot to go for the stranded crew while he remained with the trucker. Dawn took us back into the air, and once we located the stranded crew we picked them up and headed back to rendezvous at the tanker truck. It was such a relief to have everyone safe, and all in one place. One of the rescued crew then climbed out to travel back to base with the trucker, and my husband climbed back aboard our copter.

With everyone now safe and accounted for, our helicopter safely flew us to home base. When we finally landed back at the airfield we had just fifteen minutes of daylight left. The crewmember who was travelling back on board the tanker truck arrived three hours later. It was such a relief knowing that everyone would now be home safe and sound in time for Christmas.

Some may consider it a coincidence for that truck to have suddenly appeared at that exact moment on a closed road in the middle of a frozen swamp, when time was of such critical essence. And many also noticed how coincidental it was that the trucker, who had been out working on the ice road for three weeks, had only that very day decided to travel into town. But I don't accept it as "just a lucky coincidence." We rarely saw traffic of any kind out in the bush, so the appearance of that truck was considerably more than a little unusual. Personally I thanked God, because on that day, His Christmas angels were clearly working overtime in the cold northern regions!

~Ellie Braun-Haley
Calgary, Alberta

Tang's Christmas Miracle

Animals' instinctive spirituality enables them to interact with their Creator
and with creation in ways that can truly be called miraculous. Animals have
a talent for bypassing the mind and going straight to the heart.
~Allen and Linda Anderson, Angel Animals Book of Inspiration

Sometimes I think I should have named my dog Casper instead of Tang. He's a small grey and white mix of Shih Tzu and Poodle with the personality of Casper the Friendly Ghost. He's not just friendly; he is sincere. Whenever we go for a walk, he stops to greet every dog, cat, squirrel and person we meet. He loves all people young and old, babies in strollers and people in wheelchairs. He loves Canada Post letter carriers—even those without cookies in their pockets.

Tang expresses his love of life in a very vocal way. He has a special greeting where he raises his head to the sky and howls happily. Translated from dog language it means, "Joy to the World!" Nine years ago while brushing Tang's teeth I discovered blood in his mouth. My husband and I took him to the vet even though we only suspected a gum infection. The vet thought so too—at first. The antibiotics failed to reduce the swelling, and we returned to the clinic. Dr. Hall, a canine dental specialist removed the suspicious mass, and had it biopsied.

The news was devastating. Cancer. Tang was only five years old. Dr. Hall informed us that Tang's best option was radical surgery. Tang needed one third of his lower jaw removed. "Afterward he may require radiation treatment or chemotherapy," Dr. Hall said. "It might give him another couple of years. Without treatment, he will have only a few months."

Dr. Hall was honest enough to admit that the surgery was beyond his skill. He made an appointment for us at the Ontario Veterinary College in Guelph. Tang, he said, was a little trouper. At the OVC hospital, Dr. Alexandra Squires was confident she could perform the surgery successfully. But trouper or not, we were terrified to proceed. How was Tang going to eat? What would he look like with his jaw removed? What if the cancer had spread? Was it worth putting him through all this pain and suffering just so we could have him a little while longer? Were we being selfish? We did not want Tang to suffer.

Tang's response to all of the poking and prodding, X-rays and tests was a great big happy-bark song of joy. He was nervous, but he trusted us. He even trusted all of the different specialists who examined him. And for each of us there was always that howled song of joy.

By now it was mid-November. The city was decorated for Christmas. I knew I would soon have to go Christmas shopping and write cards, and there was also our annual Christmas party to organize. My husband was asked to be the chair of the anthropology department at his university. He wished desperately to decline. We were too sad. All we could think about was losing Tang. But my husband agreed to take the job of department chair. And I did not want to disappoint the students who looked forward to the annual Christmas fest in our home. We began to prepare for Christmas.

On the day of Tang's surgery heavy snow was falling. We made the drive to the hospital in just over an hour. We left Tang in the arms of one of the veterinary assistants. He twisted his little head to watch us leave, his soft round eyes curious rather than frightened. I recall thinking that this might be the last time I ever saw him. We drove home in a horrific storm, a salt truck flinging salt onto our windshield to mix with the flying snow. It was black that night—in so many ways. The highway was a booby trap of ice and blinding weather. We made it home to a cold supper and then bed. We couldn't sleep.

Tang's surgery was successful, but he wasn't out of the woods yet. He stayed at the hospital for three nights. The veterinary students were wonderful, and the girl assigned to Tang stayed by his side twenty-four hours a day. She called every evening to update us on his condition. When the doctors decided he could eat on his own, they let him come home. We picked him up on a snowy afternoon. His eyes looked bright. His mouth had been reconstructed and there were stitches in his jaw. His tongue protruded halfway out of his mouth. He wore a white cone around his neck and a morphine patch on his back.

My husband and I exchanged horrified glances. What had they done to our dog? What had we done? I remember saying afterward that I would never get used to seeing Tang like that.

Tang's jawbone was sent to the pathology lab to be tested. The pathologist was away at a convention for three days, and the wait was agonizing. By the time he contacted us our nerves were raw. But the news was good. The outer edges of the bone were clean, no sign of cancer. The following week we returned to the OVC hospital to have Tang's stitches removed. The waiting room was cheerfully decked out in Christmas lights and ornaments. A young woman sat beside me with a cage containing two ferrets. She was worried. The ferrets seemed overly large around the belly, and I asked if they were pregnant.

"No," she said, tearfully. "They have adrenal disease." Her grandfather had driven her to the hospital (clearly he loved his granddaughter) but he wore an impatient expression on his face that said "they're only animals."

Tang thought otherwise. The girl was called into the examining room with her beloved ferrets. Tang trundled over to the grandfather, and, despite the stitches under his mouth, gave his defining happy howl of joy. Even Grandpa couldn't stay grumpy with Tang around.

"That dog never stops wagging his tail," he said, cracking a smile.

By the week before Christmas all the stockings were hung. The Christmas tree was decorated, and red and green lights spiralled around the conifers outside. We welcomed the students into our home. As everyone sat down with a glass of holiday cheer, Tang greeted each and every one of his guests, tail wagging, his snout raised to Heaven howling his special song of joy.

Heroes come in many forms and I am thankful to the veterinarians who have devoted their lives to saving pets. But it was Tang that reminded us of what Christmas was really about. It wasn't just about finding the perfect gift, or cooking the perfect turkey or decorating the most festive house. It was about showing kindness to others and appreciation for the ones you love. That small furry package of joy showed us what it takes to have strength, how to find hope and courage, and how to believe in miracles.

~Deborah Cannon
Hamilton, Ontario

Lifting the Blue Shadow

If we live long enough and deep enough and authentically enough,
gratitude becomes a way of life.
~Mark Nepo

Until 2008 I had never watched the movie *It's a Wonderful Life*. The whole concept of the small town guy, George Bailey, in financial difficulty and on the verge of suicide, being saved by a guardian angel on Christmas Eve seemed too clichéd for me. But that year I gave into the holiday spirit, plunked a copy into the DVD player, sat back and enjoyed.

The next day, perhaps subconsciously influenced by the holiday classic, I decided I was due for my own Christmas miracle. I decided to give myself a gift—a Red Shadow motorcycle. I had been vacillating for weeks and now my mind was made up.

With my heart thumping I drove to the motorcycle shop. In the showroom, the Red Shadow glowed brighter than fire. I swung my leg over the side, settled into the perfectly angled leather seat, and smiled. Looking up from his desk the salesman shook his head and said, "Sorry, she just sold."

"But," he said thoughtfully, "there's a Blue Shadow upstairs, identical in every way except she's blue. Won't hurt to take a look." I reluctantly dismounted my Christmas wish and, to humour the man, I slowly climbed the stairs. There, in a dimly lit storage area my eyes came to rest on a cerulean blue gas tank—a colour as rich and pure as a midsummer sky. Even in the low light, the Blue Shadow's chrome exhaust pipes and mufflers sparkled. It made the Red Shadow look like a cheap tart. In a trance I mounted, adjusted the mirrors and squeezed the handgrips. I could feel it saying, "I'm yours."

With a deal to make, I sauntered down the stairs, forcing my wide grin into a pensive frown. "Well, I really wanted the red one," I said.

Rolling his chair away from his desk, the salesman threw down his pen and said, "How about I knock two thousand off the price, seeing as it's Christmas and all?"

We shook hands. "I'll be back to do the deal after I take care of a few things. Don't sell it to anyone else."

In truth, I was headed straight for my accountant's office. My self-employed artist-self had befallen a nasty tax audit. And as much as I wanted that bike, as much as I thought I deserved that bike, I knew I had to get the tax monkey off my back before it could be mine.

Staring across the desk at the rumpled man in the suit I was filled with annoyance. He had lost my file for over eight months and taken close to six thousand of my dollars without absolving me of anything. Now he was telling me I needed to hire a big city tax lawyer. In response to my aggressive reaction to this he interrupted, "There's a storm coming. You probably want to be off before it hits."

"So I can't be purchasing a motorcycle then?"

"Not until you pay this off," he said.

I stomped out into the snow, climbed into my truck and began to curse. With the overwhelming desire for a stiff drink, I was reminded of the movie the evening before and George Bailey who, when faced with his financial problems, headed straight for a bar and got very drunk. He then hopped into his car and drove through a winter storm contemplating suicide. He owed eight thousand dollars, a lot of money in those days, yet in today's dollars I owed about the same.

As the frost cleared from my windshield I realized that having even one drink and driving on the highway in this weather would be reckless. I decided instead to head home, and carefully pulled my fishtailing truck onto the country road—straight into a wall of sleet and gusting winds. A transport truck whooshed past me, covering my windshield with its sideways blast. I anxiously drove at a crawl, but then as I rounded the crest of a hill the howling whiteness suddenly dissolved into clear stillness. The storm had passed.

A sinking orange sun on the horizon revealed an artist's dream. Long indigo shadows glowed behind snow-laden trees, and inspiration for a new painting hit me. From a kilometre away I spotted the cab of an old rusty truck poking out of the snow. As I approached, the golden line of sinking sunlight rose up over its roof. Distracted by the suddenly dimming light, I slid sideways into the ditch with a thudding crunch.

Pulling out my cell phone I called for roadside assistance. A faint recorded message replied, "We are experiencing a high number of calls etc., etc.," Beep... beep... beep. "Your call will be..." the phone battery died. Billowy snowflakes softly and silently covered the windshield. Darkness fell.

Again the movie came to mind. After slamming his car into a tree George Bailey ran to the river bridge, leaned over the railing and contemplated jumping. While looking into the foaming water, his prayers summoned a guardian angel.

A prayer wouldn't hurt, I thought. It did offer a sense of calm in moments of darkness. Moments later, out there in the darkness, I heard faint jingling and jangling noises. Was I dreaming?

No—outside a stranger was hooking chains onto my back bumper. His large white logging truck was already positioned to pull. He refused to take any money. I shook his hand, thanked him profusely, and wished him a Merry Christmas. Unscathed, my truck fairly leapt out of the ditch.

Now full of gratitude and good cheer I headed for home. On the way, a flickering sign reading "Christmas Trees for Sale" caught my attention. I turned in. Bundled up in a quilted coat, and rocking back and forth to keep warm, a woman in her late sixties was preparing to close for the night. Feeling high on the kindness of the trucker I found myself telling her how silly I felt for spending most of the day feeling sorry for myself. Holding up the perfect tree she said, "Why would someone like you ever feel sorry for himself?"

I relayed my anguish over a huge tax bill, then landing in a ditch only to be rescued by an angel in a big white truck.

"Six years ago Revenue Canada was after me too," the woman admitted. "They don't like seasonal workers. They said I owed them a whole lot of money. I was so distraught I even contemplated suicide. As fate would have it, my first grandchild was born that year, something far more important than money troubles. And the man that pulled you out of the ditch? That would be Matthew. He's having a pretty bad year himself, but he'll always do for others."

Invigorated by the influence of my two angels, I drove home with a fragrant fir tree, and a reminder that I too was expecting my first grandchild in the New Year. I was convinced that goodness would prevail. Perhaps I'd experienced my own Christmas miracle after all.

The next night, to celebrate the decorating of our tree, our family held a dinner party for friends. Over dessert, I recounted my story of despair, then meeting the two angels. A guest, the local pastor, asked if he could tell my story as his Christmas Eve homily.

"Of course," I consented. "But could you take up a special collection at the end of the service?"

"For what charity?" he asked.

I laughed, "For my Blue Shadow motorcycle, of course!"

~Lloyd Walton
Port Carling, Ontario

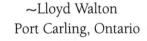

A Christmas Rescue

In Canada, the colder the winter is, the warmer the people are.
~Jean Charest

The car sputtered as we drove through the tiny, still town of Elrose, Saskatchewan. I looked over at my husband Ron and fear froze the words in my throat. His brow furrowed as he stared at the drifting snow on the deserted highway. The lone service station was closed, of course. It was Christmas Day.

I hadn't wanted to make the trip. It was dangerously cold, with the temperature dipping close to –40 degrees. Our white Plymouth had passed its best-before date long ago, and while it was usually reliable, in that kind of weather our lives depended on it. I wasn't comfortable with that.

That year, Christmas Day was the only time we could venture from our home in Martensville, Saskatchewan, for the three-hour trip to my in-laws' home in Swift Current. My husband's extended family would be waiting for us to open gifts, consume the scrumptious feast prepared by Mom and the sisters, and enjoy one another's company.

But it was freezing. Even though our three young children were safely bundled from head to toe and huddled under a blanket in the back seat, I worried about what might happen if we had car trouble. Then the old Plymouth sputtered again.

If you've ever travelled Highway 4 between Rosetown and Swift Current in Saskatchewan, you know how desolate the forty miles appeared between each of the three small towns that separate the two larger centres. Farm fields stretched from one horizon to the other, the small towns the only oases of civilization. And on Christmas Day, all businesses were closed. In fact, we seemed to be the only ones foolish enough to be travelling on such a bitterly cold holiday. In front of us and behind us, the road was empty except for our coughing, sputtering white Plymouth.

"Lord God, help us," I whispered. It wasn't my most eloquent prayer, but it was heartfelt. I knew He could change the weather, but obviously that wasn't His plan. It didn't seem right for our family to freeze to death on Jesus's birthday, but as first the car, and then its heater slowed, my faith faltered.

Our ten-year-old son spoke up from the back seat. "What's wrong with the car?"

"Are we almost there?" the four-year-old boy asked.

"I'm cold!" our daughter, age eight, chimed in.

"The car is acting up, but we'll be okay," I said, and struggled to keep my voice steady. "God sees us and knows what we need." But my anxious heart wasn't convinced.

My husband pulled over to the shoulder of the highway as our car crawled and then just died. I wondered how long it would be before anyone noticed a white car on a snowy highway bordered by flat, white fields from horizon to horizon.

As the car coughed one final time, my husband glanced into the rearview mirror.

"Where did that guy come from?"

We knew no one else had been on the highway since Elrose, but now there was a black half-ton parked behind us, and a young man was walking toward our car. He tapped on the driver's window, and Ron rolled it down.

"I noticed your white exhaust a while back and knew you were in trouble. You need some gas line antifreeze. I've got some. I'll put it in your tank, and you should be good as new."

Still puzzled, we thanked him. He opened the cap to the gas tank and pulled a small container from his coat pocket. We heard faint gurgling as the antifreeze worked its way into the tank. A moment later, the man was at my husband's window again.

"Now try it."

Ron turned the key. The car sputtered back to life, and was soon running smoothly.

"Where are you headed?" the young man asked.

"Swift Current," replied Ron.

"I'll follow you to make sure you get there."

Despite our sincere thank you, we couldn't adequately express our gratitude. He just waved his hand and headed back to his truck. As we continued toward our destination, I kept glancing in my side mirror. He was still there. For more than an hour, every time I glanced behind us, the reassuring bulk of the black half-ton truck remained in sight.

When we reached the edge of the valley where the city of Swift Current nestled, we all cheered. Just another half-mile downhill and we'd be safe in the arms of loved ones.

I glanced in my mirror one more time. The road behind us was empty.

God hadn't changed the weather for us, and He hadn't kept our car from failing. But He hadn't deserted us either. He'd sent a young man in a big, black truck to take care of us when we needed it. Was that man an angel? I don't know. But I am convinced he was sent by God, not only to put some antifreeze in our gas line, but to remind us that God is always with us.

The colourful packages we exchanged that Christmas Day have faded from my memory, but I'll never forget the gift of that young man and his truck. And ever since that day I've wondered, do angels drive black half-tons?

~Kathleen E. Friesen
Coldstream, British Columbia

Mom's Wreath

There are things that we don't want to happen but have to accept,
things we don't want to know but have to learn, and people we can't live
without but have to let go.
~Author Unknown

I wasn't looking forward to Christmas 2013. After the passing of my mom in August, and my father just two years earlier, I was finding it difficult to drum up any Christmas spirit. It was a cold December day when I left work to meet my sister Sandi at our lawyer's office to sign papers for the probate of Mom's will. We were the executors, and after completing the necessary paperwork we decided to go for coffee to regroup and address any further estate issues. We also needed to discuss the upcoming Christmas Day gathering I was hosting at my home.

With a sense of relief we sat down with our coffees and had a little celebration for what we foolishly thought was the last of the major work involved in being an executor of a will. We had done so much already, and both of us were grateful that we worked well together. I have always attributed this to the fact that we love each other very much, and are good friends as well as sisters.

That's when Sandi told me that after this year her family would probably not be coming to my place on Christmas. I was surprised and hurt. I'd simply assumed I would continue holding Christmas at my home, just as I had since 2001 when Mom had her heart attack and strokes. Our father, who had left us in July 2011, had had very strong opinions about family getting together. My parents were always grateful, and I knew Dad would want me to continue making sure the family got together. So when my sister told me this I was shocked and disappointed.

Realizing I was surprised, she explained beautifully how her own children had friends, and that she and her husband would like to have a Christmas at their place with just their immediate family. It made perfect sense. However at that moment I was in the wrong place to listen. We switched to the topic of this year's gathering and then both began to call family members to verify they'd be at my place on that day. No one was home, so we both just ended up leaving messages. We left each other with a hug and the promise to let each other know as the responses to our calls came in.

The first call back came from my mother's sister letting me know she wouldn't be coming for Christmas. A friend who knew she had no immediate family other than nephews and nieces had invited her to attend her family's Christmas gathering, and she had accepted. I said the appropriate things but I was devastated. My aunt was like a second mother to me. My mother had been her last surviving family member, and with no family of her own, she had always attended our family gatherings.

The next call came from my niece and nephew informing me they'd be going to Ontario to visit family there. I felt numb. I could understand my niece and nephew, they were both married and had family elsewhere, but I was already reeling from the news from my aunt and the earlier conversation with my sister. I was heartbroken.

Then my brother, a minister with the Mennonite Church in New Brunswick, called and suggested that I not hold a family Christmas gathering this year. I suspected my sister Sandi had called him and asked him to call me—hoping he could help me to understand that every family has its own dynamics and that her decision had nothing to do with me. With both Mom and Dad gone, things were different now; life had changed. But I resisted and defended my feelings, saying that Mom and Dad would want at least one more year, wouldn't they? It had been so important to our parents, and it felt to me like I needed to do this for them.

The next day at work I remembered my friends had booked a wreath-making course for us at the local greenhouse. But I just didn't want to go. I had tried so hard to keep my Christmas spirit, but it was gone and I was discouraged. My parents were gone, my family didn't want to come to my house, and my aunt wasn't coming. Who was I doing this for? Add to this the deep grief I still felt at the loss of both my parents, and the thought of Christmas this year was simply heartbreaking.

After work that day, when I pulled into my driveway I saw something that completely shocked me. A Christmas wreath I did not recognize was hanging on my front door. I actually couldn't move for a few moments. Where had it come from? Who put it up? But there it was, a symbol of Christmas, hanging in all its beauty on my front door. When I entered the house my husband hugged me and said, "Merry Christmas, hon." Knowing I was down about how things were working out, he'd wanted to do something special to lift my spirits. To my amazement, he had decorated the entire house, and it looked so beautiful and festive.

"Where did the wreath come from?" I asked.

"Well, it's the funniest thing," he said. He then told me how after he had picked up all the Christmas decorations from where we kept them on the lower right side of the pantry, for some reason he couldn't explain he looked over at the opposite side. "There was a plastic bag," he continued, "so I went and got it. When I opened it I discovered it was a wreath I didn't even know we had. So I put it up."

It was only then I remembered it was my mother's wreath. After she had passed away in August, and while we were clearing out her apartment, the wreath had been one of the things I brought home. But with everything else I was dealing with I had totally forgotten about it.

And with that realization, I broke down in tears. At a time when I was feeling really down and discouraged, I believe God and my mother sent me my very own special Christmas miracle to lift my spirits. I understood then that getting together with my family doesn't have to be on Christmas; it can be any day, as long as we get together in the spirit of Christmas. I believe my mom led my husband to find the forgotten wreath to remind me what Christmas really is—and that she is still with me. Now, every year when I lovingly place Mom's wreath on my door, I will thank both her and God for this wonderful gift!

~Diane Grace Driedger
Steinbach, Manitoba

Someone Watching Over You

Angels are all around us, all the time, in the very air we breathe.
~Eileen Elias Freeman, The Angels' Little Instruction Book

As usual, Christmas had been packed with presents, entertaining, food and family. It had all passed by in a blur, but now it was Boxing Day and we had a chance to catch our breath. The weather was turning cold with a strong north wind, and it was good to be inside with the heat cranked up.

The phone rang and I could see it was our youngest daughter, Kristen. I glanced at our grandfather clock and saw it was 9:30 a.m. So early for them!

"Hi Daddy. I was just calling to let you know we're heading off to Montreal for our three-day getaway."

"You've got your hotel reservations okay?"

"Everything is arranged. Brad and I are really tired so this will be a good chance for both of us to rest and have some time together. It's hard to believe we've been married for over four months!"

"Well drive carefully, honey, it's winter."

"Oh we will, don't worry. Say hi to Mummy."

"Will do. Love you."

"Love you too."

I settled back in my chair and opened my book. It was a great day to stay inside and relax. But my mind was half on Kristen's drive to Montreal.

That afternoon, a good friend was hosting a special Boxing Day get together so we could meet her fiancé from Texas. We could smell the hors d'oeuvres baking in the kitchen the minute we walked through the front door, and laughter filled the house. It promised to be a fun afternoon.

Suddenly my cellphone rang. I saw it was Kristen and my stomach immediately tightened. Why would she be calling at 3:30 p.m.?

"Hi, are you alright?"

Kristen's voice was shaking and I could barely hear her. "Daddy we had a bad accident—really bad. It's been raining for most of the drive. We must have hit a patch of black ice and then the car went sideways and slid off the highway. We rolled three or four times, I'm not sure." She stopped talking to catch her breath. I could hear the tears in her voice.

"Are the two of you okay? How long ago did it happen?"

"It just happened and I think we are alright, but I don't know. My neck's pretty sore and Brad's not feeling great."

As I was talking my eyes were on the crowd at the party, but everything seemed to be in slow motion. All the voices around me became a background buzz.

"Where are you now? Do you want me to come and get you?"

"We're just outside Cornwall, but no, don't come it's too dangerous. Highway 401 is really bad—and it's so cold. They should have closed the highway or had salt trucks out, but they didn't. We can't get into our trunk because it's jammed shut, and we don't have our warm clothes. We landed on the driver's side of the car and the back window is gone and snow has filled the rear seat. The whole car is a write-off."

"Is there anything we can do?"

"Look I've got to go. The police have just arrived. Call you soon."

As I hung up the phone I felt physically sick as I turned and explained what had happened to my wife Susan, who was now standing beside me. We so wanted to be there to help, but there was no way. Driving was out of the question, and the train would never get us there in time. I also had no idea where they were on the highway; just finding them would be problematic. I hoped they could stay safe despite the icy roads and cars passing by at 100 kilometres per hour or more.

Time dragged by, and what seemed to me to be an hour was in fact only five minutes when I next glanced at my watch. The food at the party was great but it had suddenly lost its flavour. As I talked to others at the party, my conversation was disjointed because my mind was somewhere else.

Outside the sky was turning dark and the temperature was dropping. A few passing snow showers blurred our vision of the back yard and sent chills right through me. Was it snowing on the 401? Had the ambulance come? We didn't know what was happening down the highway, and there was nothing I could do but pray.

Finally, at 7:35 p.m., my cellphone rang.

"We're here at the hospital and the doctors have checked us out. Brad has whiplash but no other damage showed up in the X-rays. I'm okay, but I'm sore and bruised all over."

"Did you get your stuff from the car?"

"We have some things. The tow truck took our car to a local impound. We'll go there tomorrow. Tonight we're staying in a motel, then taking the train back to Toronto."

"We'll pick you up. Just let us know the time."

Kristen's voice then turned quiet and thoughtful. "There was something really strange that happened after the accident, Daddy."

"What was it?"

"Well, as we were driving along we were all by ourselves on the highway. There was nobody behind us that we could see and nobody in front of us. Then we hit the black ice and lost control of the car. We slid to the right and then rolled off the road so far that no one passing by on the road could see us easily. And you know we have a white car."

"Uh huh."

"Well our car had just come to a stop in a snow bank." Kristen paused to think. "We were worried that we couldn't get out because it was on its side and the doors were jammed. It was very cold and my coat was in the back seat along with my boots. Nobody could see us from the highway. If someone did stop they would be endangering their lives because the road was so icy. And then, all of a sudden, this family appeared out of nowhere. They leaned into the car to see how we were. They pulled open the passenger door, which was now on top, and helped us get out. They called 911, kept us warm and made sure we were okay. We don't know how they found us. We don't know their names or anything about them. They left as soon as the police arrived, and we didn't even have a chance to thank them."

"Someone was watching over you," I whispered, remembering my prayers.

"I know, Dad, I know."

~Rob Harshman
Mississauga, Ontario

The Christmas Card

Death leaves a heartache no one can heal,
love leaves a memory no one can steal.
~From a headstone in Ireland

Christmas was less than two weeks away and I still had no desire to put up a tree and decorate it. Three years earlier my older sister Marie had died of lung cancer and was buried a week before Christmas. Christmas would never be the same again.

Marie had moved from her Prince Edward Island home to Tucson, Arizona where she worked as a nurse for about eleven years. She enjoyed her life in the sunny south, but was often lonesome for her three grown sons and four grandsons back in Canada. She planned to retire when she turned sixty-five, and move back home to spend more time with family. She was four years away from retirement when she died.

We grew up in rural Prince Edward Island with nine siblings. Christmas was always a magical time with massive excitement in the house. There would be one gift for each of us nine kids under the tree, and our stockings were stuffed with fruit and candies, which were rare treats for us.

How I wished I could open a door and step through it back to those simpler, happier days of Christmases long ago. But there was no door to yesterday, just the hard-to-accept reality that my sister, my friend, had been taken from us. I missed her terribly, especially at Christmastime.

On the third anniversary of Marie's death, my son Joshua called to tell me he was on the way out to the farm with Damian, my grandson. They were bringing a Christmas tree. He told me Damian was bouncing off the walls with excitement about helping Granny set it up and decorate it. I should have been happy and excited they were coming for a visit, but I wasn't. How could I be happy about decorating a tree on the day that Marie died? It didn't seem right to be having fun with Damian while Marie's grandsons would be denied decorating a tree with her.

Horrible feelings of survivor's guilt churned in my stomach. I didn't want to celebrate Christmas, let alone decorate a tree. How do you explain the sorrow of a death of a beloved sister to a six-year-old eager to help his grandmother decorate a tree? I didn't have the heart to say no, nor did I have the heart to celebrate Christmas with joy and anticipation like I'd done in the past.

It would be about an hour before Joshua and Damian would arrive with the tree. That would give me time to find the Christmas decorations and have a good long cry before they arrived. I reluctantly headed upstairs to the room where the decorations were stored. Tears began to run down my face as I dug the boxes out of the closet.

I discovered a stack of old Christmas cards I had collected over the years at the bottom of one of the boxes. Grabbing a big handful, I started reading them. I was about to throw them back into their hiding place when suddenly one of the cards fell to the floor. I was startled when I realized it was the card Marie had sent me the year before she died.

The front showed a photo of Marie and her friend John wearing Santa hats and sitting in front of a fireplace with hanging stockings. She and John were obviously in the spirit of Christmas, laughing with big silly ear-to-ear grins for the camera.

Inside the card it read: *"Merry Christmas from miles away in the sunny desert... but... see... I am only a smile away."*

Mesmerized, I sat on a chair holding the card, unable to move for what seemed like a very long time.

Some people might say that finding the card from Marie that way, and in that moment, was just a fluke. But I believe Marie had sent me a message from the spirit world. It felt like she was reaching out to comfort me and help me cope with my feelings of deep sorrow.

Later that night, after the tree had been put up and decorated, I turned on the Christmas tree lights. While sitting alone in the parlour gazing at the lights and pondering the message from Marie I felt a deep and profound peacefulness. That Christmas card from Marie changed my attitude and allowed me to get on with life.

I still miss Marie, and will grieve for her until I take my last breath, but in my heart I believe finding that card was her way of telling me to go ahead and celebrate Christmas with joy. That she was with me in spirit, and in my heart, and that she truly is "only a smile away," not just at Christmas, but always.

~Stella Shepard
Morell, Prince Edward Island

83

The Power of Christmas Memories

God gave us memories that we might have roses in December.
~J.M. Barrie

It was nothing short of a miracle. No doctor or nurse could have brought about what happened that day. The old woman had been unresponsive for more than a day and her family was sitting by her side, waiting for the inevitable.

I was visiting my good friends at the Kelowna, British Columbia retirement home, just as I'd been doing each Christmas over the last few years. I had donned my favourite red suit with the white fur trim, and my wife had brushed my white hair and long white beard so I would look my very best. My boots were shined, and I had pressed my best silk lined robe interlaced with sparkling, gold "magic" dust. As always, I entered the residence with my very best and loudest "HO! HO! HO!" A large group of the residents had been waiting patiently in the open common area of the foyer, and as they saw me, and most certainly heard me, their faces lit up. It was a wonderful reminder that we all become children again when confronted with the joy of Christmas.

I walked around the large room, flirting with some of the older ladies, and commenting on the beautiful smiles of others. The gentlemen were all complimented on their strong grips or their fancy

Christmas ties. Then I read them *The Night Before Christmas*. The smiles grew and the twinkle in their eyes brightened even more.

After finishing the poem I said my goodbyes to those assembled and set about, with the assistance of my wife Linda (my favourite helper), to visit those residents who were confined to their rooms. Each individual visit was as splendid and as enjoyable as the last. Smiles were the order of the day. In fact, as the afternoon passed, I realized I couldn't tell the difference between the smiles and twinkling eyes of these older people and the many children I see each and every year. Indeed I could honestly say this was my treat more than it was theirs.

When I had almost completed my visits I looked about for Linda and found her talking to a woman in her late sixties. A sad but caring and loving look was on the woman's face, and a tissue was at the ready. When they finished talking Linda turned and walked toward me.

The woman Linda was talking to was the daughter of the lady who had closed her eyes the day before. She told Linda her mother was going to pass any time, but that if she could just have one last visit from Santa it might help ease the pain for the family. There was no doubt in Linda's mind that I would make this visit and do all I could to make it special.

I took a moment to emotionally prepare before entering the room. It's not often I am asked to make a visit of this nature. When I entered I nodded my hello to the daughter, and gave her a warm and gentle smile as she sat at the foot of her mother's bed. I sat on the edge of the bed and looked down at a woman, very old to be sure, but also at peace. The slight rise and fall of her chest were the only signs of life left.

I softly stroked the woman's hair and I thanked her for all the gifts she had wrapped and the stories she had told involving yours truly. I thanked her for all the pies she had baked and the turkeys she had basted and stuffed. I thanked her for being a mother who showed love 365 days a year, but somehow warmed the hearts of her family even more at this special time of year.

While I was speaking, the daughter sat quietly at the foot of the bed sniffing back tears. And then it happened! It was both surprising and frightening, and for a brief second I was actually taken aback because I never expected it. This sweet, old woman suddenly opened her eyes and looked straight at me. For perhaps four full seconds we gazed into each other's eyes, and I gave her the best gift I could—a huge heartfelt smile from Santa.

"Merry Christmas, sweetheart," I said, and then she once again closed her eyes. I bent forward and kissed her forehead. I gave her daughter a hug, and then I left the room.

I continued on with my visits to those who were confined to their beds, shaking hands and giving hugs. But it was different now. I was lighter than air because of the miracle of that special moment. Then, as I finished my last visit and prepared to leave I was approached by staff and told the news. The woman had passed. It was her last Christmas, and the last thing she saw was the smiling face of Santa Claus. She walked to the light with a smile.

~Gordon Allen
Blind Bay, British Columbia

Chapter 9

Christmas in Canada

The True Meaning of Christmas

*Christmas is forever, not for just one day,
for loving, sharing, giving, are not to put away
like bells and lights and tinsel, in some box upon a shelf.
The good you do for others is good you do yourself...*

~Norman Wesley Brooks, Let Every Day Be Christmas

84

No Pressure

The best of all gifts around any Christmas tree:
the presence of a happy family all wrapped up in each other.
~Burton Hillis

When my son James was still very young he came home from school one day with one of his first crayon drawings. He had drawn our family of three sitting at the table with a giant Christmas turkey on it. The huge turkey covered the entire table; it looked like it must have been on steroids! Beside the table stood a Christmas tree gleaming with lights, complete with presents underneath it. Because it was only September, I was puzzled by the timing, so I asked James why he had drawn a picture about Christmas.

"The teacher asked us to draw a picture of something that made us happy," he explained. His simple answer brought real joy to my heart. As a young father, I felt there was no greater gift than to bring happiness to your children at Christmas. In my case, my son's words strengthened my heart, and let me know I was on track keeping a solemn promise I had made to myself some years before, when I was a young adult and my parents had recently divorced.

The first Christmas after the divorce was the first that my parents would be separated by geography. My mom was living in Burlington in Southern Ontario, and my dad was living in Sault Ste. Marie in Northern Ontario. Both were lobbying hard to have me spend Christmas with them. It was clear to me that they were motivated by more than Christmas spirit. It was a competition, and the one that snared the only son would be the winner.

But the problem with having a winner is that someone has to be the loser. In this case, the loser would be one of my parents. I knew my choice to spend Christmas with one parent would break the other's heart. Instead, I would spend Christmas alone.

Christmas morning I woke up by myself in my small one-bedroom apartment. At the time, I worked at the local YMCA and so I had keys to the building. The Y was closed for Christmas, but I went there anyway and let myself in. To kill time alone I picked up a basketball in the gym and started shooting baskets. Basket after basket, I tried to forget that it was Christmas Day, but I just couldn't. It was then that I made a promise to myself that if I ever had a son of my own I would always put his happiness first at Christmas, and never, ever, cause him to feel the sad emotions I was feeling this Christmas.

My resolution was put to the test many years later when my son and his wife had to make their own decision, with three choices: visit her mother, visit her father, or visit us. Remembering my solemn promise to myself, I let him know I wanted Christmas to be a happy time for him and his family. We told him he was always welcome to come home for Christmas, but if it turned out he needed to spend it with either of his wife's parents, that was okay with us. We let him know we understood that you just can't be in three places at once. To our surprise, my son and his young family showed up at our home for Christmas. It was totally unexpected, and turned out to be a Christmas that we all cherished. Our Christmas kindness and understanding made our son and his wife decide that this was the place they wanted to be. By letting go, we were rewarded with the great joy of spending Christmas together. It proved to us once again, that the greatest gift of Christmas is not from what you receive, but it is from what you unselfishly give.

~Chris Robertson
Stoney Creek, Ontario

I'll Be Home for Christmas

A man travels the world over in search of what he needs,
and returns home to find it.
~George Moore

In December of 2005, it seemed that everywhere I went, Bing Crosby was tormenting me with that old Christmas classic, "I'll Be Home for Christmas."

If only our kids had been singing that tune. Only one of them planned to be home for Christmas that year.

Being together at Christmas has always been way more important to me than expensive gifts, a perfectly decorated house or gourmet treats. After all these years there is still a special feeling that comes with going to Christmas Eve mass together, and lighting our candles in the darkened church as we sing "Silent Night." On Christmas morning we sit around in our pyjamas while we eat my husband Pat's cinnamon coffee cake, along with the mandarin oranges and pistachios that we pull out of our stockings. Our son Brendan's funny homemade cards cap off the morning. I cherish those precious moments together so that's why I was walking around feeling sorry for myself that December.

That fall the boys were out of town. Brendan, our younger son, had returned to the University of Guelph. Aaron our eldest child, had taken time off for travel. His plan was to fly to the U.K., travel around Europe and return by Christmas.

Our daughter Norah also had travel plans. After spending

four fun-filled years living in the Queen's student ghetto, she had moved back home with us in Ottawa, to study at Carleton. Although she redecorated her old room, the whole experience of living back with Mom and Dad was pretty boring compared to her student life in Kingston. She missed walking around to her familiar haunts at Queen's, the shops along Princess Street and most of all, living with her friends. So Norah had decided to take advantage of the Christmas break and travel with a friend. Perhaps if the trip was to Europe and she was going to meet up with Aaron, I might not have been as worried. However, her destination was Thailand. I recognized her need to have some time with friends but did she really have to go to the other side of the world?

While planning her holiday she threw us a bone. She was waiting to hear about Aaron's return date. "It would be too boring for Brendan," she declared, "if he came back from Guelph and had to endure Christmas with only you and Dad at home." She vowed not to leave her younger brother to that sad fate. She would only travel if she knew for sure that Aaron was coming home for Christmas.

Meanwhile, Aaron was having a great time playing tennis while staying in Lagos, Portugal. From there he visited Munich, Slovenia, Budapest and the Czech Republic. In November we were caught off guard when he told us his plans had changed. He and his friend were having such a good time they had decided to stay an extra couple of months. They had been hired at a ski resort in Austria to take photos of tourists. "How was this possible?" we asked. "What about winter clothing and ski equipment?"

"No worries," he assured us. They had picked up some second-hand ski clothes and the resort was supplying the equipment. It was too exciting an opportunity to pass up.

In spite of this change in Aaron's plans, Norah proceeded with her own holiday scheme. Years earlier, I had flown to Greece to spend Christmas with my then boyfriend Pat, so how could I object? We tried as hard as we could to be enthusiastic as she looked forward to elephant and tuk tuk rides, as well as the islands and beaches of

Thailand. She deserved a great holiday after all her hard work, both at school and in her summer jobs.

Still, it was with heavy hearts that we accompanied her to the Ottawa airport in the early morning gloom on December 12th. I wondered what happened to her vow not to leave Brendan alone at home at Christmas.

Later that evening, Pat left to play volleyball. I sat in the living room alone, feeling miserable. On TV, singers on a Christmas special were crooning, "There's No Place like Home for the Holidays" and I was thinking, "That's not what my family thinks." It was not my finest hour.

About 9 p.m. there was a loud knock at the front door. Before I could reach the door the knock was repeated, but this time it was louder, more insistent. I looked through the lace curtain covering the window on the door and saw a tall man wearing a baseball cap. He was turned sideways so I couldn't see who it was. It was dark. I was alone. I knew I shouldn't open my door to a stranger, especially in the dark. Why would someone be wearing only a baseball cap on a cold December night? Was this someone looking for money?

In spite of these concerns, I opened the door and as I did, the man turned to face me. It took me a few seconds to register. This tall, tanned young man, sporting a lightweight jacket and ball cap was our first-born son! It was Aaron! Aaron, the guy who was supposedly taking tourist photos on a ski hill in Austria was actually standing in front of me.

"Hi Mom. Merry Christmas!" he said with a smile.

Our kids love to play practical jokes and surprise us. He got us hook, line and sinker that time! The photo job was just a story. He had always planned on coming home by Christmas but had wanted to make it a surprise.

Norah and Brendan were in on the scheme. She had stuck to her promise and Brendan was more than pleased to have Aaron around when he came home for the holidays, a few days later. We went to Christmas Eve mass and enjoyed dinner with Pat's family and then had Christmas Day dinner with mine. Norah returned on New Year's

Day and we were grateful to have all three kids with us for a few days. The stories from Guelph, Thailand and Europe were shared enthusiastically as we admired our souvenirs. It didn't really matter whether it was on Christmas Day or not.

Christmas is, of course, a celebration of the birth of the Christ child, of love and giving. I don't remember what gifts we received that year. The gifts are never all that important. All I know was that Aaron was our gift that year. The surprise of having him appear was our special treat. It reminded me of his birth. In November of 1980 babies did not stay in the hospital room with their mothers, but spent most of their days in the nursery. At the hospital's appointed feeding times, a nurse would appear in my room, carrying Aaron, tightly wrapped in a hospital blanket. It always seemed to me that she was delivering a very special present. Now, decades later, at over six feet tall, his arrival was my special present once again.

~Mary Ellen Kot
Ottawa, Ontario

86

Chicken Soup for the Soul

From Christmas Past to Christmas Future

Christmas is not as much about opening our presents as opening our hearts.
~Janice Maeditere

Nine days before Christmas our twenty-three-year-old son was in a horrific car crash while driving home from a party. By the time Christmas arrived, we hadn't seen daylight since 2:20 a.m. that awful day. He suffered a catastrophic brain injury, and all we could do was wander the halls of Sunnybrook like zombies. We grabbed some sleep when we could, sprawled over waiting room chairs or rolled up in a fetal position, the sounds of the breathing machine and heart monitor haunting our sleep.

But how does one celebrate the joy of Christmas in the ICU? Our son's life hung by a thread and we were unwilling and unable to break ourselves from his side.

We were told that when someone is in a coma the hearing is thought to be the last of the senses to go. We decided then to push our sorrow aside and, in the only way we could, share Christmas with our son. So, leaning over his limp, lifeless body, I lovingly whispered into his ear, "Merry Christmas, sweetheart." Then, guided by the Christmas Spirit, with all the love in our hearts, we began to tell him what Christmas meant to us—the Christmases we grew up with, that he grew up with, our yearly Christmas traditions and all the variations we had passed on to our children.

First we told him about the very first Christmas Eve and the first Christmas Day. We told him about the Christmas bells chiming songs of joy to welcome the birth of Baby Jesus, of the three wise men and the Star of Bethlehem. Then we told him about the *Charlie Brown Christmas* and *A Christmas Carol*, with its three scary ghosts of Christmas past, present and future.

We told him about jolly old Saint Nick and Santa's elves in his workshop at the North Pole, located way up on top of the world. We reminded him that he sat on Santa's lap at the mall when he was a small boy, while the nice lady took pictures. We named all of Santa's reindeer and read him the story of Rudolph the Red Nosed Reindeer. We read Dr. Seuss's *The Grinch Who Stole Christmas* and *The Night Before Christmas*, where all through the house, not even a mouse was stirring. We described Tchaikovsky's *Nutcracker Suite*, with toy soldiers and sugar plum fairies, and talked about how we watched it on TV every year.

Our daughter brought videos of Christmases past to the hospital. Moments, frozen in time, of trimming the Christmas tree while the house smelled of evergreen branches mixed with the scent of freshly baked cookies; moments of gingerbread houses and big turkey dinner feasts and eggnog and of huge family gatherings at his Omi's house, where we'd see tons of relatives and open even more presents.

We quietly sang our favourite Christmas carols to him in whispers—we were, after all, in an ICU hospital ward. We sang "Santa Claus Is Coming to Town," "Frosty the Snow Man," and his favourite, "The Twelve Days of Christmas."

In his ear, we whispered the story of the time we put bales of hay out for the deer, peanuts, still in their shells, for the squirrels and seeds for the wild winter birds. That year the winter was bitter cold, and he and his sister had insisted we feed the animals that lived in the forest behind our house.

As our son lay there, silent and still, we talked of how each season we experimented with hot cocoa, sometimes adding whipped cream and cinnamon or coloured mini marshmallows or sticks of candy canes, melting in the hot chocolate. We reminded him how we placed Christmas cards from distant loved ones on the mantel, beside carefully hung stockings and plates of cookies and milk laid out for Santa. How we'd snuggle up by the roaring fire with our hands clutching mugs of steamy cocoa, while snow fell silently outside and a whisper of Christmas music danced in the air.

We reminded him of the year we drove to the farm to hunt for our Christmas tree, and took a sleigh ride with jingling bells and horses that neighed, and how that winter the snow came down gently, silently, creating a winter wonderland. We talked about snow angels and snowball fights, snow castles and forts, and the year we built the biggest snowman in the neighbourhood. We reminded him of the fun we had every year decorating the house with sparkling, twinkling lights, and of driving out at night to see the neighbourhood Christmas splendour.

Suddenly, the life support machines keeping our son alive started to bleep like crazy. Several nurses came running and pushed us aside. His heartbeat shot way up, and then dropped down really low. He was pale, grey really, and soaking wet with perspiration. These events then began to repeat themselves over and over, and it was frightening to watch. We later learned this indicated that part of his brain was waking up—the part that allowed his body to stay alive and breathe on its own, and it could be a long, drawn out process. "Prepare yourselves," we were urged. They did not think he would survive it.

I took a moment to call my mother to wish her a Merry Christmas, but when she asked me how it was going, I broke down and began to sob as I tried to describe what was happening. I think it was the first time I had let myself go.

Later that day, the nurse stationed at our son's bedside called us over with a huge grin on his face. "I have great news!" He announced excitedly. "Your son is being transferred from the ICU to Critical Care. He's not out of the woods yet, but he's definitely moving in the right direction." This wonderful news was like a gift handed to us directly from God. That day, somehow, our son managed to gather his strength and hurdle himself over the fine line between deathbed and road to recovery. Leaning into his ear I whispered, "Guess what we just found out? You're getting better, sweetheart. Great job! Keep up the good work."

Ironically, this turned out to be one of the best Christmases our family ever had. No longer would we hear "prepare yourself; he's not going to make it." Against all odds, he made it, and he made it on Christmas Day. He remained in a coma for several more weeks before he actually opened his eyes. Fully waking up was a very long process, and he still suffers from his catastrophic brain injury.

Christmas angels were definitely watching over us that day, and over our son. But it was the Christmas traditions we'd gathered up throughout the years of living in Canada that allowed us to celebrate with the mystique that had become what Christmas means to us. I believe that is why he came back—and why he lived—because of our persistent recounting of those joyous memories, with all the love in our hearts.

~Eva K. Chagnon
Barrie, Ontario

87

The Christmas Doll

It's not how much we give but how much love we put into giving.
~Mother Teresa

The weary young woman lined up several cardboard boxes and tenderly packed each with socks, panties and clean mended outfits. School was about to begin and most of the children needed to be placed in other homes. The oldest, at ten old enough to help, and youngest, just two, would stay with her. The others would be going to relatives. The next two oldest, a boy and a girl, would go to their paternal grandparents. The middle child would stay on her husband's sister's farm, and her parents would care for the remaining two girls. They would all be placed in southern Alberta, over a hundred kilometres away from the city.

She and her husband had finally found accommodation in an older home within the city of Calgary. The basement was rented out in three sections. Two other families shared the space and all had access to one shared bathroom and laundry facilities. There just wasn't room for all seven children, and there was no other choice. It was all they could afford. She prayed it wouldn't be for long—that soon things would be easier.

The children excitedly clamored into waiting cars to embark on their new adventures. They were going on holidays! Waving excited goodbyes, they didn't see the tears or pain in their mother's face or hear her cry to God as her hands clutched her swelling abdomen.

"Oh Lord, I can't even take care of them. How will I be able to care for another?"

That young woman was my mother and I, the middle child. At six, I was too young to realize the hard times my parents were facing, but as weeks turned into months, I longed for my family. My aunt, uncle and cousins were kind, but it wasn't the same. I felt like an outsider.

One snowy evening, my aunt drove me to my maternal grandparents' home. It was Christmas Eve, and I was overjoyed when I discovered that Mom, Dad, my brother and all my sisters were there. What a commotion! A cardboard carton with Kellogg's Corn Flakes printed on the side was tucked in beside a chair in the corner, and sweet cooing sounds emerged from it. I approached the makeshift bassinet and for the first time I saw my beautiful baby sister. What a doll! She reminded me of the baby in the nativity scene outside the church, where people quietly stood around gazing at Baby Jesus lying in a wooden box. Now I had my own baby in a box. I felt our family was special.

Before long we were sent off to bed. Four of us found our spots in one bed by alternating heads and feet. Giggles, tales of what was happening in our lives, talk of Baby Jesus and Santa Claus kept us awake for hours. It was good to be together again and we were content.

Christmas morning brought us scrambling to the tree to see if there were any gifts. For me there was the most beautiful doll I would ever own. She had a wood putty head with blue eyes that opened and closed and a cloth body attached to wooden arms and legs. There were scuffs on her face and some of her toes and fingers were chipped, but she was special. She was mine! I tenderly kissed her and promised to love her forever.

Relatives began to arrive. The smell of turkey roasting and festive goodies filtered through the air. We children packed ourselves into an old church pew that served as a bench behind the table and shared Christmas dinner. Unfortunately, all too soon it was over, and once again we went our separate ways with promises we would be together again soon. At least now, I had my Janet doll to love.

When I returned to my aunt and uncle's home that evening they too had a present for me—a brand new doll with long blonde hair and pretty lacy clothes. She was a smaller version of my cousin's new doll, but I never took her anywhere with me. All I needed was my Janet doll. I later learned that the city's firefighters knew of my parents' plight. The toys we received were used toys people had donated for the Calgary Fire Fighters to repair and distribute to needy families. They helped make my Christmas unforgettable. Never was a used doll more loved.

By the time Christmas rolled around again my family was reunited. Things were not always easy, but at least we were together. As time passed, we saw our parents extending help to other families in need, giving even though it made things tighter for us. Mom filled boxes with preserves, carrots, potatoes and even home raised chicken. Each of us would scamper off to find a jacket, shoes, sweater, outfit or toy that some other child might treasure. Dad would repair things on their cars, inspect our offerings and pack them into their vehicle before returning it.

Through the kindness of others, family, friends, and even people we didn't know, we learned that love is about unselfish giving. We came to understand the importance of living our lives by helping others. We also learned that although Christmas is considered the season of love and giving, real love gives in all seasons. Over fifty years later it is not a lesson we have ever forgotten.

My precious Janet doll stayed with me into marriage until she fully disintegrated. Then sadly, I put her to rest, but I learned a lesson from her too. You don't have to be perfect to be loved. We are all blemished and flawed. This lesson I later realized was also part of the true meaning of Christmas.

~Irene Bastian
Okotoks, Alberta

88

Hand-Stitched Love

From home to home, and heart to heart, from one place to another. The
warmth and joy of Christmas, brings us closer to each other.
~Emily Matthews

Snatches of holiday music hit me from all sides as I walked through the mall. It was two weeks before Christmas, and I wasn't sure how I was going to make it. Try as I might, I hadn't been able to figure out a way to make my meagre budget as a second-year grad student yield up the cash for a trip home. The distance from Halifax, Nova Scotia, to my parents' house in Simcoe, Ontario, might as well have been measured in light years rather than kilometres. For the first time in my life, I wasn't going to spend Christmas at home with my family.

I was going to have to cope, that was all. But privately, when I allowed myself to admit it, I realized the whirlwind of part-time work, research, sports and social activities I had plunged myself into couldn't make up for the bare, honest fact that I was homesick.

About a week before Christmas, I received a notice to pick up a parcel from the post office. When I arrived to claim my prize, a box of gratifyingly large proportions, wrapped in brown paper and bound with twine, was thrust into my arms.

I scurried home to my apartment, placed the box on the kitchen table, and painstakingly undid the knots in the twine. A pair of scissors would have done the job more quickly, but I wanted to savour the moment.

Finally, the string fell aside and I stripped away the paper wrapped around the cardboard box. I opened the flaps to reveal a bulky cloth object. When I unfolded it, I gasped in surprise when I realized it was a quilt, lovingly crafted by my mother. But it was not the normal patchwork kind. No, this one was definitely different.

On a green background my mother had recreated, with a combination of sewing and embroidery, an image of home. There was our house, right down to the three white front pillars and the number 80 on the middle post. There was the redbud tree, with clouds of purple blossoms painstakingly hand-embroidered, and a tartan blanket spread below it like the one on which my mother and I would lie during lazy summer afternoons to read our books.

There was more: boldly orange tiger lilies at the base of a big pine tree; green shrubs with flowers embroidered on them; and the grey shed that housed the lawn mower and assorted garden implements. A badminton net was represented by a broad strip of lace spanning the space between two brown fabric posts, a croquet course serpentined across the yard and an image of Tiny, our Toy Terrier, was embroidered beside the blanket.

I pictured my mother bent over her handiwork on the dining room table at home, her brow furrowed as she concentrated on her work, her bent fingers holding the needle while her hands moved steadily as she made the painstaking, tiny stitches. How many hours of work this must have taken!

This quilt was more than material, batting, and thread; there was love sewn into it as well. As I wrapped it around me, I felt a warmth that was more than physical.

So what if I wouldn't be home this Christmas? Home had come to me. More than that, I realized now that home and the love that resided there would always be a part of me, no matter where I went. And in that moment, I knew that this Christmas, and all the Christmases I might have to spend away, would be okay after all.

~Lisa Timpf
Mulmur, Ontario

Driving Home to Canada

By hook or by crook this peril too shall be something that we remember.
~Homer, The Odyssey

On my daughter's first Christmas, I drove fourteen hours through the night, arriving at daybreak on Christmas Day for my father's first look at his granddaughter. After lunch I headed out to drive again for another nine hours to the other grandparents' house. By the time my second daughter was born, driving home for Christmas had become my way of keeping the family together.

After my divorce, I stopped driving home for Christmas. The girls were never there to wake up in my house on Christmas Day, so I slept until noon. There was no early morning scuffle of feet, no opening presents at dawn, and once the girls became teenagers, I stopped putting up a Christmas tree.

Eight years later I was sitting at work during the second week of December planning another holiday alone when I received an invitation to spend Christmas with someone. I had recently started dating again and the thought of spending Christmas with her was appealing. There was only one thing: this was a long distance relationship, as she lived in Toronto and I lived in Australia. Throwing caution to the wind, I booked my ticket for an eighteen-hour flight to Baltimore, with a connecting flight to Toronto.

Late in the evening of December 23rd, I took off from Brisbane. A winter snowstorm delayed my arrival in Baltimore for an additional two hours, and while my baggage made the connecting flight to Toronto, I was caught in the Christmas Eve backlog. By the time I cleared U.S. Customs, the storm had moved in and all remaining flights to Canada were cancelled.

A rental car was my only choice, and I exited the Baltimore airport just in time to join rush hour traffic. No one was moving, the snow was already axle deep, and the crawl to the interstate took hours. As I started putting miles behind me, traffic thinned out, and by 8 p.m. I saw my last car of the night. It was Christmas Eve; everyone was where they were supposed to be… except me.

I turned on the radio and listened to the football games being broadcast. Between quarters, local stations gave the ominous weather reports. Bridges and highways were being closed behind me, record snowfalls were being recorded in towns as I passed through, and the rental car was struggling to keep ahead of the storm.

Shortly after midnight, I finally arrived at the Canadian border.

"Purpose of visit?" the agent asked me.

"Home for Christmas," I answered with my thick Australian accent.

The agent looked at me twice perplexed, before finally stamping the passport. I drove onwards, and in the rear view mirror, watched the "Bridge Closed" barricades go up as I entered Canada. It was a downhill run from there, across the Queen Elizabeth Way into Toronto and then north to the 401. After twelve hours driving and a twenty-hour flight, I arrived at my girlfriend's home at 3:00 Christmas morning, and parked on the street.

The snow was falling heavily and the house was unlit. Sliding over to the passenger seat I curled up for some long overdue sleep. About twenty minutes later I was still awake and I saw the porch light go on and a silhouette step into the darkness.

I got out of the car and slogged my way across the street, knee deep in snow.

"Merry Christmas, babe," I said, hugging her tightly. Her flannelette pyjamas felt warm against my still cold skin, and I could feel her heart against mine, racing.

"Welcome home for Christmas," she whispered, while kissing me on the cheek. She took my hand and led me inside where I saw my luggage, which she had already collected from the airport, sitting under the Christmas tree, now adorned with a gift tag and a red bow.

I picked up the phone and called my father back in Australia.

"I heard about the snowstorm; how were the roads?" he inquired.

I looked across the room at the woman who had waited up all night for me to cross the globe. She was making me a hot beverage.

I told my father that I was glad to be driving home for Christmas again.

~Grant Madden
El Cajon, California

Scrooge No More

We cannot live only for ourselves.
A thousand fibers connect us with our fellow men.
~Herman Melville

I was not going to let a citywide blackout stop me. Millions were without power, but the mall had it and that's where I was driving. It was the thirtieth anniversary of my annual Christmas Eve tradition of going to a mall, and even the crippling ice storm that had hit Southern Ontario wasn't going to stop me. Traffic, on the other hand, might. I scanned the radio looking for a station not playing Christmas music. Not so easy on Christmas Eve.

The mall was fifteen minutes away on a good day, but not in this mess. I wasn't going to make it. But I needed to make it. I also really needed to find one radio station, just one, that wasn't playing carols. I shut off the radio.

Power lines were down. Traffic was being diverted. Was that pain in my chest something serious or just a cramp from holding the steering wheel so tight for an hour and a half? I thought I had given myself enough time to get to the mall before it closed. All I really needed was an hour. Even a half hour, but it was closing in less than forty-five minutes.

I managed to work my way across the lanes to take an earlier turn, pulled to the side, grabbed my smart phone and opened my map app. I couldn't believe my eyes. A clear route presented itself—bright green lines on the road map, with no traffic! The other roads were mostly covered in red, indicating massive traffic jams. I memorized the route, put away the phone, and headed down the side street.

The radio had talked about the people working for the power company who were out in the mess, trying to get as much power back on as they could. I tried to imagine what they were thinking about their own Christmases. Were they thinking about the people watching them work from their front windows, as they tried to save Christmas? Or were they thinking of their own families, waiting for them to come home?

I drove cautiously. Every house I passed was dark. Nobody was out walking. Everywhere lay broken ruined trees. Some split in half, some devastated by the weight of the ice and lying in heaps on the ground. As my car turned a corner, the headlights lit a house with a tree cutting it in half. Where were all the people who lived in these homes? I pressed on.

We had power at home, having only gone without it for six hours in the middle of the day. For all the towering old trees growing in our neighbourhood, we were fortunate to have had little damage.

I couldn't believe my eyes when the mall came into sight. Thirty minutes left to closing. I could make it. I could make it. The parking lot was jammed. I could sense the desperation coming from every vehicle competing for a parking spot.

Snow and ice had obliterated the lines indicating where to park. People took advantage of that. Was that a spot? No. That? No. Then after reaching the end of a row, as far from the mall entrance as I could possibly be, I saw brake lights on a parked car. Then back up lights. I put on my turn signal, claiming the spot. Then a car came down from the other side and the driver saw the same thing. But I was there first. Why was he waiting? Didn't he see I was there first? Typical aggressive Christmas shoppers, I thought. Was it going to be war? This was the kind of thing I really disliked about the season.

The parked car began to back out. My heart raced. Which way would it turn? Luck was on my side and it backed out toward me. I pulled in, parked, and joyously headed for the mall with twenty minutes to spare.

Once inside, I was swept into the current of stressed, aggressive shoppers. I bought my chai latte to soothe my nerves and, with much relief, began my annual Christmas tradition of strolling a mall to watch all the mayhem die down. Up until those last few minutes passed, people's faces were full of angst. But then when it was over, when the stores finally closed their gates, smiles began to appear.

Now don't get me wrong, I'm no Scrooge. Okay, I am. But only for the lead up. I find those months almost unbearable. The pressure. The competition. I revel in watching firsthand as it all stops, and that is when Christmas really begins for me.

I wandered, watched and waited. As the minutes ticked away, the crowds thinned. But something wasn't right. I checked the time.

It was ten minutes past closing and there were still a lot of people milling about. In all the years of my tradition, I had never experienced this. The malls would usually empty within minutes. When I walked out, it would be into a nearly empty parking lot. But this year, 2013, a half hour later, the mall still had people in it. It had to clear for the tradition to be fully realized. I had to feel like the last one out.

I rounded the corner and entered the food court and discovered hundreds of people sitting there! Food vendors were still open. After a moment of confusion, I realized these were the people who had abandoned their homes. This is where they had come. These were the people who had no power, and because of that, no Christmas. At least not the one to which they were accustomed. This Christmas, they were grateful for a mall they could keep warm in for a few hours more, for food vendors choosing to stay open to sell them a hot meal. Their traditions had been seriously interrupted, and yet here they were, smiling and laughing and letting their children race about the place in youthful exuberance.

Suddenly, my own tradition didn't seem all that important. This year, if the urge hits me to carry on with my long-standing, Scrooge-like ways, maybe I will head out to the mall, and maybe I won't. That night, though, I walked to my car, got in, and looked around at all the other vehicles parked where for thirty years it had usually been desolate. I turned on the radio and the first thing I heard was a

Christmas carol. I laughed, cranked up the volume, and sang along all the way home.

~William Leskevich
Etobicoke, Ontario

A Canadian "Family" Christmas

*We only need to look at what we are really doing in the world and at home
and we'll know what it is to be Canadian.*
~Adrienne Clarkson, former Governor General of Canada

My mother lost her battle with breast cancer right before Christmas when I was twenty-one years old. Losing your mother is never easy. But being an only child, without a father, and losing your mom only two days before Christmas is just awful.

Christmas is, by all accounts, a time for family. The dining room table is decked out with the good china and piled high with the home-cooked dishes that make Christmas so special. One is surrounded by warm smiles on the faces of mother, father, siblings, aunts, uncles, cousins, and grandparents. A familiar and friendly mix of laughter and Christmas carols fills the air and creates a feeling of good cheer for this annual tradition. Outside, snow falls softly and adds to the ambience. This is the stuff memories are "supposed" to be made of.

But what happens if your family is all dead? How then do you orchestrate the perfect Christmas scene?

We were a small family, it was true, but we had always spent Christmas together, opening gifts on Christmas Eve, eating traditional German food based on recipes my mother had brought with her to Canada from her homeland, and enjoying one another's company.

Each year we decorated a real tree. The stars which my great-grand-father had made of straw in Berlin almost a hundred years ago were now wrapped carefully in paper and packed away each year until my mother and I decorated the tree and delighted in these family heirlooms once again.

How would I manage without her?

That first Christmas without my mother was a pretty dark and miserable one. I was determined not to let my mother's untimely death steal this most special part of the season from me forever, so I set out to create a new kind of Christmas in my home, one that honoured her memory and the spirit of the season.

At the time, my husband and I were volunteering at a local refugee reception centre and around the middle of the following November, an announcement was made at church that families were being sought to invite a refugee into their home for a Canadian Christmas dinner. The idea was that we'd extend the hand of hospitality to our new friends, many of whom had never experienced an authentic, home-cooked turkey-and-cranberries-and-pumpkin-pie dinner before. Most of the would-be guests were separated from their own families—some by thousands of kilometres and others by death, thanks to whatever vicious war was raging in whatever country they had managed to escape before arriving safely in Canada.

After consulting with my husband we decided to open our table to as many families as were able to make the trek on Christmas Day from the downtown refugee centre to our small West Toronto home.

A large turkey had been donated by someone at our church. A volunteer stepped forward to cook and deliver the turkey, if my husband and I would prepare the rest of the food. We agreed we would. And of course we invited the turkey cook and her family to join us.

On Christmas Day, our little house was fairly bursting at the seams! With the approximately twenty-five refugees who had accepted the invitation, along with our friends and volunteers who were on hand to help cook the feast and clean up afterwards, the total count was over thirty!

At the last minute, a number of local businesses had opened

their hearts as well and donated enough gifts that each person had at least one parcel to open at dinner. (Don't ask how we managed to get everything wrapped and under the tree on time!)

Oddly enough, sharing my house with thirty-two strangers turned out to be the best Christmas experience I'd ever had. So often in the past I'd been caught up in the anticipation of receiving. I would eagerly tear open my presents, only to be disappointed at the junk bought in haste by someone who had felt obligated to give me a gift at Christmas. But this year was different. There was something extraordinarily fulfilling in sitting back and watching so many people, whose families were scattered all over the world, come together courageously to make a new, Canadian "family" theirs for a day.

As I ate the wonderful meal, I looked up briefly at our Christmas tree, adorned with the straw stars made so long ago by my mother's grandfather in Germany. I thought then about how I missed my mother's presence at the table on this special day. But I knew that she, too, must be enjoying this scene from her place in Heaven, along with the other mothers, fathers, sisters and brothers who were looking down on their own beloved family members starting a new life here in Canada, and sharing a traditional Christmas dinner in their new country.

That was the year when I learned that it truly is better to give than to receive.

~Vera C. Teschow
Toronto, Ontario

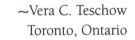

Christmas Comes Everywhere

*Mankind is a great, an immense family. This is proved by
what we feel in our hearts at Christmas.*
~Pope John XXIII

A week before Christmas we put up the tree, hung decorations and wrapped gifts. On the coffee table the nativity scene included camels and sheep, donkeys and cows, shepherds and the holy family, some worked in wood and others made of sisal. After supper we sang carols by candlelight. And we dreamed of our loved ones, imagined driving up to my parents' house in snowy Ontario, walking up the driveway with snow crunching underfoot and knocking on their door. They would appear with open arms to envelop us with joy and love.

But when the Christmas break began we packed up our sleeping bags and drove to a tented camp many hours north of the house where we were living in Nairobi. No snow, just sand and savannah scrub in a game reserve. We would spend part of our holiday with giraffes and zebras. We would cook on a camp stove and sing carols while sitting around a campfire. We would try very hard not to be sad that we were so far from our home in Canada.

Kenya is a beautiful country. But at Christmastime we longed for fat flakes of snow, rosy cheeks, warm scarves and snowmen. We pictured my parents' tree decorated with decades-old ornaments and remembered the presents that once spread across their living room floor. As we sat in the dark in our canvas safari chairs with our young daughters we sang "I'm Dreaming of a White Christmas," but the only snow at the Equator was at the top of Mount Kenya.

The camp was comfortable; we had permanent tents with real beds and mattresses, not our usual foam on the ground. We cooked in the dining pavilion under a grass roof that would protect us if it rained. The rainy season had missed this area so the land was dry, cracked and dun-coloured, vegetation dust-covered and stream beds exposed.

But the nights were cool and the sky so clear we could see an astounding number of stars. At dusk a very bright planet, Venus, rose above the pale blue line along the horizon. Our older daughter wondered if this was the starry light that the shepherds and wise men saw so long ago near another desert. So we sang again "O Little Town of Bethlehem," and felt closer to the reality of what it must have been like on that first Christmas where there was no snow.

Morning was hazy with soft light filtering through the branches of the flat-topped acacia trees. Out of the mist stepped a man with a spear, our guide who would escort us on a game walk. We hiked around thorny bushes, avoided tufts of spiky grass and kept an eye out for snakes. The guide silently pointed when he spotted animals. Herds of impala kept their distance, periodically moving in unison as we approached. We startled a thin jackal that scrambled away. A towering giraffe loped off to join its companions.

When the sun grew hot we made our way back to the camp. The children were disgruntled because of thirst, heat and fatigue. Just then, as we crossed a dirt track, we spotted the shimmering mirage of approaching figures. As they drew closer we made out a herd of camels strutting along with their regal snouts held high. Behind the herd a young man led a donkey that carried a woman sitting side-saddle. A cotton veil was draped over the woman's head and shoulders as protection from the sun. Running along beside the donkey was a small, curly-haired boy, a tan-coloured cloth wrapped around his lean body. The procession moved slowly, looking straight ahead as though we were not there. In silence we watched their retreat, their transformation back to shimmering mirage, lost in our own thoughts.

Our younger daughter broke the spell. "Christmas is here!" she announced. "We saw Christmas right here."

Smiles now replaced long faces.

Into our day had somehow appeared a tableau of the scene repeated in thousands of greeting cards and window displays and church altars, a simple spontaneous reminder that Christmas was special no matter where we celebrated its ancient rituals. Our spirits lifted and we sang with vigour as we tramped back to our campsite.

~Tanya Ambrose
Mallorytown, Ontario

Chapter
10

Christmas in Canada

The Spirit of Giving

Christmas, my child, is love in action.
Every time we love, every time we give, it's Christmas.

~Dale Evans Rogers

Half Full

The manner of giving is worth more than the gift.
~*Pierre Corneille*, Le Menteur

When I attended school as a child in Montreal, it was customary to give your teacher a Christmas gift on the last day of school before the holidays. I was never able to participate. Instead I would watch sadly as my classmates eagerly waited for their offering to be pulled and opened from the staggering pile on the teacher's desk. There was no extra money in our house to splurge on presents. Often there was barely enough for my parents to feed and clothe their rapidly growing four children.

I adored my fourth grade teacher, Mrs. Brennan. Always optimistic and encouraging, she made every student feel special. Early in the year she noticed that I had some ability to write, and encouraged me in that direction. I and wanted so badly to give her a token of my admiration.

As that last day approached, I feverishly tried to come up with anything in our tiny home that she might like. Just once, I wanted to feel that warmth and satisfaction of giving someone a present—to see their eyes light up with joy as they unwrapped something special that I'd carefully selected.

I searched frantically through my meagre belongings. The few items I owned were cast off toys that no one else wanted. They were treasures to me, but were pathetically worn out, and there was no sense going through them anyway; Mrs. Brennan had long ago stopped playing with toys. It didn't take me long to abandon my search through the room I shared with my three brothers. I owned nothing that could be re-gifted to an adult.

Next, I began digging through cupboards, hoping to find something my mother might be willing to part with. It was fruitless. She needed every pot, pan and chipped dish or cup we used every day. Now all that remained was a recessed dark cubicle of bathroom shelves that always smelled musty. Even in the dead of winter it was inhabited by spiders, which terrified me. Putting my fears aside, I continued on my quest. I pushed aside towels, facecloths, medications, shampoos and thin slivers of leftover soap we saved "just in case." Suddenly I felt a familiar item.

I pulled out a miniature flat bottle of hand cream that had been there forever. It was half gone, and the vivid pink colour had long since changed to a ruddy hue. When I opened it and sniffed it smelled rancid, but I was excited! Perhaps I could fill it to the top with a little water and a few drops of Mom's special perfume!

I did exactly that. The scent was strong and somewhat unpleasant. No matter how much I shook, it resisted blending with the old dried cream. I poured out the added liquid and decided it was still better than nothing and would have to do.

I washed the outside carefully until it gleamed. Next, I carefully tore a sheet of paper from a copybook. I grabbed my red and green crayons and coloured until no white or lines showed through. Finally, a wrinkled piece of ribbon from our junk drawer completed the wrapping and I placed it in my school bag. I couldn't wait to put it with the other packages my classmates were bringing in.

On that last afternoon of class, I watched Mrs. Brennan open her gifts. She cooed over every one equally and, as she displayed each treasure, I began to squirm in my seat. She received glistening new decanters of cologne, cosmetic sets, soft flannel pyjamas, a watch, earrings—someone even bought her a beautiful fake fur jacket.

I shrank into my chair as the pile diminished and my pathetic, makeshift parcel came into view. It looked cheap and ugly tucked in between the remaining gaily decorated boxes. What had I been thinking? I wanted to run up and snatch it away before she got to it. I even prayed that she would knock it over so it would roll away unnoticed, hoping I could retrieve it on my way out. Of course, none of that happened. Instead, I could only sit there and wait, knowing someone was sure to jeer at my offering.

Finally, her fingers closed around it. She announced who it was from and proceeded to open it. Pulling out the glass container, she stared at it for a long time before holding it up to the cries of "Let's see! Let's see!"

My eyes filled with tears when someone shouted out, "It's half empty!" Another giggled and said, "It's used up shampoo or something. What a stupid—"

Silenced by a rare penetrating glare from our teacher, the last word never left his mouth.

"This," she began holding it up again, "happens to be my very favourite hand cream—and it comes all the way from Paris, France," she informed the mocking heckler. "It's not half empty. It's half full," she corrected, "and that's how they sell it because it's so expensive. A little goes a long way."

With that, she twisted off the cap, turned over the container, and made it seem like she was dabbing a scant amount on her wrist. She palmed the bottle in such a way so that no one could see nothing was coming out. She pretended to rub it over her skin, then raised her hand to her nose and inhaled deeply, spreading a blissful smile over her face as if it truly was an outrageously costly lotion.

"I love it," she said looking at me with a huge grin, as the tension and embarrassment slowly left me. "Thank you so much, dear." Several moments later, she dismissed the class, wishing us all a Merry Christmas.

For the next two years I often passed Mrs. Brennan in the school halls. She always had a warm, beaming smile for me. As much as I wanted to, I never found the courage to thank her for saving me from humiliation that day.

When I was in grade six our teacher told us that Mrs. Brennan had been sick with cancer, and it had now recurred and she was undergoing treatment. When I learned this I was very sad. I wrote her a poem, and asked my teacher to give it to her. Mrs. Brennan died not long after, having continued to teach almost to the end.

The entire school went to her viewing. While I was there, her sister began asking around, "Which one of you is Marya?" When I identified myself, she took me aside. First she mentioned the poem, and said, "My sister asked me to tell you to never stop writing." Then she tucked a small bag into my pocket, and told me to open it when I was alone. I recognized it immediately. Nestled in the wrapping paper I'd coloured were the familiar bottle and crumpled ribbon I had given her. Included was a short note in her immaculate handwriting:

"Dear Marya," she wrote. "This lotion was all you had to offer, and you chose to give it to me. That beautiful gesture meant more to me than all the expensive gifts I received that day, because it told me you loved me. I am returning it to you so you never forget that it's the small things given with pure love that matter at Christmas. May every one of your future Christmases be as special as the one you gave me when you gave me this gift."

Each December, that little bottle, still half full, is unwrapped carefully and placed under my tree as a reminder that the true spirit of Christmas is the gift of love.

~Marya Morin
St. Lin des Laurentides, Quebec

Being Santa

Love has nothing to do with what you are expecting to get,
only what you are expecting to give.
~Katherine Hepburn

For several years now I have happily taken on the task of helping Santa by writing personalized Santa letters to children all over the world, for the pure pleasure of doing it. And I really mean personalized! I write each child every year until they are ten, and longer if they have special needs. It is the grandparents who generally send me three highlights of the child's previous year, and Santa comments on them. Parents keep the letters to preserve a running history of the child growing up through the eyes of Santa Claus.

Eventually my letter writing activities came to the attention of the management of a huge mall in Western Canada. Helping out Santa in such a place allows me to talk about the magical season with literally thousands of children every year. There is a great deal of commonality in these visits, but I always try to make each one special, for not only the children, but for the parents or grandparents who brought them. I get to perform my duties forty-two hours a week for five to six weeks every season. The mall takes such good care of me, Santa's helpers, and the children and families who wait in line for two hours each day, that I decided to offer my services free of charge for any special visits.

That happy day came when a member of the Public Relations office asked if Santa would visit some special children on behalf of the mall. Along with the visit and the usual photos, I would receive information on each child in order to write them their personalized letters from Santa.

On the appointed day, before I changed into my "uniform of joy," I chose the best place for the photos. In a traditional family room, Santa's comfortable easy chair with wide armrests sat next to the most beautiful Christmas tree I'd ever seen. With my love of being Santa always at the fore, I began what turned out to be the greatest evening of my life. I was especially thrilled to see a number of children from different cultures waiting to see Santa Claus.

The first youngster was a little girl of about eight. To describe her smile would be to redefine the words beautiful and radiant. We talked about Christmas, had our picture taken and shared a number of laughs. What a sheer joy she was! Her mother sat on the couch taking in the visit and the happiness, and it was so easy to see where this young girl got her smile.

Next were two boys about twelve and fourteen. Their continuous laughter raised the fun of their visit to a level that went through the roof. Everyone who was also in the room was laughing along with us. What great boys they were!

Then came the infant. Only four months old, he was as cute as he was tiny, and of course, he had no clue he was in Santa's arms. When I speak to newborns I'm actually speaking to the new parents. I remind them what a special season Christmas is for everyone who believes in love and magic. The baby doesn't care, but you see the excitement rise in the mother, thinking of all the Christmases to come. Tears fill her eyes, but seeing these tears combined with her smile, I know I'm seeing tears of sheer love and joy. A life to look forward to.

Have you ever looked at the innocent face of a five-year-old-boy knowing the spirit you see within should be shared with the world? That was Joel! He climbed into my lap with a quiet confidence. His mother teared up immediately and whispered in my ear, "He's never sat in Santa's lap before. He's been too frightened." What an extreme honour this was! Joel and I had a serious talk about Christmas, and what he would eat for supper, and what his favourite gift would be. He kept looking from me to his mother, forming a connection that seemed to bring me into his family. I loved Joel immediately!

There were other children who visited Santa that night, and they were all special to be sure, but these four stood out. Once the photos were all taken, and I had read *The Night Before Christmas* with Joel hanging over the armrest of the chair listening intently, it was time for Santa to leave. I bid farewell to those assembled and thanked them all for spending treasured time with me. I was then overjoyed when sweet, young Joel took me by the hand and walked me down the hall to the front door. I shook his small hand and, when I realized that wasn't enough, I bent down and gave my new friend a huge hug. A Christmas present for all time!

With the information from the children in my hand, I immediately called my wife, Linda, at home in British Columbia, and told her about my wonderful evening. While talking to her I started reading the letters I'd been given about the children. We both cried as we learned what these incredible children had been through, and still maintained their joy of living.

The first little girl had just had an artificial heart implanted and was awaiting a complete heart transplant. The twelve-year-old-boy was connected to an oxygen tank and was hoping for a donor for a double lung transplant. The infant child had been born four months premature, and was going home for the very first time in his young life. And Joel? Over the previous year, he had undergone five heart surgeries.

Once the tears had stopped, I began writing the answers to these children. It took a great deal of time because once again the tears flowed. I couldn't get out of my mind their strength, their attitude, and their sense of pure joy during this Christmas season. Once I managed to finish them, the letters from Santa were delivered to children in time for Christmas.

When answering letters to children who have gone through what these had, it is essential to stay upbeat and not refer to their ailments. I told them how lucky they were to have such well-trained doctors who dedicated their lives to helping, and nurses who cared for each one of them as if they were their own child. But I also made sure they were aware of the professional staff and all the volunteers at Ronald McDonald House of Northern Alberta. It's a place where they can live with their families, play with other children, and where their parents can talk to and help other parents who live through life's greatest fear. This is not only a temporary home but, to Santa Claus, a monument to love and care.

~Gordon Allen
Blind Bay, British Columbia

No Gifts for Christmas

Remember there's no such thing as a small act of kindness.
Every act creates a ripple with no logical end.
~Scott Adams

My first husband, Rick, was born with asthma and suffered many severe attacks as a child. But when we married he was in a good, healthy cycle, seemingly hale and simply happy to be thriving. As asthma goes though, another cycle came around resulting in many trips to the emergency room where I often feared the outcome. It was a roller coaster at times, but when specialists controlled the medications and oxygen was in place, he seemed to flourish and be full of jokes.

If only he could have felt like that every day. After a few years of missed time from work, and more frequent trips to the hospital, his employer asked that he step away from his job. They knew the dusty workplace wasn't making his life any easier, and of course, they needed an employee who could be there for every shift. We didn't panic, but we did struggle.

With Rick living on a disability pension and taking computer courses to learn a new career, we didn't have much. But we believed that all things happen for a reason, and perhaps this change would be the best thing for his health.

When Christmas came along we needed a strict financial plan to help make ends meet. We began shopping earlier than usual and got as much as we could for our loved ones. We stocked up on groceries to make a special dinner. And lastly, we agreed to not buy gifts for each other unless there was money left over. We weren't the first couple to fall on hard times, and we wouldn't be the last. But Christmas was our favourite holiday and we did feel disappointed to be in that position.

As the big day drew near we finally had our gifts, our food and a small turkey for our Christmas dinner. There was just enough left over for us to get each other something small to put under the tree. We'd both worked hard at sticking to our budget. We were as excited as kids again to know our sacrifices had paid off and our plan was finally coming together.

On December 23rd we went off separately to buy something special for each other. Relying on city buses to get us to our respective shopping spots, I went downtown and Rick went to the mall. I knew exactly what I was after, and was home soon enough to wrap my gift and get it under the tree before my hubby returned. But as the time passed and he did not return, I began to worry. Then the phone rang.

It was frightening to hear my husband's asthmatic rasp on the other end. He was so worked up he could hardly speak. Then a policeman came on the line to explain how my husband's shopping trip had turned into a mugging! When Rick had gone down a hallway to use the restroom he was poked from behind by a knife and his wallet demanded. He begged the man not to take what little he had because it was for the gift he planned to get me. But the guy ripped the wallet from his pocket and took off running through the mall.

Undaunted, Rick took chase. He couldn't bear to see the money we'd struggled so hard for taken without a fight. But the asthma prevented him from getting very far, and soon some bystanders took up the pursuit. They followed as the thief raced out the exit toward the field behind the mall. While running through some bushes, the mugger took the bills from the wallet and threw it to the ground. The good Samaritans returned the billfold to Rick as he panted and gasped on a bench outside a store. Then they called the police. All his identification cards were intact. The only thing taken was the cash.

I tried my best to reassure him that the only Christmas gift I needed was for him to be safe and unscathed from this ordeal. The outcome could have been much worse. He saw and felt the knife the robber had used to threaten him. It was a boon that all we lost was the cash. But deep inside, for both of us, it was more than just the money. It was the fruition of our personal commitment and struggles.

As we considered the events, we realized we weren't the only ones feeling needy this Christmas. We began to wonder who the thief might have been—a struggling single parent, an unemployed man with a family, or even a homeless person. With that we counted our blessings and committed ourselves to making our own Christmas as warm and joyful as possible. We had a roof over our heads, groceries in our cupboards and family with whom we would celebrate.

On Christmas Eve my sister and a few friends gathered in our living room to enjoy the lights and music we all loved to share. Rick had to retell his story a few times with each new person who arrived. But the tale always ended with our true gratitude that he came home safely, and we still had each other and our loved ones adding to this special night.

Another knock came on the door, and when I opened it a total stranger stood on the porch. A young woman asked if I was Lea Ellen, and when I said I was, she handed me an envelope and wished me a very merry Christmas. Off she went back to a car where others were waiting. They were gone before I could see who it was. Not sure what to expect, I opened it to find a card containing some cash—more in fact than had been taken from Rick, and a note wishing us the very best. I was flabbergasted! Who was it? Why would they do this for us? How did they know?

It wasn't until Christmas Day that we learned our benefactors had been gathered together by a neighbour of my sister. She had mentioned Rick's encounter at the mall to her friends and family, and word had spread fast. These fine ladies decided if they each gave a little it would quickly add up to cover the lost money. And indeed it did!

These two life-changing events had both occurred in less than forty-eight hours, and we became overwhelmed with all the mixed feelings. We'd had such a scare and loss one day, followed by our own mini-Christmas miracle the next! When something like this happens you read about it and think it's only going to happen to "the other guy." And when a selfless act of giving occurs, that, too, rarely hits so close to home. I decided to write a letter to the editor of our local newspaper, and thank our benefactors publicly. Hopefully, they would recognize how not only had they helped us with the money, they had also redeemed our faith in people. I wanted to reassure our friends and neighbours in town that the spirit of Christmas was still very much alive right here where we all lived, and most especially in the hearts of those who gave Rick and me the true gift of Christmas.

~Lea Ellen Yarmill Reburn
Barrie, Ontario

The Most Beautiful Ugliest Gift Ever

You don't raise heroes, you raise sons. And if you treat them like sons,
they'll turn out to be heroes, even if it's just in your own eyes.
~Walter M. Schirra, Sr.

I t was ugly. It was, in fact, the worst Christmas present I had ever received. I quickly feigned delight. After all, the giver was Michael, my four-year-old son, who had purchased the distasteful item at his school's Christmas bazaar. No doubt from the white elephant table, I surmised.

"I bought it for you Mama," he proudly exclaimed, offering it up to me, arms outstretched, face beaming, eyes big, blue and bright. At his young age, he had no way of knowing that this cheap-looking, off-white, ceramic, semi-circle thing (stuffed with unattractive plastic greenery), was the antithesis of all I valued about Christmas decor. And did I mention that it was ugly? Really, really ugly!

"We'll... put it... here... on... on the... kitchen table," I sputtered.

The rest of the house was bedecked with beautiful, natural materials from the garden. In the summers, I operated a garden gift shop out of the shed at the bottom of my yard. I also hosted an open house on the main floor of our Victorian-style home in late November, featuring high-end gifts for gardeners as well as natural items for the discriminating Christmas decorator (Ilex berries, rosehips, dogwood, etc.). And each year, I demonstrated unique and attractive ways to bring the outdoors in with wonderful, creative decorating ideas.

How awkward and out of place my son's addition looked in the midst of all this natural beauty. He must have noticed my captivation with decorating and thought I would be pleased with such a gift.

Soon my older children burst through the back door, excited to relay the adventures of their day and display their precious purchases. Within seconds, the kitchen table was laden with treats: festively decorated cupcakes; cereal and marshmallow squares sprinkled red and green and wrapped in cellophane; a couple of flattened, muddied packages of homemade fudge; candy cane reindeer with pipe cleaner antlers, black, wiggly eyes and red Rudolph noses; and a few of the small crafts some of the moms had prepared for the kids to purchase with their allowance money.

"Where are the rest of the things you bought?" I turned and queried Michael, hoping he hadn't eaten them at school or on the way home.

"I spent all my money on your present," he said proudly, not the least bit bothered by the chatter and delight hovering in the air as the others admired their booty.

Suddenly, this ugly, lacklustre gift took on new significance.

"You spent all your Christmas bazaar money on me?" I asked, incredulous that a four-year-old boy would bypass candy and cupcakes and crafty creations designed with kid-appeal in order to buy a present for his mom. Ugliness suddenly blossomed into beauty. I was delighted. No. Overjoyed. Wholeheartedly, I embraced both my son and his gift.

~Judi Peers
Peterborough, Ontario

A Song for Dedi

When we give cheerfully and accept gratefully, everyone is blessed.
~Maya Angelou

As soon as my husband, Andy, suggested we give Dedi a gift from the heart I knew exactly what I wanted to give her. I sat down and tapped out an e-mail to her son:

Hi George,

I hope all is well. I've been playing around with my ukulele, trying to write a few songs of my own. Andy mentioned that Dedi loves gifts from the heart. I thought it might be fun to try writing a song for her. I know the basics of her life story, but maybe you could help fill in the gaps? Please don't tell anyone, in case I can't come up with anything. If I do it would be a nice surprise for everyone, me included. :)

Marla

I smiled when I read his reply later that day.

Sure! Would be happy to help. What tempo calls to you? Happy, whimsical, a ballad? Like the theme of The Beverly Hillbillies *with a Hungarian twist?*

What did I want to say to the lady who was like a grandmother to my husband? Who had welcomed me into the family with open arms?

I knew she had an interesting story to tell. More than once she had picked up and moved on, starting over.

A few days later a line popped into my head as I thought about Dedi as a young mother rocking her newborn. *You don't know what the future holds, the miles you'll travel, or the places you'll call home.*

I e-mailed George a few questions.

Hi George,

I was thinking maybe something reflective—a toast, somewhat sentimental but hopefully not too sappy.
- *When (and how) did they leave Hungary to come to Canada?*
- *Why did they move from Montreal to Kelowna?*
- *What jobs did Dedi have?*

His reply gave me all I needed:

Hi Marla,
- *We sneaked through the Hungarian border into Austria in the dark of a November night in 1956.*
- *We crossed the Atlantic in ten days (which she spent most of throwing up) on a really old ship.*
- *Had an interesting encounter wondering what Jell-O pudding was.*
- *Arrived in Canada in Saint John, New Brunswick, wondering if we'd made the right decision.*
- *Were given a total of $10.00 to start a new life in Canada. No further contributions were received.*
- *Arrived by train in Montreal on Christmas Eve, in the middle of a snowstorm and -20 degree C, again wondering if we'd made the right decision.*
- *She found employment as a maid in Westmount, Montreal.*
- *Learned how to prepare poached eggs that didn't run and cook bacon crisp.*
- *Worked hand-to-mouth (manicurist hahaha) at the Ritz Carlton Hotel beauty shop until retirement.*
- *Packed all the furniture (cat included) on a bought mileaged out*

Hertz truck and came to Calgary in 1979 to escape exploding mailboxes (or more precisely the continuing political tension and separatism).

- *Five days later moved to Kelowna, BC, and found paradise.*
- *Paradise consisted of buying a motel and going back to being a maid.*
- *Finally settled down to the good life when the motel was sold.*

Don't know how this helps, but you are the creative one. When you get it set to music, send me the chords. We'll do a duet.
George

The weeks that followed were full of researching, writing, revising, playing, and singing. I read stories about the Iron Curtain, the Hungarian revolution, Hungarian refugees, and the October Crisis in Quebec. Slowly and surely the story became a song.

A few days before Christmas I slipped my ukulele into my suitcase, hidden amongst clothes and other gifts. I carefully slipped the printed song lyrics into my carry-on bag. I had already e-mailed George a copy, but it still seemed too precious to risk losing.

On Christmas Day, after enjoying a traditional family breakfast of Icky Sticky Ooey Gooey Buns and crispy bacon, I announced that I had a special gift for Dedi.

I pulled out my humble ukulele and George sat beside me with his twelve-string guitar. Knowing how difficult it can sometimes be to understand song lyrics the first time through, I read it first, my voice shaking.

Tanks are back in Budapest
ending revolution
with a crushing iron fist.
You sneak across the border
in search of better life
on a cold November night.

Ten dreadful days to cross the ocean,
ten dollars to start again.
Welcomed to Montreal on Christmas Eve
by a bitter winter snow.

Another tense October,
endless talk of separation
Twenty-two years of Quebec politics,
the truck is packed and headed west
for paradise
across the Rocky Mountains.

You don't know what the future holds,
the miles you'll travel or the places you'll call home,
how you will get there or if you'll grow old.

When I am old will I be wise?
Will my life story be worth being told?
How many tears will I cry?
How many smiles?

George and I strummed while I sang my heart out. Dedi dabbed her eyes with a tissue while her grandsons recorded the moment on their smart phones. Everyone joined in on the chorus. Afterwards, the family huddled around Dedi to listen to stories we hadn't heard before. I hadn't hit every note with perfect pitch but I knew that the song and this moment had been a very special gift for everyone, myself included.

~Marla Lesage
Lincoln, New Brunswick

Love in a Christmas Card

The simplest acts of kindness are by far more powerful than a thousand heads bowing in prayer.
~Mahatma Gandhi

Times were tough for our family of five. I was a stay-at-home mom with three young children. My husband was working two jobs, but in spite of all his efforts we often had trouble making the money he earned stretch from one paycheck to the next.

In the weeks leading up to Christmas we had been extra careful, determined to have at least one store-bought gift to put under the tree for each child on Christmas morning. Careful planning and a little ingenuity (allowing our children to think they were eating steak when it was actually... liver, for example!) had provided the money needed to purchase a toy or book for each child to go along with the gifts we had made for them.

Now, it was the Friday before Christmas. And despite all the corners we'd cut, when we finished our shopping we realized there was nothing left to put gas in our vehicle for the trip to my parents' home. Tears flowed as I realized there was no way we'd be able to see them on Christmas. I dreaded the thought of calling and telling them, but I knew it had to be done. I also knew I couldn't call until after 6:00 p.m. Daytime long distance calls were a luxury we could not even consider.

The day dragged on as I waited to make my call. Each minute seemed like an hour and each hour like an entire day. I was working in the kitchen when I heard a noise outside. Glancing out the window I saw the mail carrier walking away from our house. When I checked the mailbox I found a stack of envelopes waiting—the last rush of Christmas cards before the break for the holidays.

I took my time opening the cards, enjoying reading greetings from friends and relatives across the country. It was a welcome way to divert my mind from the sorrow I felt at the thought of making the call to cancel our trip. I knew it would bring disappointment to both our parents, and to our children.

When I came to the last envelope I stared at the handwriting, unable to identify it. I turned it over, but there was no return address. The postmark was blurred, making it impossible to tell where it had been mailed. As I opened the envelope, a twenty-dollar bill fluttered to the floor. I reached for the card, anxious to know who had sent this timely gift. At the bottom of the card, below the printed greeting, was just one word, printed in block letters—LOVE. There was no signature.

Twenty dollars was not a lot of money, and it may not have been enough to fill our gas tank. But it was enough to get us to my parents' home and back. My day instantly took on a totally different feeling as my heart lifted knowing I no longer had to make that call.

On Christmas Day we had a joyful time watching the kids open their gifts, playing games together and feasting on the meal Mom had prepared. What we didn't know, and couldn't have known was that it would be my father's last Christmas with us. He passed away the following summer, making the memories of that Christmas gathering—that almost didn't happen—especially meaningful.

After Christmas we made some discreet inquiries, hoping to thank whoever had sent us the money, but we never did discover who it was. Although we were unable to personally thank the person who sent it, I still think of him or her every Christmas and today, more than thirty years later, I'm still so very grateful for that gift!

~Gloria V. Phillips
Collingwood, Ontario

The Barbie

*Mother love is the fuel that enables a normal human being
to do the impossible.*
~Marion C. Garretty

Hanukkah came early to our family in 1963. My mother,
nine months pregnant with her fourth child declared
we would celebrate the festival of lights right now,
tonight. She knew that in all likelihood she would be in the hospital
when the first day of Hanukkah arrived and she didn't want us to
miss out.

Back then Hanukkah wasn't a big deal. We all knew the story
of how a small group of Jews led by Judah Maccabee had fought the
Romans. Even though he was badly outnumbered, Judah and his fol-
lowers had won the battle and were able to once again practice their
religion. They needed enough oil to burn for eight days to make the
temple holy again, but they had only enough oil to burn for one day.
A miracle happened and the oil burned for eight days. That night, as
we lit the first candle, we all thought of the story and of course of the
present we would get to celebrate the first night of Hanukkah.

I was seven and the oldest. I couldn't tell you what my brother
and sister got but I can tell you every detail of my gift. It was my
first Barbie, and she was beautiful! She had long blonde hair, perfect
features and a red bathing suit. Ever so carefully I took her out of
the box, knowing I was the luckiest girl in the world. I had a Barbie!
Then, as I surveyed my new friend it occurred to me, she had no

other clothes! Wasn't the whole point of having a Barbie doll being able to dress her up?

My mother sensed my growing disappointment. What could she do? She understood, but with all the preparations for the new baby it hadn't occurred to her that Barbie needed a wardrobe. She promised me she would sew an outfit for Barbie, and it would be ready when I got up in the morning. I went to bed excited and looking forward to playing with my Hanukkah gift.

The next morning I woke early and ran downstairs looking for my mother. The house was quiet. I peeked in my parents' room, and there was Barbie sitting in the middle of the dresser and wearing the most beautiful dress I had ever seen! The material was a blue print, not unlike the drapes my mother had recently made for the basement windows.

My brother, now awake due to the racket I had been making, came running into my parents' room as well. He noticed that my dad was sound asleep in bed but my mother was nowhere to be found. We both jumped on the bed and then on Dad.

"Where's Mom?" we demanded.

"She's in the hospital," a groggy Dad shared with us.

We jumped on him again. "Did she have the baby?"

"Yes," he replied, "soon after we got there."

"What did she have?"

"A baby girl! Now let me sleep!" he replied.

I found out later that Mom hadn't quite finished making Barbie's dress when she went into labour. She knew how disappointed I would be, so she somehow managed to finish the dress before heading to the hospital. Of course the self-centered seven-year-old who spent the day playing with her new Barbie had no idea of the determination and love her mom had shown. It wasn't until I had children of my own that I thought back to the day of my sister's birth.

Mom always commented that when you have children you don't divide your love between them—you multiply it. She had shown me this truth so well that night. Even though all of her energy should have been focused on bringing her new baby daughter into the world, she made sure her three other children did not miss the first night of Hanukkah and were taken care of in every way. And of course she gave us the best Hanukkah present ever, my sister Marla.

~Cindy Armeland Clemens
Lambton Shores, Ontario

Brighter than Any Christmas Lights

Nobody can do everything, but everyone can do something.
~Author Unknown

I can't actually remember Wally's face. I only remember certain details, like how he cast down his head when he stood up to shake my dad's hand. Out of the corner of my eye, I saw poor Wally's free hand try desperately to close the gap, the broken zipper in his threadbare pants.

For weeks we'd nagged Dad: "When are we going?" Every year he drove the three of us to see the Christmas lights around our hometown of Port Arthur. When the big night arrived, I felt impatient when Dad turned the wheel of the Chrysler New Yorker away from the edge of the suburbs onto a bumpy snow-caked path into what I thought was a junkyard. Dad had told us kids that we had to make a detour.

"Got a gift for an old friend," he said.

I looked up to see a weather-beaten boxcar shack. Smoke floated out of a small stack in the roof. I wondered aloud: "Does somebody live here?"

"Yes, his name is Wally," said Dad. "You call him Mr. Wilson." Dad opened his car door allowing cool air to waft in.

My little brother in the front seat said, "Yuck."

"Shhh," said my sister Jane sitting next to me.

"Be polite," my dad said.

"Yes, Dad," Jane said.

I frowned. Jane was almost two years younger than me, but acted older.

Dad set Wally's gift down on a wobbly table, careful to lay the brown paper bag flat. Wally watched, and then turned his eyes away. He offered my dad the only chair. My sister and brother sat on either side of Wally on a bed that was covered with ragged blankets. Several of Wally's bare toes stuck out from his slippers. Standing by a wall, I managed to avoid brushing up against anything. Tattered seemed a good word to describe everything there.

As we got up to leave, Wally stood, still talking with his hands. This made it awkward to hide the opening of his trousers. He lowered his eyes, head down. I guess he opened the gift after we left.

Walking down the path my dad explained that wealthy neighbours were trying to get the government to bulldoze Wally's house.

"That's not fair," my sister said.

I spun my head around to see Dad smile her way.

"Well, Janie... these rich people pay a lot of taxes."

"Humph," she said. My dad put his arm around her laughing softly.

I kicked snow her way.

As we cruised by the big suburban houses my dad cried out, "Wow... look at that one."

But for me, the bright lights of Port Arthur no longer had the same sparkle they usually did.

When my dad turned the car onto our street, illuminating for a moment my sister's face, I caught a strange look in her eyes.

Back home we got ready for bed. I was almost asleep, when through the darkness of the bedroom, words floated over to me from Jane's bed on the other side.

"I know what we can do."

I said nothing.

"We'll have a circus."

She really had me awake now. She began talking about how we could raise money for Wally. I turned my head on the pillow and sighed. She talked about decorating the garage. Then she said, "You can make up games that we could play. You're good at that."

My ears tuned in immediately.

Jane said, "You're good at spreading the word too. Kath, you're kind of artistic, right?"

I lifted my head and said, "Yes. I'll make posters."

"That's great."

I said, "Okay... but please go to sleep. We have school tomorrow."

By 3 p.m. Saturday, we had raised $1.80 from circus admission alone. We took in $5.60 from games of chance like Ring Toss. I invented a game that I called Ball Throw. For twenty-five cents a pop, if you hit and broke an old 78 LP record album hung by a string from the garage ceiling you won a prize. If you hit it dead centre it created great smashing noises. When Jane had to call out, "Watch it," one too many times because of razor-edged shards flying about, she cancelled Ball Throw.

We made the most money from my next game. We charged fifteen cents for jumping off the garage roof into the next-door neighbour's backyard snow bank. This was very popular. When we were up another $4.35, Jane hugged me. "You always have the best ideas," she said. "I wish I could be more like you."

Hearing her words, I felt like something inside cracked. In its place warmth flooded in.

Soon, our neighbour Mrs. Novak came home and phoned our father to make us stop. Total fundraising efforts for the day: $11.75—which back then was a nice haul.

On Monday Janie was in charge of buying Wally's present.

"They're nice," I said, when she showed me the slippers. "I hope they're the right size!" When I looked at the other items—safety pins, a plastic washbasin, a fluffy yellow towel and a bar of white soap—it set my stomach in a knot. What would he think?

Four days before Christmas, as we drove to Wally's boxcar home, I watched my dad's head bob and shake like you see one of those toy dogs on a car dashboard.

"I'm so proud of you kids," he said, letting his hands fly off the steering wheel. "I feel like the richest man in the world, like I have three million dollars!"

My little brother beamed.

I said aloud, "Dad, it's not fair they're going to make Mr. Wilson move. When I'm in government, I'm going to make new laws."

At that, Dad said, "I forgot to tell you... Town Council didn't approve the eviction notice. Wally gets to stay."

My heart leapt. My sister nudged me and smiled.

Dad held the door for the three of us as we stomped our boots and trudged into the boxcar house. Being the oldest, it was my job to hand the large brown shopping bag to Wally.

"This is for you, Mr. Wilson," I said simply. Then, not being able to think of anything else to say, I put an arm around my little brother's shoulder.

"Merry Christmas," Jane said.

I saw Dad attempt to hide a smile as Mr. Wilson tried on the slippers. They looked about two sizes too big.

Mr. Wilson then pulled the other things out of the bag one by one. With the dim light from the table lamp I noticed the grey in the stubble on his chin. Gently, he set down the pins, washbasin, towel and soap next to the shoebox, making a straight line along the edge of the bed. He smiled. I breathed out deeply.

When Wally turned around, he had his left hand holding his trouser gap closed and his right reaching out to me. Suddenly, I lifted my arm. In turn, Wally shook each of our hands the way I saw our parish priest greet us when Dad finally brought us back to the church.

I looked down at the contrast of Mr. Wilson's old bed covers and the objects lined up along the edge. Their shiny newness reflected in his wet eyes. It was a display that lifted up to my heart and burned brighter than any Christmas lights.

~Kathy Ashby
Bracebridge, Ontario

Santa Knows Best

To ease another's heartache is to forget one's own.
~Abraham Lincoln

It was Christmas Eve and I could barely contain myself. Decked out in my new flannel pyjamas, I knew I looked my festive best and this was going to be the best Christmas ever. This was the year I would get a Mrs. Beasley doll. I had sent my letter to the North Pole with very specific requests, and Mrs. Beasley was at the top of the list. I had also given detailed instructions to the mall Santa when I had my annual photo shoot with him. I didn't like waiting in line with other screaming children, and I wasn't a particularly photogenic child, but I knew that the mall Santa, though merely a helper, had a direct line to the real Santa. Keeping my eye on the prize, I had endured wearing a purple velvet frock and sleeping with rollers in my hair so it would look fluffy in the photo.

Mrs. Beasley was a doll on a sitcom called *Family Affair*. Buffy, the impossibly cute little girl on the show, had a doll named Mrs. Beasley, with a plastic face and body, soft flaxen hair, a blue dress and wire glasses. She was atypical because she was an old lady rather than a cute baby doll. I was obsessed. Maybe I thought having my own Mrs. Beasley would make me cuter, like the pigtailed Buffy, rather than the gangly kid with a bowl cut that I was. I like to think that my attraction to Mrs. Beasley was because I was an old soul drawn to the wisdom that an old-lady-doll could impart. I was solitary and shy, more drawn to books than playing with the neighbourhood kids.

Mrs. Beasley would be all the companionship I needed. She would be a confidant and give sage telepathic advice that I would decipher from her kindly, all knowing expression. One more fitful sleep and she would be under the tree, delivered by Santa at last.

It was a particularly cold December. The wind howled and rattled the windows as we listened to Christmas carols on the radio. The tree looked glorious, although the coloured lights were a trigger for my grandmother to declare, as she did every year, that Canadian Christmas trees were inferior to the trees from her childhood in Latvia. She disapproved of us opening presents on Christmas morning like Canadians instead of on Christmas Eve as they did in Europe. She would sulk on the couch, engulfed in the blue smoke of her Rothman's cigarettes and inform us that Latvian Christmas trees were adorned with real candles, unlike the tacky coloured bulbs we had draped across our tree. Lest the evening become too cheerful, my grandmother would reminisce about a woman she knew whose tree had caught on fire from the candles. As the unfortunate woman attempted to carry the burning tree out of the house to extinguish it in a snow bank, the wind blew the flames onto her nightgown and set her on fire, creating a pine scented towering inferno. My grandmother's story was an annual tradition, much like I imagined other families read Dickens or *The Night Before Christmas*.

After my grandmother stalked off to bed, my dad decided to light a fire. "Now when Santa comes down the chimney he is going to get all burnt up," he quipped. He found this hilarious. I became hysterical. I was too young to realize that Santa would be prepared for such hazards. It wasn't his first time dealing with chimneys, after all. All I could think was that we were the family that would send Santa to a fiery death, much like my grandmother's tree hoisting acquaintance. How would I get Mrs. Beasley if Santa was reduced to ash?

Eventually I was reassured that the fire would die down long before Santa visited. I set out a plate of cookies and my dad added a bottle of beer instead of a glass of milk—we were Canadian after all. Dad threw a piece of sausage on the plate as well. "We don't want Santa to become diabetic with all those cookies," he said, which almost sent me into hysterics again. Santa could get diabetes? Maybe we should be leaving him a light salad instead. Obviously, I needed Mrs. Beasley. There were far too many anxieties in life to handle on my own.

A few hours later, I awoke with the house quiet and dark. I sensed that Santa had already visited, which meant Mrs. Beasley had arrived. I crept out of bed, my bare feet like icy blocks against the cold floor. Despite my tiptoeing, my mother heard me and appeared as I entered the living room. 'It's too early," she whispered to me, "you should go back to bed."

"I just need to see Mrs. Beasley," I whispered, unable to wait a second longer. I looked at the tree and saw a doll that was not Mrs. Beasley. Instead of being plastic, she was a rag doll version with wool hair and a limp body. Her glasses were painted on rather than being real wire. I stopped in my tracks. This imposter was not the Mrs. Beasley I wanted. I had been very specific with my instructions. I had sent my letter and endured mall photos. I did not want to go near this shabby impersonator. My mother cleared her throat.

"I heard that the elves ran out of the other Mrs. Beasley, so Santa brought you this one who is very excited to meet you." I tried to keep my face impassive as I stared at the crumpled doll, my fantasies of parading around with my glamorous doll shattered. I felt my mother shifting nervously at my side. I stared at the doll some more. I saw her painted face and frail body. She looked so hopeful and vulnerable. I imagined how excited she must have been to arrive with Santa, thinking that she was going to bring joy to a little girl on Christmas morning. I wondered if she felt self-conscious that she wasn't as flashy as the true Mrs. Beasley. She probably felt like a bit of an awkward outsider with her floppy body and glasses. I knew how that felt. How could I be disappointed in something that wasn't the shiniest or the prettiest, but still wanted to be loved?

I resolved then and there that I would love her with all my might. I rushed to her, hoping that the fake Mrs. Beasley couldn't read minds and know that I had been ready to dismiss her. I squeezed her scrawny body and kissed her woolly hair. I heard my mom let out a sigh of relief. The rag doll Mrs. Beasley and I would be awkward, bespectacled best friends. We wouldn't be the belles of the ball, but we didn't need silky hair or plastic bodies to be special and worthy of love. I realized then that Santa knew better. He brought me what I truly needed, not what I thought I wanted. He really was a wise, all knowing elf.

I am so relieved we didn't burn him to a crisp.

~Kristine Groskaufmanis
Toronto, Ontario

Meet Our Contributors

Gordon Allen retired as a constable on the Toronto Police Service and now writes children's novels in British Columbia. He and his wife Linda have four children, four grandchildren and one great-grandchild. His children's book about a mermaid meeting Santa Claus, *Celesta's Magical Journey*, can be purchased at www.aspirebooks.ca.

Tanya Ambrose is a retired teacher. She lives in rural Eastern Ontario, where she enjoys gardening, walking, cycling, snowshoeing and cooking. Occasionally she even writes, and has had several short stories and essays published. She continues to travel the world for adventure and enlightenment.

Kathy Ashby is the author of *Carol 'A Woman's Way'* published by DreamCatcher Publishing. Her book was nominated for the 2010 Muskoka Chautauqua Reading List and she was chosen to participate on the We Wise Woman website: www.wewisewomen.com/stories/kathy-ashby. E-mail her at ashbykathy@gmail.com.

With a camera around her neck and a notebook in her backpack, recently retired **Barbara Baker** spends her free time racing up and down the Rocky Mountains to capture their story. Her passion for writing is dedicated to finishing a YA novel, unless of course a bird flies by her window.

Ardy Barclay is a retired teacher whose career started in Lobo Township, near London, Ontario. It was there she met her husband

Robert. She likes to fish, garden, and be outdoors. Ardy has had many life experiences, and likes to share them with others through her writing.

Irene Bastian lives with her husband and daughter on a farm in the Municipal District of Foothills near Okotoks, Alberta. A former high school teacher, Irene is moving into semi-retirement, which she hopes will bring her more time for writing, painting, and spending time with family and friends.

Luanne Beresford is a wife and mother to two brilliant kids. She loves to spend time writing, gardening and working with animals. She also has published a children's story, "Lady the Light Brown Dog."

Barbara Black's articles, columns, book, film, and theatre reviews have appeared in numerous North American publications. Her award-winning writing also appears in *CV2*, *FreeFall*, and *Poems from Planet Earth*, fiction in *The New Quarterly* and poetry in *What Can't Be Contained*. She lives in Victoria, BC. Learn more at www.barbarablack.ca.

Ellie Braun-Haley, a former newspaper correspondent, has three children. She designs greeting cards, presents talks on miracles, and writes. She and her husband publish a newsletter. E-mail her at milady@evrcanada.com.

Michael Brennan, a veteran runner of sixty marathons, left a job where he commuted two hours each day to start his own business organizing running races. A home office means time to walk his young daughter to school, walk the dog and plan events with his wife's able assistance. This is his third story published by Chicken Soup for the Soul.

Deborah Cannon is a fiction writer. She recently won an honourable mention for her story, "Twilight Glyph," published in *Canadian*

Tales of the Fantastic (2014). She is best known for her archaeological suspense novel series, The Raven Chronicles. She lives in Hamilton, Ontario with her archaeologist husband and two dogs.

Janet Caplan lives near Victoria on Vancouver Island. Her work has appeared in *Dogs in Canada*, *Animal Wellness*, *Ocean* magazine and *Tiny Lights*, as well as in several print and online anthologies.

Linda Carpentier received her Bachelor of Arts degree from the University of Manitoba and her Associate of The Royal Conservatory diploma in Piano Pedagogy. Now retired from music teaching, she has more time to devote to her lifelong interest in writing.

Eva Chagnon has spent her working life as an independent entrepreneur. However, since her son's tragic accident in December 2007, she has begun to work from home and intends to utilize her lifelong writing passion in future endeavours. E-mail her at evachagnon@ hotmail.com.

Elynne Chaplik-Aleskow, a Pushcart Prize-nominated author, is Founding General Manager of WYCC PBS and Distinguished Professor Emeritus of Wright College. Her stories, which she has performed throughout the USA and Canada, are published in numerous anthologies and adapted to film. Lean more at LookAroundMe. blogspot.com.

Cindy Armeland Clemens graduated from the University of Windsor. Her story "Shoe Shoe Train" appeared in *Chicken Soup for the Soul: O Canada The Wonders of Winter*. She's had a diverse career, but her most important title is Jacob and Jonathan's mom. She and her husband Mark live on a hobby farm. E-mail her at cindyclemens@hotmail. com.

Deborah Janes Collins was born in St. John's, Newfoundland, and grew up in the small town of Paradise. After completing high school, she acquired a diploma in early childhood education, and worked in that field for twenty-two years. She now resides in Bolton, Ontario with her husband.

Harriet Cooper writes essays, humour, creative nonfiction and health articles for newspapers, newsletters, anthologies and magazines. She's a frequent contributor to the Chicken Soup for the Soul series. She writes about family, relationships, health, food, cats, writing and daily life. E-mail her at shewrites@live.ca.

Lynn Dove's stories have appeared in several Chicken Soup for the Soul books. Her award-winning blog, "Journey Thoughts," has a worldwide audience. She enjoys writing, teaching, and spending time with her family and friends. Connect with Lynn on her blog at lynndove.com and on Twitter @LynnIDove.

Diane Driedger grew up on a family farm in rural Manitoba. Diane rode and broke in horses, milked cows and took care of all the farm cats and dogs. Diane is married and has two boys, two dogs and a cat. She loves swimming, camping, reading and telling stories.

Donna Fawcett is a freelance writer, an award-winning novelist, songwriter and poet. She received two university writing certificates, which led her to teach creative writing at Fanshawe College in London, Ontario. Donna continues to write for magazine and book markets.

Lori Feldberg's first joy is writing, followed by "necessary exercise!" She writes fiction as well as nonfiction, and has dabbled in poetry. Lori works with writing groups in her central Alberta hometown and surrounding area, and is always looking for a writing contest to enter.

Denise Flint is a freelance journalist based outside St. John's, Newfoundland on the edge of the North Atlantic. She's lived in four provinces and three countries, and her interests are diverse. Denise's articles have appeared in newspapers and magazines across the country, and she has received several awards for her work.

Liz Maxwell Forbes writes for a local newspaper, tends her garden, and cherishes time with her life partner and blended family. A charter member of the Chemainus Writers Group, she is published in a number of anthologies as well as being a third time contributor to Chicken Soup for the Soul.

John Forrest has sixteen stories in nine Chicken Soup for the Soul books about the exceptional events and wonderful people who have enriched his life. Scrivener Press has published his Christmas anthologies *Angels Stars and Trees* and *Home For Christmas*. He lives in Orillia with his wife Carol. E-mail him at johnforrest@rogers.com.

Kathleen Friesen loves reading and writing stories that encourage faith in God. She especially loves sharing them with her five wonderful grandchildren. Kathleen enjoys visiting with family and friends, travelling, kayaking, and puttering in her garden. She is currently working on her third novel.

J.A. Gemmell spent most of his working life in industrial settings. Possibly as a result of this, he now spends as much time as possible outdoors hiking, fishing, snowshoeing and walking continental camino routes. To date, he has racked up more than four thousand kilometers hiking in Spain and France.

Robyn Gerland is the author of *All These Long Years Later*, a recently published book of short stories, and is also a contributor to various magazines and newspapers. She is the past editor of the glossy, *Hysteria*. As a graphic artist, her work has been shown in several Canadian cities, London, England, and Sydney, Australia.

Paula Gillis received bachelor's degrees in arts and education from

St. Francis Xavier University in Nova Scotia in 1980 and 1981, and immediately moved to Alberta. She taught briefly and then worked as an employment specialist for people with disabilities. She volunteers, practices yoga, reads and is trying snowshoeing.

Pam Goldstein is a seasoned writer with short stories published in more than a dozen books; many are in the Chicken Soup for Soul collections. She edited *Chicken Soup for the Soul: O Canada The Wonders of Winter*, has written several children's stories, three adult manuscripts, and two plays. One was professionally workshopped in 2013.

Anita Grace is a writer and mother who spends many winter evenings buried in knitting projects and books, and many winter days romping in the snow with her kids.

Peter Green is a native of Toronto. He and his family operate Encounter Niagara Tours, a tour company showcasing the best of Canada and the U.S. in Niagara Falls. Formerly a professional musician, Peter lives with his wife Danielle and daughter Maddie in Kenmore, New York.

Ross Greenwood has degrees in sociology, theology and education from the University of Toronto. He is a retired teacher. He lives with his wife Jennifer in Orillia, where he is the president of the Mariposa Writers' Group. Ross's interests include gardening, tropical fish, travel, writing and spending time with his five grandchildren.

Kristine Groskaufmanis has been scribbling in her journal since she was eleven years old and needed an outlet for her childhood angst. She lives in Toronto with her husband and favourite playmate, Andrew. She is currently trying to figure out how to make a fortune as a full-time pet cuddler.

Gloria Jean Hansen has been writing for most of her life, in between working as a nurse, enjoying four children and a growing number of grandchildren. She has published several novels and is always working on the one book that will be the bestseller. Gloria also plays in a bluegrass band. E-mail her at glowin@persona.ca.

Rachel Lajunen Harnett is a teacher with a passion for writing short stories. She runs (often chasing her husband, two kids and Great Dane!), bikes and plays Ultimate Frisbee. Rachel is a graduate of Carleton University's Journalism Program. She lives in Toronto. E-mail her at rachelharnett@yahoo.ca.

A retired teacher with two grown daughters, **Patricia Harrison** enjoys reading, traveling, and entertaining friends. She loves historical fiction, and has had five Regency novels published. Her nonfiction work, *A Quiet Hero*, was self-published. At present, she is writing a mainstream novel of Scottish immigrants in Canada.

Rob Harshman has been a social science teacher for over forty years and has traveled to over forty countries. He is married, and has two married daughters and a grandson. Rob's hobbies include travel, gardening and photography. He plans to continue writing short stories.

Cheryl-Anne Iacobellis is a mother of four and lives in Barrie, Ontario. She enjoys writing short stories, camping, gardening and kayaking. She is currently studying with the Institute of Children's Literature.

Don Jackson is the former host of Canada's #1 evening FM radio program, *Lovers and Other Strangers*. He now produces a unique webcast about life, love and relationships on his website heartbeatoftheinternet. com, where he can also be reached. He plans to write inspirational books and novels. He is married and a father of two.

Donna Janke lives in Winnipeg. She enjoys reading, traveling, wintering in Arizona, and playing her piano. She writes both fiction and nonfiction, and blogs about travel and the writing life. She believes in love, miracles, and looking after each other. She laughs a lot.

Tanya Janke has worked in three schools, two shopping malls, a theatre, a market research company, and a berry patch. Now she spends her days writing. Her first play, an adaptation of *The Little Prince*, was produced in Toronto in 2010.

Shannon Kernaghan has published two books as well as hundreds of stories in anthologies, journals and newspapers. She's still waiting to find that "singing clock" in her Christmas stocking! Connect with her at www.shannonkernaghan.com.

Deborah J. Kinsinger is a psychotherapist in private practice, a writer, a mom, a traveller and a lover of all things Christmas. She has been writing forever and is delighted to share this Christmas memory.

Mary Ellen Kot is an Ottawa freelance writer and retired teacher whose work has appeared in the *Toronto Star*, *Ottawa Citizen* and *The Globe and Mail*. She is currently working on a book of humorous vacation mishaps. Follow and contact her at maryellenkot.blogspot.ca and kotmaryellen@gmail.com.

Liisa Kovala is a writer and teacher living in Sudbury, Ontario with her husband and two children. Her fiction and creative nonfiction work has appeared in a variety of Canadian publications. Liisa's current project is a family memoir about her father's experiences as a Finnish merchant marine imprisoned by the Nazis.

Stephen Lautens is a writer and lawyer who has written a weekly column for a number of major Canadian newspapers, including the *National Post*, *Toronto Sun*, *Calgary Sun* and *The London Free Press*. When not writing he can be found on Twitter. E-mail him at stephen@lautens.com.

Mark Leiren-Young is the author of two comic memoirs, *Free Magic Secrets Revealed* (Harbour) and *Never Shoot a Stampede Queen: A Rookie Reporter in the Cariboo* (Heritage), which won the Stephen Leacock Medal for Humour. He is also a playwright, performer, filmmaker and journalist.

Marla Lesage is an aspiring author and illustrator from New Brunswick. She enjoys reading, writing, sketching, painting, and playing ukulele. Her favourite mornings are spent catching rainbows with her children.

William Leskevich has worked in the entertainment industry for more than two decades. Currently a theatre scenic artist, he's been learning and exploring the craft of writing for almost just as long and is working at completing his first novel.

Ruth Levenstein is a professor, with a PhD in Electrical Engineering from the University of Toronto. She has five boys, who keep her quite busy whenever she is not working. In her "spare time," she also plays violin in an amateur string orchestra and is an avid hobby photographer. She also loves the great outdoors.

Suzanne Lindsay lives in Toronto with her two children and works as a freelance producer in the world of commercial photography. Her favourite quote is by Jodi Hills: "She wasn't where she had been. She wasn't where she was going… but she was on her way."

Julia Lucas is a freelance designer, specializing in needlework designs published by embroidery magazines, fabric companies and craft catalogues. She lives with her retired husband, has two stepsons and two grandchildren.

Catherine MacKenzie writes all genres but mostly dark fiction women can relate to—stories perhaps bizarre, yet ominously real. A published author, she's also self-published several poetry and short story collections on Amazon and Smashwords. Cathy lives in Halifax, Nova Scotia, and winters in Ajijic, Mexico. E-mail her at writingwicket@gmail.com.

The award-winning author of thirty-two published books, **Gail MacMillan** is a graduate of Queen's University. Her stories and articles have appeared in magazines across North American and in Western Europe. Gail lives in New Brunswick with her husband and two dogs.

Marie MacNeill is an interior designer in the Toronto area. She enjoys travelling, power walking, gardening and writing, and is currently working on an authorized biography. Marie is looking forward to carrying on her Christmas traditions with her new grandchild.

Australian-born author **Grant Madden** immigrated to the United States in 2005 and currently resides in San Diego, CA. He writes for the *Eugene Daily News* in Oregon, and has cover stories in *Sailing*, *Catamaran Sailor* and the *San Diego Reader*. He can be reached at www.grantmadden.com.

Lesley Marcovich, biography coach, believes everyone has a story to tell. And she is always "all ears." She runs a writers' group, biography workshops, and volunteers at hospice. She lives near Toronto with her husband Bruce and an ever-growing family, all great fodder for her own life story. E-mail her at marco7579@rogers.com.

Brandy Lynn Maslowski follows her passion as a quilt teacher, speaker, judge and the host of *Canadian Quilt Talk*. She just published her first picture book called *Kristy's Quilt*. Learn more at www. brandylynndesigns.com.

Nancy Koruna McIntosh is a Food Bank Community and Development Coordinator. She's been a radio announcer, newspaper columnist, clothing and art designer, and won numerous marketing awards for corporate window displays, merchandising and advertising campaigns. She hopes to travel, paint more and illustrate children's books. E-mail her at nancymcintosh4@hotmail.com.

Sally Meadows is a freelance writer and recording artist. She began her career in the sciences, segued into education, and now passionately pursues the arts full-time. She is a two-time national award-nominated lyricist, aspiring children's book author, and Ambassador for Compassion Canada. Contact her at sallymeadows.com.

Sharon Melnicer is a writer, artist and teacher in Winnipeg, Manitoba. She has frequently aired her "Slice of Life" pieces on CBC radio. A retired high school English teacher and university instructor, she continues to teach life-story writing to adults and is a recognized artist who shows and sells throughout North America.

Patricia Miller is an author, wife, and mother of two living in Bradford, Ontario. She loves lakes and cottaging in the Haliburton Highlands. Her first adult romance novel, *The Mausoleum Road Affair*, is a sizzling love story arriving Fall 2014 from Swoon Romance. Visit Patricia at www.patriciamillerwriting.com.

After a life of school teaching, **Joyce MacBeth Morehouse** decided to put down some funny episodes that had occurred over her lifetime. As a twelve-year-old, Joyce published her first poem, and poetry has always been a "first love." Over the years, several writings have found their way into periodicals.

Marya Morin is a freelance writer. Her stories and poems have appeared in publications such as *Woman's World* and Hallmark. Marya also penned a weekly humorous column for an online newsletter, and writes custom poetry on request. She lives in the country with her husband. E-mail her at Akushla514@hotmail.com.

Bob Mueller is a self-taught artist and writer. Achieving a seventh-degree black belt in karate, he became a pioneer in teaching children martial arts across Canada. At age forty-seven, he discovered his passion as an artist. He and Steve Sabol at NFL Films made *Finding Your Butkus*, a movie about Mueller's life story that won the 2008 Sports Emmy Award for Outstanding Long Feature.

Janette Oke is celebrated for her significant contribution to the Christian book industry, including books such as *Love Comes Softly* and *Where Courage Calls*. Her novels have sold more than thirty million copies, and several have been made into Hallmark Channel original movies. Janette and her husband live in Alberta, Canada.

Born in Grand Bank, Newfoundland and Labrador, **Robert C. Parsons** continued his career in education after his first year teaching in Philips Head, completing thirty years in the elementary classroom. He has three children and four grandchildren, and is the author of over thirty books of marine related stories of eastern Canada.

Alexa Danielle Patino is a young aspiring writer, filmmaker, songwriter and musician. Attending an arts school in Toronto, she majors in vocal, plays the piano, guitar and left-handed bass. She enjoys skateboarding, mixed martial arts, making YouTube videos and fashion! Alexa hopes to write full-length novels one day.

Danielle Mathieson Pederson is a part-time working mom of two toddlers. Her husband accepts their overflowing bookshelves as part of the home decor. She loves to read fantasy, science fiction and romance. She is also an active blogger and book reviewer. She started writing her first novel in grade nine and has loved writing ever since.

Judi Peers has published many children's books (*Brontosaurus Brunch*; *Home Base*; *Shark Attack*; *Sayonara, Sharks*; *Guardian of the Lamp*) and contributed to several anthologies. She is also a speaker and literacy advocate, who just happens to love Christmas. Judi and her husband Dave make their home in Peterborough, Ontario.

Born in northern Alberta, **Gloria V. Phillips** lived in various locations throughout Alberta and Saskatchewan before settling in Ontario. Her interest in genealogy and history led her to write two historical fiction novels—*A Pilgrim Passing Through* and *A Pilgrim's Daughter*. Her writing was also featured in *A Second Cup of Hot Apple Cider*.

Jan Piers lives on the Canadian Prairie in Edmonton, Alberta, where the winters are long, cold and dark. Yet she describes Christmas as her favourite time of the year. Jan is ecstatic to have her story included in *Chicken Soup for the Soul: Christmas in Canada*. She is working on a novel and hopes to have it published soon.

Lea Ellen Yarmill Reburn resides in beautiful central Ontario and was born and raised locally. Lea Ellen loves to write true-life experiences—some typical and some not! Previously published in *A Cup of Comfort for a Better World*, *Chicken Soup for the Soul: O Canada The Wonders of Winter* and other periodicals.

Kim Reynolds received her B.A. degree in Journalism from Concordia University in Montreal. Her essays have appeared in newspapers, online and in *Chicken Soup for the Soul: The Multitasking Mom's Survival Guide*. She lives in Ottawa with her husband and two children. Visit her blog at BookGiddy.ca.

Kendra Rice received her Bachelor of Science in Nursing from the University of Alberta in 2004. She currently resides and works in Tofino, British Columbia. She has two children—Lela and a two-month-old girl—and a loving husband. She enjoys travelling, surfing, camping, hiking and working with the First Nations.

Annie Riess farms with her husband in Saskatchewan. She also teaches piano lessons and does freelance writing. She enjoys spending as much time as possible with family and friends. E-mail her at anneriess@yahoo.ca.

Chris Robertson is an author and award-winning speaker. The diary of his historic first journey from the bottom of mainland Canada to the top has been published in the book *To The Top Canada*. Order autographed copies of the book or get Chris as a speaker for your next meeting at www.chrisrobertson.ca.

Encina Roh lives in British Columbia with her parents and two siblings. In her spare time, she enjoys reading, writing, photography and painting flowers.

Caroline Sealey's life consists of the 4F's—faith, family, friends and farming. She is a freelance writer, works at a local newspaper and is excited and thankful to be published in a Chicken Soup for the Soul book for a second time. Her future plans include an inspirational children's farm book. Check out her blog at afarmersheart.blogspot. ca.

Ritu Shannon has had her stories published in numerous Chicken Soup for the Soul books. She has recently accepted a major promotion to become a sales manager within her company and is now learning to balance work/travel with family life. The loves of her life are her children, Priya and Keegan, and her loving husband of nine years, Jamie.

Stella Shepard is a journalist whose stories were published in *Chicken Soup for the Canadian Soul, Chicken Soup for the Soul: Like Mother, Like Daughter* and *Chicken Soup for the Soul: O Canada The Wonders of Winter*. "The Christmas Card" is in memory of her beloved sister, Marie Shepard. Contact her at rphelan@pei.sympatico.ca.

Laura Snell, her husband Dave, and their dog Gus Gusterson live in Wasaga Beach, Ontario where they operate their web development and online marketing firm, GBSelect.com. Her son Ryan lives in Melbourne, Australia. E-mail her at laura@gbselect.com.

John Stevens, a man with a wandering soul, has pursued many roads in life. He has worked in TV, as technical director of Softball Canada, executive director of the Canadian Association of Journalists, a computer instructor, and supply teacher. He is currently teaching ESL and running his B&B with his wife in St. Marys, Ontario.

Vera C. Teschow is a certified Ontario teacher and mother of monozygotic twins. She also holds a Private Pilot License (PPL). Based in Toronto, Vera spends her summers on the north shore of Prince Edward Island. Visit Vera online at www.verateschow.ca.

Crystal Thieringer is blissfully retired, yet busier than she has ever been. Writing stories was something she dreamed of as a child but didn't pursue until she bid adieu to her career. Now she lives in Ottawa, Ontario with her husband. Together they are the live-in people for their stubborn and rather opinionated cats.

Jayne Thurber-Smith is an award-winning freelance writer for various publications, including *Faith & Friends*, *Sports Spectrum* magazine and *The Buffalo News*; she has also written for cbn.com. E-mail her at jthurbersmith@cox.net.

Lisa Timpf is a graduate of McMaster University in Hamilton, Ontario. Lisa enjoys writing, nature walks, and organic gardening, and has published a collection of creative nonfiction and poetry entitled *A Trail That Twines*.

Lori Twining is a writer, blogger and social media guru. She's an executive member of the Writers' Community of Simcoe County, a key organizer for the Muskoka Novel Marathon and Owen Sound's Ascribe Writers' Group. She's a lover of books, sports and birdwatching, and a hater of slithering reptiles and beady-eyed rodents.

Lloyd Walton, as director-cinematographer, has won over thirty-five national, provincial, and international film awards. Reflecting on extraordinary experiences all over Canada, his autobiography, *Positively North Street*, is a collection of encounters with extraordinary people like Pierre Trudeau, Neil Young, Bob Dylan and a 108-year-old Ojibwa elder.

With a background in vocal performance, **Kyla G. Ward** brings a creative and relational approach to all she does, including her storytelling. Though she originally hails from Winnipeg, she considers herself an island girl, having lived in Victoria since she was two. Kyla enjoys serving as a pastor, wife, and mom of two.

Brian Wettlaufer was born and raised in Canada, travelled extensively throughout the world on his student loans and now lives in Wisconsin re-paying his debts. He enjoys a good cigar with a cold martini by a warm fire. And oh, he loves his wife, eh? E-mail him at bwettlaufer@wi.rr.com.

Deborah K. Wood is a writer, a mom, a life coach, and a Christmas enthusiast. Many of her best memories, stories and adventures are centered around the Christmas season.

Meet Our Authors

Amy Newmark was a writer, speaker, Wall Street analyst and business executive in the worlds of finance and telecommunications for more than thirty years. Today she is publisher, editor-in-chief and coauthor of the Chicken Soup for the Soul book series. By curating and editing inspirational true stories from ordinary people who have had extraordinary experiences, Amy has kept the twenty-one-year-old Chicken Soup for the Soul brand fresh and relevant, and still part of the social zeitgeist.

Amy graduated *magna cum laude* from Harvard University where she majored in Portuguese and minored in French. She wrote her thesis about popular, spoken-word poetry in Brazil, which involved traveling throughout Brazil and meeting with poets and writers to collect their stories. She is delighted to have come full circle in her writing career—from collecting poetry "from the people" in Brazil as a twenty-year-old to, three decades later, collecting stories and poems "from the people" for Chicken Soup for the Soul.

Amy has a national syndicated newspaper column and is a frequent radio and TV guest, passing along the real-life lessons and useful tips she has picked up from reading and editing thousands of Chicken Soup for the Soul stories.

She and her husband are the proud parents of four grown children and in her limited spare time, Amy enjoys visiting them, hiking, and reading books that she did not have to edit.

Janet Matthews is a bestselling author, freelance editor and inspirational speaker. After spending the first twenty years of her professional life in Toronto's fast paced fashion-photography and advertising industry, in 1997 she became involved with producing *Chicken Soup for the Parent's Soul*. When Jack Canfield invited her to coauthor *Chicken Soup for the Canadian Soul*, she jumped at the chance. When it was released in 2002 it shot right to the top of the bestseller lists all across Canada. Since 2002, Janet has been inspiring audiences across Canada with her heartfelt journey of creating this unique Canadian book. With her stories, anecdotes and passionate delivery, Janet lights up a room.

Since 2003, Janet has utilized her editorial expertise to help other authors bring their books of personal or spiritual growth to publication. Working with American coauthor Daniel Keenan she completed a book-sized version of *The Navy's Baby*, an amazing story first appearing in *Chicken Soup for the Parent's Soul*. She has stories in seven Chicken Soup for the Soul books and, with the release of *Chicken Soup for the Soul: O Canada The Wonders of Winter*, and *Chicken Soup for the Soul: Christmas in Canada*, Janet is thrilled to once again be part of the Chicken Soup for the Soul family.

An eclectic individual with diverse interests and talents, Janet is a certified Love Yourself Heal Your Life workshop leader with training based on the philosophy of Louise Hay. She is a certified canoeing instructor, a couturier seamstress, and a passionate skater. She also plays the violin.

Now living in Aurora, Ontario, Janet has been a guest on countless television and radio talk shows across Canada, and gives a very dynamic interview. She is generally available for guest speaking spots and interviews, and you may contact her through www.janetmatthews.ca or www.canadiansoul.com.

Thank You

Thank you, Canada. We owe huge thanks to every one of you who shared your story about the wonders of a Canadian Christmas. It was very hard to narrow the list down to 101 stories, and even the stories that didn't make it into the final manuscript had a big influence on us and affected the final manuscript. Some of them may appear in Chicken Soup for the Soul's next Christmas book, scheduled for 2015!

We want to thank Chicken Soup for the Soul's VP & Assistant Publisher D'ette Corona for her input, her editing, and all her work with our contributors as we worked with them to perfect their stories. Managing Editor and Production Coordinator Kristiana Pastir oversaw the long journey from Word document to finished manuscript to proofs to cartons of finished books and Senior Editor Barbara LoMonaco oversaw the story submissions and proofread the final layout.

We owe a very special thanks to our creative director and book producer, Brian Taylor at Pneuma Books, for his brilliant vision for our cover and for the interior design. And we are grateful to the whole sales team at Simon & Schuster Canada for enthusiastically presenting our book and making sure that it gets on store shelves all over Canada.

~Amy Newmark and Janet Matthews

Sharing Happiness, Inspiration, and Wellness

Real people sharing real stories, every day, all over the world. In 2007, *USA Today* named *Chicken Soup for the Soul* one of the five most memorable books in the last quarter-century. With over 100 million books sold to date in the U.S. and Canada alone, more than 200 titles in print, and translations into more than forty languages, "chicken soup for the soul" is one of the world's best-known phrases.

Today, twenty-one years after we first began sharing happiness, inspiration and wellness through our books, we continue to delight our readers with new titles, but have also evolved beyond the bookstore, with wholesome and balanced pet food, delicious nutritious comfort food, and a major motion picture in development. Whatever you're doing, wherever you are, Chicken Soup for the Soul is "always there for you™." Thanks for reading!

Share with Us

We all have had Chicken Soup for the Soul moments in our lives. If you would like to share your story or poem with millions of people around the world, go to chickensoup.com and click on "Submit Your Story." You may be able to help another reader, and become a published author at the same time. Some of our past contributors have launched writing and speaking careers from the publication of their stories in our books!

We only accept story submissions via our website. They are no longer accepted via mail or fax.

To contact us regarding other matters, please send us an e-mail through webmaster@chickensoupforthesoul.com, or fax or write us at:

Chicken Soup for the Soul
P.O. Box 700
Cos Cob, CT 06807-0700
United States of America
Fax: 203-861-7194

One more note from your friends at Chicken Soup for the Soul: Occasionally, we receive an unsolicited book manuscript from one of our readers, and we would like to respectfully inform you that we do not accept unsolicited manuscripts and we must discard the ones that appear.